EVALUATING DECISION SUPPORT AND EXPERT SYSTEMS

WILEY SERIES IN SYSTEMS ENGINEERING

Andrew P. Sage

ANDREW P. SAGE and JAMES D. PALMER
Software Systems Engineering

WILLIAM B. ROUSE
Design for Success

ANDREW P. SAGE
Decision Support Systems Engineering

LEONARD ADELMAN
Evaluating Decision Support and Expert Systems

EVALUATING DECISION SUPPORT AND EXPERT SYSTEMS

LEONARD ADELMAN
Department of Systems Engineering
School of Information Technology and Engineering
George Mason University
Fairfax, Virginia

A Wiley-Interscience Publication
JOHN WILEY & SONS, INC.
New York / Chichester / Brisbane / Toronto / Singapore

In recognition of the importance of preserving what has been
written, it is a policy of John Wiley & Sons, Inc., to have books
of enduring value published in the United States printed on
acid-free paper, and we exert our best efforts to that end.

Library of Congress Cataloging-in-Publication Data

Adelman, Leonard, 1949–
      Evaluating decision support and expert systems/Leonard
Adelman.
            p. cm.—(Wiley series in systems engineering)
      "A Wiley-Interscience publication."
      Includes bibliographical references.
      1. Expert systems (Computer science)—Evaluation. 2. Decision
support systems—Evaluation. I. Title. II. Series.

QA76.76.E95A329 1992
006.3'3—dc20   91-19337
ISBN 0-471-54801-4   CIP

Printed in the United States of America

10 9 8 7 6 5 4 3 2 1

To my father

Contents

Preface

Decision support systems and expert systems hold great promise. Unfortunately, this promise has yet to be fully achieved. One reason for this state of affairs is that development is currently technology driven instead of requirements driven. Things are, however, changing. Methods are evolving for implementing a requirements-driven develoment process. Evaluation is a critical part of the process. Formal evaluation methods are tools that sponsoring and development team members can use to obtain the feedback and, thereby, improve the judgments and decisions inherent in system development. For that reason, evaluation represents the control mechanism that keeps the decision support system and expert system development process on track.

The audience for this book includes developers of decision support and expert systems, managers of such development efforts, and personnel tasked with evaluating these technologies. The purpose of this book is to show readers how to perform formal evaluations of decision support and expert systems. The goal is to impart an understanding of the methods required to perform effective evaluations, and how to incorporate these methods into the design and development process.

Chapter 1 is introductory in nature. We define decision support systems and expert systems, and consider the role of evaluation as well as test and evaluation personnel. Moreover, we point out that evaluation is often the forgotten step in the development process. This is not meant to imply that it is not found in decision support system and expert system development diagrams; it is. Nor is it meant to imply that computer scientists do not test and evaluate their code as they develop it; they do. What it does imply, however, is that formal and systematic evaluations of decision support systems and expert systems and, for that matter, most software products—are not performed throughout the development process. As a result, we lose the opportunity to gain valuable information about what potential users think about the system, how well its code is written, and the extent to which the system really does support decision making early in the development cycle, when changes are, relatively speaking, easy and inexpensive to make.

Chapter 2 presents a general framework for considering evaluation issues and a multifaceted approach for selecting classes of evaluation methods. The multifaceted approach is composed of a technical evaluation phase for "looking inside the black box"; an empirical evaluation phase for assessing the system's impact on performance; and a subjective evaluation phase for obtaining users' opinions regarding the system's strengths and weaknesses. A case study is presented to illustrate how the approach can be used to evaluate decision support and expert system technologies.

Chapter 3 describes a prototyping blueprint for developing decision support systems and expert systems, and provides a general discussion of how subjective, technical, and empirical evaluation methods can be integrated into this development process. In addition, Chapter 3 provides a brief overview of specific subjective, technical, and empirical evaluation methods as a means of introducing the reader to them prior to their detailed consideration. Finally, this chapter considers the relative importance of subjective, technical, and empirical evaluation methods for different steps in the development blueprint.

Chapters 4, 5, and 6 present detailed discussions of subjective, technical, and empirical evaluation methods, respectively. Specifically, Chapter 4 describes five subjective evaluation methods in detail, provides an example illustrating how two of them were used in a development effort of the U.S. Air Force, and discusses how to construct questionnaires to obtain users' opinions about the strengths and weaknesses of a decision support system or expert system. Chapter 5 discusses four classes of technical evaluation methods: those for evaluating the appropriateness of the analytical methods selected by the design team for incorporation in the decision support system; those for estimating software development costs; formal software testing and verification methods; and methods for evaluating the logical adequacy and predictive accuracy of a knowledge base. Chapter 6 considers the use of experiments, quasi-experiments, and case studies to assess empirically whether the system actually improves performance.

Chapter 7 discusses how to manage the multifaceted evaluation approach presented herein so as to ensure project control. The chapter is divided into two sections. The first section overviews basic issues in managing the test and evaluation process, including the evaluator's responsibilities, the key elements for effective testing, and using test documentation as a control tool. The second section again focuses on the importance of selecting different evaluation methods at different steps in the development process in order to answer questions cost effectively throughout development. In addition, multiattribute utility technology is presented as a method for both more effectively managing the test and evaluation process, and obtaining an overall assessment of system utility throughout development.

We make three points in closing this preface. First, this book assumes that the reader has some working knowledge of what decision support systems and expert systems are, and how to build them. This is not an introductory text on these technologies, but, rather, one on how to evaluate them. Second, this is a methods book. The goal is to present an overview of the different methods required to perform effective evaluations of decision support and expert systems, and how to incorporate them into the development process. And, third, we emphasize a decision making perspective to system evaluation. The evaluator's job is to produce information that can improve the judgments and decisions inherent in system development. The better these judgments and decisions are, the higher the probability that an effective system will be developed and implemented. Evaluation is the control mechanism that keeps development on track.

LEONARD ADELMAN

Acknowledgments

Preparation of the majority of this book was made possible by a subcontract from Science Applications International Corporation (SAIC) to George Mason University (GMU). The funds for the subcontract were from the Ft. Leavenworth Field Unit of the U.S. Army Research Institute of the Behavioral and Social Sciences (ARI) as part of a major effort to design, develop, and evaluate the role of decision support and expert system technologies for enhancing command and control performance. Additional support was also provided by the Center for Excellence in Command, Control, Communications and Intelligence (C3I) at George Mason University. The center's general research program is sponsored by the Virginia Center for Innovative Technology, MITRE Corporation, the Defense Communications Agency, CECOM, PRC/ATI, ASD(C3I), TRW, AFCEA, and AFCEA NOVA.

I want to thank Dr. Stanley Halpin, Chief of ARI's Ft. Leavenworth Field Unit, Mr. Paul McKeown, Manager of SAIC's Ft. Leavenworth office, and Dr. Harry Van Trees, Director of GMU's C3I Center, for their support throughout the preparation of this manuscript. I also want to thank Dr. Michael Donnell, former Vice President of SAIC's Behavioral Research and Artificial Intelligence Operation, for his support of my initial ideas for the manuscript. Without their support, this book would not have been possible. Consequently, they deserve credit if the research presented here improves the development of decision support and expert systems. In light of any criticism, however, it should be remembered that the views and opinions expressed herein are those of the author and should not be construed to represent those of the above individuals or their organizations.

I also want to express my appreciation to a number of other people who were influential in the preparation and publication of this work. First, I want to thank

Dr. Stephen Andriole. Without Steve's gentle prodding, I probably would never have started this manuscript. Second, I want to thank Dr. Andrew P. Sage for his enthusiastic support of the publication of the manuscript as part of the Wiley-Interscience series on systems engineering, for which he is the editor. Third, I want to acknowledge Mr. George Telecki and Ms. Jimin Han, the Editor and Assistant Editor of the Wiley-Interscience Division, for their support and assistance. In addition, I want to thank Dr. Jon Fallesen and Dr. Sharon Riedel at the Army Research Institute for their helpful comments on an earlier version of the manuscript, and Mr. Robert Harder of the U.S. Army Electronic Proving Ground and Dr. Jacob Ulvila of Decision Science Consortium, Inc., for their support on a related effort. And, last but certainly not least, I want to thank Ms. Mary Fran McDavitt for her secretarial support in preparing this work.

I also want to acknowledge the influence of my major professor, Dr. Kenneth R. Hammond, who has studied human judgment and decision making for his entire career. Hammond was one of the first scientists to begin building and evaluating decision support system technology back in the late 1960s. His tutelage greatly affected the perspective of this book.

I also want to thank my wife, Lisa, and my two children, David and Lauren. They have had to endure many countless refrains of "Daddy has to go upstairs to work on his book" over the two years it has taken me to write it. Without their constant love and encouragement, I am certain that I would never have completed this book.

Finally, I want to thank my father, mother, two sisters, their families, and Lisa's family for their constant support from afar. This book is dedicated to my father, Solomon Joseph Adelman, who died when the first draft was less than half completed. The memory of his love kept me going through some dark hours; it will never be forgotten.

LEONARD ADELMAN

Chapter 1

Introduction

Why should one evaluate decision support systems and expert systems? The answer is, quite simply, to increase the probability that they will be used and effective.

1.1 WHAT ARE DECISION SUPPORT SYSTEMS AND EXPERT SYSTEMS?

Ironically, it is necessary to begin this text about evaluation by defining the entity one plans to evaluate. The reason for this is that the term *decision support system* has all too often been used to refer to any computer-based system that supports the thought inherent in decision making. This definition is, however, much too general. It connotes everything, but denotes nothing. More importantly, it conceals the fact that successful decision support systems (and expert systems) are extremely difficult to develop, and that evaluation methods can be used to increase their success rate.

The definitional problem can be traced, in part, to the latter half of 1970s and early 1980s, when "decision support systems" was a new concept coined to capture how technology would revolutionize managerial decision making. According to Morton [1980, p. 77], for example, "The term 'decision support systems' (DSS) refers to the use of computer-based systems, often interactive, to support humans as they make certain types of partially structured decisions." And, according to Keen [1980, p. 35], "It supports, rather than replaces their (managers') judgment. The overall aim is to improve the effectiveness of their decision making." And Wagner [1981, p. 81] concluded, based on the results of a survey conducted with users of a modeling language for building and using decision support systems, that ". . . the real substance of DSS is Executive Mind Support."

All of these definitions are true, in part. The basic assumption is that a decision support system refers to a computer program designed to support the decision-making process by assisting decision makers in thinking about the various aspects of the decision problem(s) facing them, and this is true. But the assumption and the definition are not synonymous. If they were, a management information system, or perhaps even a simple database program, would be a decision support system. After all, the information provided by such programs does help decision makers think about various aspects of their decision problems. And given the ever-increasing power of personal computers and networking capabilities, these programs are now routinely interactive ones. But they are not decision support systems.

Decision support systems are herein defined as interactive computer programs that utilize analytical methods, such as decision analysis, optimization algorithms, program scheduling routines, and so on, for developing models to help decision makers formulate alternatives, analyze their impacts, and interpret and select appropriate options for implementation. This definition is not new. It was inherent in the perspective of Sprague and Carlson [1982], and recently emphasized by Andriole [1989a] and Sage [1986; 1991]. The definition does suggest, however, why successful decision support systems are so difficult to build. The development of software using analytical methods with which the users are often not familiar, and which typically structures problems differently than people do, is not an easy task.

An analogous statement can be made for expert systems. Such systems are interactive computer programs designed to emulate the problem-solving process of one or more experts in a particular problem domain. The typical user of an expert system is not the expert, but more inexperienced personnel. The desire is that less experienced personnel perform up to the level of the expert. The expert system contains a knowledge base, and an inference engine for controlling the processing of this knowledge on the basis of the data under consideration. The output is a conclusion. It, plus the expert system's underlying process, is colloquially represented by if–then rules: If this, then that. The expert system interface has an explanation or tracing capability to help the user understand the system's reasons for its conclusions.

This all sounds easy, and the development of an expert system seems so straightforward. However, the ability to capture expertise, which often cannot be articulated by the experts themselves, and package it in a piece of software for use by individuals without the knowledge to critically evaluate the system's recommendations, has been anything but an easy task. The development period has often been measured in years and costs in tens of person-years. And still the vast majority of expert systems never get past the prototyping stage.

Decision support systems and expert systems have evolved from different disciplines; information systems versus computer science, respectively. They use different types of analytical methods, are often implemented on different types of hardware, and often use different types of software languages. Companies that develop one type seldom develop the other. Developers and researchers alike belong to different professional societies and publish in different journals. In sum, in many ways decision support systems and expert systems represent very different forms of technology.

Yet, decision support and expert systems also have many similarities. First, and foremost, both represent technologies for decision support. They represent a means for aiding the decision maker's problem-solving process. The appropriateness of one versus the other depends on the problem. For example, if the problem requires substantial quantitative reasoning and empirical data, it is more suitably supported by a decision support system containing, for instance, optimization algorithms than an expert system containing judgment heuristics. However, an expert system would be more appropriate than a decision support system if the problem required substantial symbolic reasoning and subjective data.

Because decision support systems and expert systems represent technologies for decision support, they have many other similarities. Three are critical for our purposes. First, both technologies utilize a development approach emphasizing user involvement, iteration, and prototyping. Second, the same general evaluation approach, and many of the same evaluation methods, can be used to evaluate decision support systems and expert systems. And, third, both technologies hold great promise that has yet to be fully realized. We consider the last point now; the other two will be considered throughout this book.

1.2 GREAT PROMISE BUT, THUS FAR, LIMITED SUCCESS

The decreasing cost of hardware and the increasing power of software are making it possible for decision makers to use sophisticated problem-solving techniques. Off-the-shelf decision support system packages and expert system shells are much more affordable than they were just five years ago. Many are now available on personal computers, thereby decreasing the implementation costs and problems that existed, particularly when one needed expensive expert system hardware.

There are clear commercial successes. For example, a decision support system using optimization and scheduling procedures will probably help schedule the dates and times for different events for the 1992 Olympics [Andreu and Corominas, 1989]. Weyerhauser Corporation uses a decision support system employing pattern recognition, optimization, and simulation procedures to cut trees into lumber of various sizes so as to maximize profit [Hehnen et al., 1984]. IBM purchasing personnel use a decision support system employing mixed integer optimization techniques to analyze purchasing strategies under a range of plausible contract conditions [Bender et al., 1985]. Citibank uses an expert system to process loan applications as an experienced administrator would [Keyes, 1989]. Blue Cross/ Blue Shield of South Carolina uses an expert system to process insurance claims [Weitzel and Kerschberg, 1989]. Ford Motor Company uses expert systems to diagnose functional problems with robots [Smith, 1988]; Sumitomo Metal Industries of Japan uses them to monitor on-line network performance [Newquist, 1988].

Moreover, indications are that decision support systems and expert systems have barely impacted their potential market. To quote Wolfgram et al. [1987, p. 21], "Many industry analysts estimate that currently only 10% of potential expert system applications are being recognized . . . " And even after 1988, which Chapnick [1988, p. 5] indicated "won't be considered a banner one for AI . . . , everyone is still predicting relatively high compounded growth rates (greater than 30%) through the mid-1990s." And this estimate does not appear to include mass-market expert systems applications, which combine expert systems technology with traditional applications-oriented software for the mass market. Examples of currently available mass-market expert systems include AskDan for tax preparation, SELL-STAR for sales tracking and advice, Ex-Sample for determining the appropriate sample size for a research project, and STS/Expert for stocks. To quote Eliot [1989, p. 9], "Mass-market applications are the future of the expert-systems industry and will affect applications everywhere."

Yet, the "state of the art" has not yet matched the "state of the expectation" [Andriole, 1989a]. Although there have been successes, the sad fact is that many, if not most, decision support systems and expert systems that are developed are simply not used. According to Casey [1989, p. 44]:

> For every success story, however, many expert-system development projects have failed or are in deep trouble. Many expert systems end up either "dead on arrival" (never work), among the ranks of the unemployed (never used), or serving a life sentence in research and development (never finished).

The Department of Defense has spent millions of dollars on decision support and expert system technology with minimal transfer to operational personnel. Private industry has spent millions of dollars developing expert systems with minimal impact on the size of the work force these expert systems were to replace.

The reasons for this state of affairs lie of course, on both sides of the fence. "Vendors have vested interests in overselling, and users are inclined to want to believe that a solution to all their problems can be found on one or two floppy disks" [Andriole, 1989a, p. 7]. However, a focus on motives obscures the bigger problem. For as Andriole [p. 7] points out, "The truth of the matter is that the state of the art of decision support systems technology is unbalanced and evolving."

What is imbalanced is the fact that decision support system and expert system development is currently technology driven instead of requirements driven. What is evolving is the development of methods for increasing the probability that the system design process will be requirements driven and that, in turn, the system will be used. Evaluation is a critical link in the application of a requirements-driven development cycle, for it provides the information that keeps the development process on track.

1.3 EVALUATION: OFTEN A FORGOTTEN STEP

Evaluation is often the forgotten step in developing decision support and expert systems. That is not meant to imply that it is not found in decision support system and expert system development diagrams; it is. Nor is it meant to imply that computer scientists do not test and evaluate their code as they develop it; they do. What it does imply, however, is that formal and systematic evaluations of decision support and expert systems are not performed throughout the development process. As a result, we lose the opportunity to gain valuable information about what potential users think about the system, how well its code is written, and the extent to which the system really does support decision making early in the development cycle, when changes are, relatively speaking, easy and inexpensive to make.

Andriole [1982] estimated that reliable evaluations were conducted on about only 1 in 10 government-sponsored decision support system development projects. Unfortunately, things are not much better now. There are a variety of reasons for this, as Andriole [1989a, p. 187] indicates:

First, there are always those who are inherently distrustful of structured analyses of any kind, particularly when they challenge conventional wisdom. Many decision support systems have not been evaluated because their designers and users *felt* that the systems were working fine and that everyone *liked* them. If you listen carefully to vendors, you hear these kind of "soft" testimonials all the time. Other systems have gone unevaluated because the projects simply ran out of money.

Unfortunately, some of the evaluations that are performed are undertaken for political, not developmental reasons. In particular, Ruttman [1980; see also Andriole, 1989a] has identified five types of politically oriented evaluations: "eyewash" when the evaluation deliberately focuses on the superficial to make the system look good; "whitewash" when the evaluation attempts to cover up system limitations and/or failures; "submarine" when the evaluation is purposefully negative; "posture" when the evaluation is a ritual with little substance but is required for further funding; and "postponement" when the evaluation is used as a ploy to delay or postpone needed action. Although Ruttman presents these types of evaluations tongue-in-cheek, the development team should determine and be concerned about who set the requirement for an evaluation, and the reasons for it. As Riedel and Pitz[1986, p. 980] point out, "All of this suggests that utilization of evaluation results should be explicitly addressed in the evaluation design. By utilization of evaluation results we mean that the evaluation should have some impact on future development or deployment of the DSS.''

1.4   THE ROLE OF EVALUATION AND THE EVALUATOR

There are two groups of persons that utilize and, indeed, require the results of decision support system and expert system evaluations. The first is the development team. It should include user(s), designers, programmers, and evaluators. For expert system technology, it would also include domain experts and knowledge engineers.

The second group is the sponsoring team. If a decision support system or expert system is being developed only for the use of a particular decision maker, then s/he is both the user and financial sponsor of the system. However, for many decision support system and expert system development efforts, especially those funded by the federal government, the sponsors and users are different groups of people. Satisfying the requirements of one group does not necessarily imply that those of the other group will be met.

Unfortunately, it is often not possible to incorporate sponsors into the development process systematically. In fact, it is often difficult to get users to actively participate as members of the development team, although both research and common sense have demonstrated its importance to successful implementation. Many reasons are given for users' (and sponsors') lack of involvement, including busy schedules, a belief in a hands-off policy during development, lack of desire to be involved,a lack of money, and so forth. Evaluators need to be conscious of this problem and do what they can to solve it in order to increase the probability of successful system development and implementation.

Users and sponsors have specific requirements for the decision support system or expert system under development. For example, they might want the expert system to be totally reliable, easy to use, fast, accurate 90% of the time, and so on. These ''requirements'' represent evaluation criteria or measures of effectiveness (MOEs). Users, sponsors, and developers need to know how well the system is doing in terms of these criteria. To put it simply, is the system measuring up or not?

Answering this question is often problematic because users, sponsors, and developers have different concepts of what a successful system will look like. Sometimes they have different assumptions of what constitutes success on one or more of the criteria; sometimes they will disagree on the definition for the criteria themselves. However, the answer to the above question is critical, for it provides the information that lets everyone know whether the development process is on track. By integrating evaluation methods into the development process, the development team is capable of performing course corrections that will increase the probability that the decision support system or expert system will be used and effective, and decrease the time and cost of development.

The specific evaluation or measurement approach depends on the criterion. Different evaluation criteria require the use of different evaluation methods. For instance, the evaluation method might be (1) logic-based, for testing the logical consistency of the rules in an expert system's knowledge base; (2) empirically based, for testing the predictive accuracy of the knowledge base against the judgmental accuracy of experts or ground-truth measures of accuracy; or (3) subjectively based, such as in using questionnaires to assess users' opinions of the system's strengths and weaknesses. The evaluator must know how to implement different methods in order to provide the required information on different criteria.

In addition, the evaluator must know how to use subjective evaluation methods for identifying and aggregating evaluation criteria. Identifying evaluation criteria is a subjective process. What one user might consider to be a critical criterion, another might fail to mention. Moreover, it is a difficult step, for users are often uncertain of exactly what their decision requirements are. As a result, the identification of evaluation criteria is often a forgotten step early in the decision support system or expert system development process. This can be disastrous, for the development team would be without its guide posts for defining success.

Central to the concept of evaluation is the concept of relative importance weights, or alternative decision rules, for combining good test scores on some evaluation criteria with bad test scores on others. Relative importance weights represent personal judgments. Such judgments should be made by the decision makers, or their representatives, who are sponsoring the development effort, not by the evaluators. This initially might be disturbing to and difficult for members of the sponsoring, development, and evaluation teams, for it emphasizes the subjective process decision makers go through when evaluating the overall value of a decision support system or expert system. However, "there is no way to avoid the fact that the overall MOE [measure of effectiveness] must be based on such judgments, or the fact that no mechanical procedure can replace this subjective assessment . . . "[Riedel and Pitz, 1986, p. 988]. Again, subjective evaluation methods are essential.

User satisfaction is a necessary, but insufficient criterion for evaluation. There are numerous other factors, such as the quality of the decisions made with the system, the logical soundness and appropriateness of its analytical methods, the effectiveness of the match with personnel and organizational characteristics, and so forth, that go into making a good decision support system or expert system. User satisfaction is, however, a necessary condition for use of the system. After all, a system that is not used is of little practical importance regardless of its technical sophistication.

Similarly, user satisfaction is a necessary condition for assessing the adequacy of an evaluation. An evaluation of a system that does not provide information that will significantly help the development team determine if the users of the system will be satisfied with it is an inadequate evaluation. Again the focus is on the user. To quote Riedel and Pitz [1986, p. 994]:

> Similarly, the purpose of the evaluation is to produce information that is useful. This concern for impact on design or policy decisions is the determinant of what evaluation information to obtain. How to obtain that information in a valid manner is left to the expertise of the evaluator.

Good evaluations use explicit methods for helping members of the development and sponsoring teams make the numerous judgments and decisions inherent in system development. This does not imply that developers do not evaluate their systems during development. Informal evaluations are a pervasive activity; developers are always examining and judging system quality and trying to improve it. But these evaluations are often idiosyncratic and ad hoc. And although a small project with technically knowledgeable users and developers might be successful with informal evaluation methods, a large project with technically naive users must rely on formal evaluation methods for success. What is essential to emphasize about the above definition of good evaluations is the systematic application of "explicit and appropriate methods" for making the judgments and decisions inherent in system development.

Most decision support system and expert system development efforts do not use explicit evaluation methods. Doing so will increase the probability of the successful implementation. The evaluator's job is to select the method(s) that are most appropriate for the decision maker's questions, stage of the development process, available funds, and so on. The basic requirement is for an eclectic approach that is based on the evaluation purpose and situation. The goal throughout is to provide guidance in making the judgments and decisions inherent in building decision support and expert systems. It is for this reason that evaluation has been referred to as the control mechanism that keeps the development process on track.

1.5 THE PURPOSE OF THIS BOOK

This is a methods book. The goal is to present an overview of the different methods required to perform effective evaluations of decision support systems and expert systems. The goal is to give readers an understanding of the different methods required to perform effective evaluations, and how to incorporate these procedures into the development process. Perhaps as importantly, it will provide a general perspective on test and evaluation that can also be applied to other system development efforts that are beyond the scope of this text.

It is necessary to make three introductory points in closing this chapter. First, this book assumes that the reader has some working knowledge of what decision support systems and expert systems are, and how to build them. This is not an introductory text on these technologies but, rather, one on how to evaluate them. Most texts on these technologies spend minimal space on how to evaluate them and, therefore, this text can be seen as a companion volume designed to overcome this deficiency. Readers interested in book-length treatments of decision support systems are referred to Andriole [1989a], Sage [1991], and Turban [1990], just to mention a few. Readers interested in expert systems are referred to recent texts by, for example, Harmon et al. [1988], Liebowitz and De Salvo [1989], and Wolfgram et al. [1987].

Second, this is not a cookbook. This is not to say that we will not show you how to perform formal evaluations of decision support and expert system technology; we will. Moreover, we will provide illustrative examples of how to utilize formal evaluation procedures, as well as guidance for helping you apply these procedures to ongoing decision support system and expert system development projects. The last chapter discusses general issues in managing the decision support system and expert system evaluation process. However, we will not offer a step-by-step description of how to perform decision support system and expert system evaluations. Our goal is to present an overview of the range of evaluation methods; provide you with a general understanding of how to implement them; and point you in the right direction for learning more about them.

Third, because evaluation serves as a control mechanism for the development process, readers also need a broad perspective for considering evaluation issues, as well as specific evaluation methods, in order to keep the development process on track. This book will provide readers with such a perspective. Moreover, the text will show readers how the broad perspective and specific methods can be integrated with the decision support system and expert system design and development approach (or "blueprint") being developed by researchers and practitioners alike. Again, pragmatism is the reason for doing so. The goal of evaluation is to produce information that can be used to increase the probability that an effective system will be successfully developed and implemented.

Chapter 2

Evaluation Perspective and Approach: Overview and Case Study

The purpose of this book is to show you how to perform formal evaluations of decision support and expert systems. Such evaluations are eclectic; the selection of evaluation methods is dependent on the stage of the development process, the decision maker, the type of information s/he needs, and so forth. In order to make these choices, evaluators need a broad perspective for considering evaluation issues, as well as specific evaluation methods. We now provide such a perspective, present an overview of the evaluation approach, and offer a case study.

2.1 A DECISION-MAKING PERSPECTIVE

When evaluating decision support systems and expert systems, it is important to remember the obvious, which is that the overall aim of these systems is to improve the effectiveness of the organization using them. Improved organizational effectiveness can occur in many ways, such as through decreased personnel costs, greater access to expert knowledge, or improved decision making. The latter focus is the one emphasized throughout this book.

2.1.1 Decision-Making Paradigms

Simon [1960] has used three categories to describe decision-making activities: intelligence, design, and choice. Intelligence refers to the activities inherent in problem identification, definition, and diagnosis. It is the conscious process of trying to explore the problem in an effort to find out the current state of affairs, and why it does not match our desires. Design refers to those activities inherent in generating alternative solutions or options for solving the problem. It involves ". . . identifying items or actions that could reduce or eliminate the difference between the actual situation and the desired situation" [Huber, 1980, p. 15]. And choice refers to those activities inherent in evaluating and selecting from the alternatives. It is the action that most people think of when one makes a decision.

As Huber [1980] and others [e.g., Andriole, 1989a; Sage, 1986; Wohl, 1981] have pointed out, decision-making activities are a subset of problem-solving activities. Figure 2.1 presents Huber's five-step problem-solving paradigm. The first three steps are those activities that require (1) problem identification, definition, and diagnosis; (2) the generation of alternative solutions; and (3) evaluation and choice from among these alternatives. These steps are conceptually identical to Simon's three decision-making categories. The fourth step in Huber's paradigm involves those activities required to implement the chosen alternative. The fifth step involves reviewing or monitoring the implemented action to see that the alternative was implemented in the way wanted, and that it had the desired results— that is, solved the problem. If there is a significant mismatch between the actual and desired state of affairs, we are back to step 1, exploring the problem.

Although it is presented within the context of military tactical decision making (and aiding), Wohl [1981] has presented a problem-solving paradigm that explicitly identifies the evaluation functions inherent in decision making. Figure 2.2 illustrates Wohl's [1981] SHOR (simulus–hypothesis–option–response) paradigm. Intelligence activities are differentiated between the stimulus and hypothesis elements of the SHOR paradigm. The stimulus element includes data collection, correlation, aggregation, and recall activities; it naturally includes many of the activities also included in Huber's last problem-solving stage, that of monitoring the situation. The hypothesis element is that aspect of intelligence that involves creating alternative hypotheses to explain the cause(s) of the problem, evaluating the

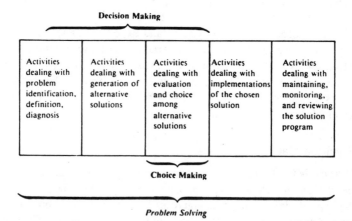

FIGURE 2.1 Huber's five-step problem-solving paradigm

Generic Elements	Functions Required
Stimulus (data) S	Gather/detect
	Filter/correlate
	Aggregate/display
	Store/recall
Hypothesis (perception alternatives) H	Create
	Evaluate
	Select
Option (response alternatives) O	Create
	Evaluate
	Select
Response (action) R	Plan
	Organize
	Execute

FIGURE 2.2 The SHOR paradigm

adequacy of each hypothesis, and selecting one hypothesis as the most likely cause of the data.

On the basis of the selected hypothesis, or hypotheses if one cannot differentiate between hypotheses because of the uncertainty and/or ambiguity in the data, the decision maker generates alternative options for solving the problem. As in Simon's and Huber's paradigms, the option element in the SHOR paradigm differentiates between option creation, evaluation, and selection activities. Finally, on the basis of the selected option, the decision maker takes action. This includes the planning, organization, and execution of a response to the problem, analogous to the fourth step in Huber's problem-solving framework.

The SHOR paradigm deals explicitly with two types of uncertainty in the decision-making process: (1) information input uncertainty, which creates the need for hypothesis generation and evaluation; and (2) consequence-of-action uncertainty, which creates the need for option generation and evaluation. Different elements of the SHOR paradigm become more or less important depending on where uncertainty exists. For instance, if options are clearly prescribed once one knows the cause of the problem, but the meaning of available input data is uncertain, then a premium is placed on creating and testing hypotheses. In contrast, if the cause of the data is clear, but the decision maker is not certain about what to do, then a premium is placed on creating and analyzing options and their consequences.

When evaluating decision support technology, it is important to remember that the decision maker and/or other members of the sponsoring group are in a tactical or strategic decision-making situation, depending on the forecasting and planning horizon under which they are operating. Moreover, the situation can be represented by the SHOR paradigm. For on the basis of available and projected data, members of the sponsoring team are making hypotheses about the nature of the environment that they and their organization will face in the future. That is, they are forecasting the future state of affairs and trying to assess whether their current actions will be effective or not in achieving their future goals and objectives. And they are generating options to deal with their hypotheses regarding potential future performance shortfalls. Given all the stimuli about the dynamic nature of future business and government (particularly military) environments, the ever-increasing role that decision making will play in organizational success, the decreasing financial cost of computer hardware, and the ever-increasing power of computer systems to support decision making, it is not surprising that decision makers in many organizations think that decision support and expert system technologies will be an effective response to their hypotheses about the future.

2.1.2 Evaluation From This Perspective

As decision support system and expert system evaluators, it is critical for us to keep this "big picture" in mind, and to remember that hypotheses about the problem environment and judgments about the relative effectiveness (or utility) of various options are often made under both information input and consequence-of-action uncertainty, respectively. It is necessary to realize that, at the time that it is made, the decision to develop a decision support system or expert system is, in fact, nothing more than a hypothesis that this option will be an effective response to the problem environment. This may or may not be true. Other options, either singularly or in combination with the development of such technology, may actually be better options.

It is easy to assume that decision support systems and expert systems will improve a decision-making group's interaction process and, in turn, organizational performance simply by providing advanced communication and computational capabilities. However, empirical research [e.g., Adelman et al., 1986b; Steiner, 1972; Stumpf et al., 1979] has demonstrated that simply providing the capability for a good interaction process will not ensure high levels of group performance.

Other factors, such as the characteristics of the individual members of the group and the group's composition and reward structure, can have a significant (if not greater) impact on the group's interaction process and performance. Such research findings are, of course, consistent with real-world findings that many decision support systems and expert systems are often not used. Therefore, at the highest decision-making level, the evaluator's job is to help members of the sponsoring team decide whether the option of developing a decision support system or expert system, either singularly or in combination with other actions, is an effective organizational response for dealing with the present and/or future problem environment.

Once the development process is under way, the application of formal evaluation methods helps members of the sponsoring and development teams monitor the perceived utility of the decision support system or expert system under development, and take corrective action to increase the probability of its use and effectiveness. This can be seen by using the SHOR paradigm to represent the development process. Specifically, the development team's job is to plan, organize, and execute the selected option, which in this case is the development of a specific decision support system or expert system. The evaluator's job is to systematically gather, filter, and aggregate data (i.e., stimuli) about the system under development in order to test the hypothesis that all is going well; that is, that the decision support system or expert system will do what decision makers and/or other members of the sponsoring team want it to do. If all is not going well, then one needs to identify the cause of the problem. If it is not clear what action to take, then options need to be generated, evaluated, and selected for correcting the problem(s) so that the development process can be kept on track.

2.2 A MULTIFACETED EVALUATION APPROACH

Evaluation is an iterative process, and one that is consistent with the prototyping approach used in decision support system and expert system development. Moreover, it is one that involves members of both the sponsoring and development teams to various degrees at various stages of development. Consequently, the evaluator needs to be able to use different methods to answer different questions. This requires a multifaceted evaluation approach.

2.2.1 The Approach

The approach has three facets: technical, empirical, and subjective. The technical evaluation facet looks "inside the black box." The empirical evaluation facet assesses the system's effect on performance. The subjective evaluation facet obtains users' opinions regarding system strengths and weaknesses.

The technical phase focuses on evaluating the decision support system or expert system from both an internal (algorithmic and/or heuristic) perspective and an external (systemic input/output) perspective. For example, someone considering the technical evaluation of an expert system might focus only on testing the adequacy of its knowledge base. That is, is the knowledge base logically consistent, functionally complete, and accurate in its predictions? However, one also needs to be concerned with conventional test and evaluation issues. For instance, can the system be effectively and efficiently integrated with other software and hardware systems? Can its data requirements be met? Was it designed consistent with the organization's design and coding standards? And, more generally, was the best analytical modeling method (i.e., artificial intelligence technique) chosen to support the user's decision-making process?

The empirical evaluation focuses on obtaining objective measures of the system's performance. The goal is to assess, for example, whether persons make significantly better or faster decisions or use significantly more information working with rather than without the system, and to identify mechanisms for improving performance if the system fails to measure up on these criteria. It is important to note that the potential users of expert system technology may not be experts in the substantive domain. In these cases, one needs both experts and users to participate in the evaluation. The experts are needed for the technical evaluation of the knowledge base; the users for the empirical evaluation of system performance. If possible, experts should also participate in the empirical evaluation in order to systematically assess whether system performance is a function of user type. In addition, as will be illustrated in the case study presented later in this chapter, participation of domain experts in the empirical evaluation often provides insight into the functional completeness and predictive accuracy of the knowledge base.

The subjective evaluation phase focuses on evaluating the decision support system or expert system from the perspective of potential users. The goal is to determine whether the users generally like the decision support system or expert system; what they consider to be its relative strengths and weaknesses; and what changes they would suggest for improving it. Most of the suggestions will focus on improving the user interface, both in terms of its ease of use and compatibility with the background, training, and needs of the user. Also, as will be discussed below, evaluators should anticipate that a number of suggestions will be directed toward improving the system's fit into the organization. If the system is not tailored to fit into an organization's formal and informal operational procedures, it can seldom be used effectively and is often not used at all.

2.2.2   Verification and Validation

For definitional purposes, it is essential at the outset to compare the multifaceted approach with the terms *verification* and *validation*. Technical evaluation methods, which are directed toward looking inside the "black box," represent verification methods. Empirical evaluation methods, in contrast, are directed toward assessing whether the system actually improves the decision maker's performance; consequently, they represent validation methods. And subjective evaluation methods have a role in both verification and validation, although their use is primarily reserved for the latter.

There is not, however, uniform agreement with the definitions for verification and validation. Part of the reason for the confusion is that, in terms of general usage, the words verify and validate mean the same thing. *Webster's Dictionary* [1966] lists the single word *confirm* as the synonym for both. Computer scientists and system engineers have chosen to use the words to refer to different points of reference. To quote Kirk and Murray [1988, pp. 5-5 and 5-6, capitalizations and italics theirs]:

> VERIFICATION refers to *internal correctness*. It pertains to the absence of coding bugs and logical flaws, as well as other mistakes made by the builders in translating their original plan into a detailed design and coding it. . . . VALIDATION, on the other hand, refers to *external correctness* which is manifest in correct or desired output when the system is operating in a realistic environment.

The problem is that it is often unclear what point of reference represents "external correctness" (versus "internal correctness") and, thus, the dividing line between validation and verification. For example, software engineers often use the term validation when referring to whether or not the system meets technical system requirements, not whether it actually improves user performance in an operational setting. Similarly, they sometimes use validation to refer to the collection of empirical data for assessing technical performance characteristics of the software, such as system response time, not whether users can perform the task faster with the new system. System response time and task performance time are not always correlated. In addition, knowledge engineers use the terms verification and validation to refer to assessing the adequacy of different aspects of a knowledge base.

Therefore, in an effort to avoid confusion, we will try to refrain from using the terms verification and validation. Instead, we will simply focus on the three classes of evaluation methods, and discuss how they can be used to evaluate the system on different criteria.

2.2.3 Three Conceptual Interfaces

Research over the last decade or so indicates that evaluators must monitor the compatibility of the decision support system or expert system under development with the characteristics and needs of the broader organization, as well as that of the individual user for which it is being developed. Huber [1986] and others have emphasized this point. To quote Huber: "A number of conceptual and prescriptive articles advance the perspective that the designs of management information systems and decision support systems should be compatible with the structures and processes of the organizations in which these systems reside. . . ." The classic article by Ackoff on "management misinformation systems" [Ackoff 1967] was perhaps the first to make highly visible the need to develop management information systems (MIS) that fit the organization's decision and control systems. Another article critical of the incongruity between organizational needs and the then-current information systems technology was Dearden's "MIS is a Mirage" [Dearden 1972]. "Pieces more explicit in their approaches for designing information systems suited to the organization's processes have appeared in the last decade (cf., King and Clelland, 1975; Markus, 1984)" [Huber, 1986, p. 580].

Consistent with this research, Adelman et al. [1982] have pointed out that the decision support system and expert system development process needs to be monitored from the perspective of three interfaces: the extent to which the system fits the characteristics of the individuals who are going to use it, the structure and processes of the organization within which it will reside, and the demands of the problem environment affecting the organization's performance. This is represented pictorially in Figure 2.3.

The first interface is between the system and the user. Here the issue is the extent to which characteristics of the decision support system or expert system facilitate or hinder its usability. The second interface is between the user (and system) and the larger decision-making organization of which both are a part. Here the issue is to what extent the decision support system or expert system facilitates the decision-making process of the organization. The third interface is between

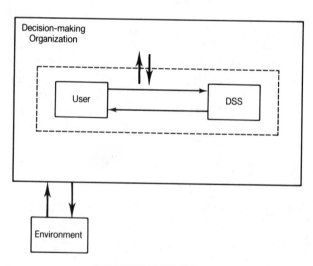

THREE INTERFACES TO BE EVALUATED

FIGURE 2.3 The three interfaces to monitor and evaluate when developing decision support and expert system technology

the decision-making organization and the outside environment with which it interacts. For instance, if the organization was a company, then its "environment" would be its competitive environment, including other companies, the state of the economy, the demand for its products, and so on. If it was a military, combat organization, its "environment" would be its combat environment. The critical issue is whether the decision support system or expert system improves the organization's decision making and, in turn, its overall performance.

These three types of interfaces are not independent; in fact, they are nested. The effectiveness of the organizational interface is necessarily influenced by the effectiveness of the user interface; the effectiveness of the environmental interface is necessarily influenced by the effectiveness of the other two. Nevertheless, the three interfaces do have different implications for the measures of effectiveness used to evaluate them. These measures of effectiveness represent the evaluation criteria.

2.2.4 Measures of Effectiveness

If an evaluation is to be effective, the evaluator must decide in advance what is to be tested. This is done by identifying measures of effectiveness designed to answer the evaluator's questions. These questions depend on who needs the information—that is, whether it is a member of the development or sponsoring team—the type of information needed, the stage of the development process, the interface being evaluated, and so forth. The resulting effectiveness measures may be either objective or subjective variables depending on the selected evaluation method, a point that will be returned to later in the chapter. The only restrictions are that each measure of effectiveness must be measurable and that it must provide the required information. Alternatively, these effectiveness measures must be correlated (positively or negatively) with the overall utility of the decision support system or expert system.

Table 2.1 presents the hierarchy of subjective measures of effectiveness used in the case study presented later in this chapter. This hierarchy was developed by Adelman and Donnell [1986] in order to evaluate the adequacy of five different decision support system prototypes, including three expert systems, developed to support U.S. Air Force tactical decision making. We use the term *subjective measures of effectiveness* because a questionnaire was used to assess each prototype's performance on the effectiveness measures.

The effectiveness measures presented in Table 2.1 are organized into a hierarchy such that the three uppermost levels represent the three interfaces in Figure 2.3: user interface, organizational interface, and environment interface. The topmost level of the hierarchy represents the decision support system's or expert system's overall utility or value to the decision maker and organization for whom it is being built. Each of the three uppermost levels of evaluation categories is subdivided further until it is easy to identify distinctly measurable "measures of

TABLE 2.1   Hierarchy of Measures of Effectiveness (MOEs) and the Number of Questions Assessing Bottom-Level MOEs[a]

0.0   Overall Utility (6)

1.0 DSS–User Interface	2.0 User-DSS-Organization	3.0 Organization–Environment
1.1 Match with personnel	2.1 Efficiency factors	3.1 Decision accuracy (8)
1.1.1 Training and technical background (3)	2.1.1 Time	3.2 Match between DSS' technical approach and problem's requirements (7)
1.1.2 Work style, work load, and interest (4)	2.1.1.1 Task accomplishment (3)	3.3 Decision process quality
1.1.3 Operational needs (5)	2.1.1.2 Data management (2)	3.3.1 Quality of framework for incorporating judgment (2)
1.2 DSS's characteristics	2.1.1.3 Setup requirements (2)	3.3.2 Range of alternatives (2)
1.2.1 General	2.1.2 Perceived reliability under average battle conditions (2)	3.3.3 Range of objectives (2)
1.2.1.1 Ease of use (4)	2.1.2.1 Skill availability (3)	3.3.4 Weighing of consequences of alternatives (2)
1.2.1.2 Understanding (3)	2.1.2.2 Hardware availability (2)	3.3.5 Assessment of consequences of alternatives (3)
1.2.1.3 Each of training (2)	2.2 Match with organizational factors	3.3.6 Reexamination of decision-making process (3)
1.2.1.4 Response time (2)	2.2.1 Effect on organizational procedures and structure (2)	3.3.7 Use of information (3)
1.2.2 Specific	2.2.2 Effect on other people's position in the organization	3.3.8 Consideration of implementation and contingency plans (2)
1.2.2.1 User interface (2)	2.2.2.1 Political acceptability (2)	3.3.9 Effect on group discussions (3)
1.2.2.2 Data files (3)	2.2.2.2 Other people's work load (2)	3.3.10 Effect on decision makers' confidence (2)
1.2.2.3 Expert judgments (2)	2.2.3 Effect on information flow (2)	
1.2.2.4 Ability to modify judgments	2.2.4 Side effects	
1.2.2.5 Automatic calculations (2)	2.2.4.1 Value in performing other tasks (2)	
1.2.2.6 Graphs (2)	2.2.4.2 Value to SAC[b] or other services (2)	
1.2.2.7 Printouts (2)	2.2.4.3 Training value (2)	
1.2.2.8 Text (2)		

[a]From Adelman and Donnell [1986].
[b]SAC stands for Strategic Air Command.

effectiveness.'' By assuming that each terminal node in the hierarchy could be translated into a measure of effectiveness, the task of evaluating a decision support system or expert system is translated into one of assigning scores to the bottom-level nodes of the evaluation hierarchy. By then weighing the relative importance of the individual measures of effectiveness and the broader effectiveness categories moving up the hierarchy, one obtains an explicit, retraceable process for evaluating the overall value and relative strengths and weaknesses of the system.

The measures in Table 2.1 will be considered in more detail in the case study. For now, it is important to make three points. First, the specific measure(s) of effectiveness you select as criteria for evaluating a decision support system or expert system should be determined from a decision-making perspective. What information is needed? Who needs it? What stage is the system development process in? In addition, you need to consider how these questions, as well as potentially limiting factors (e.g., funds, time, personnel, etc.) affect the selection of testing methods. Remember, the selection of a particular method is a decision in and of itself, for methods themselves differ on various dimensions, such as the generalizability of their data to real-world settings, their costs, the amount of control the evaluator has in implementing them, and so forth. Evaluators need to consider systematically the technical trade-offs, limiting factors, and decision-making perspective when selecting test and evaluation methods.

Second, an eclectic approach is required to test and evaluate decision support systems and expert systems effectively. As Riedel and Pitz [1986] point out, many people erroneously assume that objective, empirical measurement is the most valid and, therefore, preferred type of data to collect. However, the preference for a particular type of data depends on the relative importance of the individual "measure of effectiveness'' being measured by that data. If the user's performance in solving test cases with—versus without—the system is the most important effectiveness measure, then objective empirical data will be the most important type of data to collect. However, if the user's opinion of the system is the most important effectiveness measure, which it often is early in development, then subjective data will be the most crucial type of data to collect at that time. Moreover, aggregation of all the test data to make an overall evaluation of the system is inherently a subjective judgment.

Decision support systems and expert systems can be tested on many different kinds of MOEs. Different testing methods and, thus, types of data are appropriate for different measures of effectiveness. The methods used to test the logical consistency of the knowledge base are different than those used to test the user's performance with the expert system or how well the software is written or what the users think of the reasoning trace. The multifaceted approach presented herein represents the kind of eclectic approach required to test and evaluate expert systems comprehensively. This book reviews a range of subjective, technical, and empirical methods for testing decision support systems and expert systems on measures of effectiveness that are routinely important to members of the sponsoring team.

Third, the hierarchy of measures of effectiveness presented in Table 2.1, when combined with relative importance weights, represents an application of multiattribute utility technology (MAUT). MAUT, as well as other subjective evaluation methods, will be considered in detail in this text. What is important to note here is that the MAUT framework helps delineate the evaluator's job. In particular, the evaluator's job should be limited to three distinct roles.

First, the evaluator needs to work with users and members of the sponsoring team to define the measurement of effectiveness hierarchy. This is not as difficult a technical task as it may appear, for it is primarily one of definition and clarification; that is, defining exactly what it is one wants to know, and clarifying imprecise general terms into precise and highly specific ones. Moreover, there are techniques for structuring multiattributed hierarchies, and these will be considered in Chapter 4.

It can, however, be surprisingly difficult persuading users and members of the sponsoring team to perform this task. Just like "user involvement," there is often some legitimate reason for why some other activity is more important. It is all too easy for them to say that you, as the evaluator, should go off and define the evaluation criteria, that is, measures of effectiveness. However, as with the requirements analysis—with which this first evaluation task should go hand-in-hand—do not be put off if at all possible. It is essential that the evaluator work with the users and sponsoring team members to define the criteria for assessing the system's overall value, for in the end, they and not you will determine whether the decision support system or expert system is acceptable.

Second, the evaluator needs to test the system on each of the bottom-level measures in the hierarchy. For this reason, evaluation personnel are sometimes referred to as "testers." You will have to select the evaluation methods for assessing how well the system is doing on each bottom-level measure. As has been emphasized throughout, different methods are appropriate for measuring evaluation criteria.

With this knowledge in mind, evaluators need to work with users and sponsoring team members to define the bottom-level measures in the hierarchy. For, to a large extent, the bottom-level measures are defined by the measurement method. For example, one could define response time objectively as the amount of the time, on the average, between the user's inputs and the system's outputs. Or one can define it subjectively, as was done in the evaluations represented in Table 2.1, in terms of the (averaged) judgment of users. The distinction is important and, whenever possible and appropriate, made in conjunction with users and sponsoring team members.

And, third, the evaluator needs to combine the decision support system's or expert system's scores on all the bottom-level measures into an overall measure of system utility or value to the users and sponsors. Notice the emphasis on overall system utility, not overall system performance. A system's overall performance could be exceptionally good and, yet, the system might be considered of low utility because it was not well tailored to the characteristics of the personnel who would use it and/or the organizational context within which it would reside.

All the effectiveness measures in the hierarchy, moving from the bottom level up to the top, need to be assigned relative importance weights (or some other decision rule) to obtain an overall assessment of the system's utility. If the bottom-level measures combine to form some technical measure of effectiveness, then the evaluator's technical expertise is required to weight or, in some other manner, combine the system's scores on the individual bottom-level measures into a score on a general evaluation criterion moving up the hierarchy. However, in most cases, it will be the sponsoring team (and user's) job to assign the relative importance weights to the general evaluation categories of which the bottom-level measures are a part. For instance, with respect to Table 2.1, the users and sponsoring team members should indicate the relative importance of match with personnel (node 1.1) and the quality of DSS [decision support system] characteristics (node 1.2) in determining the quality of the DSS–user interface (node 1.0). Similarly, they should indicate the relative importance of the DSS–user interface (node 1.0), the user-DSS–organization interface (node 2.0), and the organization–environment interface (node 3.0) in determining the overall utility (node 0.0) of the system.

Here too, users and sponsoring team members may be reluctant to participate fully. After all, they may require that all the requirements be met; that the system score perfectly on all measures. However, this requirement is seldom satisfied for the finished product, let alone for prototypes. Moreover, as will be discussed in detail in the concluding chapter, the relative importance weights represent importance guideposts for managing both the evaluation and development process. They convey to all involved what aspects of the system are most important to users and sponsors and, consequently, in which areas the system must shine.

An application of the multifaceted evaluation approach will now be described.

2.3 A CASE STUDY

The first subsection below describes the background for the case study. The remaining three subsections describe the technical, empirical, and subjective evaluations, in turn.

2.3.1 Background

Over the 24-month period from September 1981 to September 1983, PAR Technology Corporation was the prime contractor to the Rome Air Development Center (RADC) on a contract designed to develop five decision-aiding prototypes for supporting U.S. Air Force (USAF) tactical decision making. Two were decision support system prototypes using decision analytic procedures as their principal analytical method. Three of the prototypes were expert systems; one of these also employed an optimization algorithm and, therefore, could be considered a "hybrid" system.

Four tasks were performed on this project. Task I was a detailed study of the various activities, and their functions, performed in USAF tactical decision making. The study was performed with a view toward defining potential aiding situations in which the technologies of artificial intelligence, decision analysis, and operations research might be applied to aid decision making. In Task II, 28 prototypes were proposed for development. The proposals were subjected to a two-phase utility analysis and to a cost-benefit analysis in order to identify the five prototypes that would be developed on the project. These five decision support prototypes were developed by PAR and its subcontractors (Decisions and Designs, Inc. and Systems Control Technology, Inc.) in Task III. Different companies built different prototypes on the basis of the match between the technical requirements of the prototypes and the technical skills of company personnel. All five prototypes were evaluated in Task IV by a test and evaluation team led by the author.

This section overviews the technical, empirical, and subjective evaluation of the Duplex Army Radio/Radar Targeting (DART) prototype. DART was an expert system built by PAR [see Figgins et al., 1983] to assist intelligence personnel identify different types of activity nodes for subsequent air strikes. An activity node might be a command post or any of a number of various weapon systems containing radars that might be detected by sensors belonging to friendly forces. Activity node identification is extremely difficult to perform because of the many kinds of nodes of interest on the battle field, and the tremendous volume and speed with which relevant data is received about them. Because of limited time and potential information overload, experience has become increasingly critical to accurate activity node identification.

There are, however, few analysts with the necessary experience. An expert system represented a means of capturing activity node identification expertise, and making it available to less experienced analysts. The DART prototype was to contain enough expert knowledge to identify (with a degree of certainty) 13 different types of activity nodes. More importantly, the DART prototype had to be able to communicate the rationale for the identification effectively, because it was to support the analyst's decision-making process, not replace it.

The results for each of the three evaluation facets are now considered, in turn. Three general points must be emphasized at the outset. First, there were limited funds and time to perform the evaluations. The evaluation activities for all five prototypes—from initial planning, to conducting the tests and performing the analysis, to documenting the results—had to be conducted for approximately 10% of the project's total cost.

Moreover, the actual testing of all five prototypes had to be conducted in seven months. The prototypes had to be evaluated sequentially, consistent with the participating contractors' development schedule. For example, DART was the second prototype developed and evaluated; it was evaluated in the second month of the testing period. Thus, the evaluation process had to be designed, conceptually, like an assembly line in order to evaluate all five prototypes within time and funding constraints. Furthermore, the process needed to be kept as similar as possible for all five prototypes so that developers could not argue that they had been treated differently or, perhaps more accurately, unfairly if their prototype did not score well.

Second, consistent with the perspective of integrating test and evaluation results into development, each prototype was tested twice. The first test was with engineers at RADC who were novices in the prototype's domain area, but who had a college degree emphasizing computer science or engineering. The second test was with experts in the substantive domain that the prototype was designed to support. There were always at least two weeks between the two tests to provide the development team with some time to enhance the prototype based on the feedback obtained in the first test session.

And, third, the overall purpose of the evaluation of DART and the other four prototypes developed on the contract was to determine which ones showed the greatest potential value to the Air Force and, hence, should go on to further development. Consequently, efforts were made to standardize the evaluations of the five prototypes as much as possible. This fact, plus time, money, and scheduling constraints for the evaluations, resulted in the decision to emphasize the subjective and empirical evaluation phases over the technical one.

Each prototype was subjected to an experiment to test whether the system improved users' performance. Second, the table of subjective measures of effectiveness presented in Table 2.1 was used to obtain participants' opinions of the prototypes' strengths and weaknesses. Last, each evaluation session concluded with a roundtable meeting between sponsoring team members and the experts who evaluated the prototype. This further helped the sponsors determine whether the prototype was good enough to warrant further funding. This illustrates that the evaluation team saw their overriding purpose to be providing the sponsors with the stimuli necessary to test the hypothesis that the prototype would (or would not) improve organizational effectiveness and, consistent with the SHOR paradigm, to select the appropriate option(s) for proceeding in the future.

The following overview is based on Adelman and Donnell [1986]; more specific details can be found in Adelman and Gates [1983].

2.3.2 Technical Evaluation

The technical evaluation of the DART expert system prototype took place at PAR's corporate headquarters in New Hartford, New York, in late January 1983. The first issue, which was actually considered early in the development process [Rockmore et al., 1982] was whether artificial intelligence was an appropriate analytical method to select for the activity node identification problem. The answer was an affirmative one. Consistent with the SHOR paradigm, the user's job is to evaluate and select hypotheses regarding activity nodes. Artificial intelligence is ideally suited for this requirement.

The technical evaluation focused primarily on the system characteristics of DART's many modules. These modules are represented in Figure 2.4 from a functional perspective. The most visible portion of the system is the executive, which assists the user in managing the aid. The executive consists of

- The inference engine
- The advice interpreter
- The model manager
- The display manager

Based on a selected goal hypothesis (one of the 13 identifiable activity nodes), the inference engine accesses that portion of the inference network that will analyze the pertinent, available information concerning the goal. The rules contained in this selected segment of the inference network use the data (or evidence) found in the message and associated degrees of belief from the evidence manager to identify the most likely activity node. The advice interpreter advises the user of the degree of belief for this identified activity node. Additionally, the user can consult the advice interpreter for the evidence used in reaching this decision.

Once advised, the user can call the graphics display via the display manager or

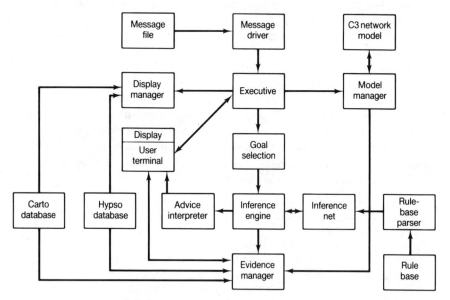

FIGURE 2.4   DART functional overview

call the model manager to update the activity node identification model. The display manager provides the means to display terrain data; the model manager places identified activity nodes on this terrain. The message file and driver provide a time-sequenced list of reports that the analyst can use to correlate multiple reports of the same activity node, thereby increasing the confidence in the activity node recommended by the system.

In brief, the evaluation team concluded that, from a technical perspective, the DART prototype contained all of the modules necessary for a consultative expert system to support the activity node identification, decision-making process. The experts who participated in the empirical and subjective evaluations supported this position, for although they recommended many improvements, they neither recommended additional modules nor deletions of those already developed for the DART prototype.

The logical consistency, functional completeness, and predictive accuracy of the knowledge base were considered as part of the empirical evaluation with the experts. Ideally, the evaluation team would have measured DART against these evaluation criteria using the methods for evaluating the knowledge base described in Chapter 5. Again, however, the timing and funding constraints of the project did not make this possible.

2.3.3 Empirical Evaluation

The goal of the empirical evaluation phase was to assess objectively whether DART significantly improved the accuracy of analysts performing the target identification process. To accomplish this goal, an experiment was performed. The three independent variables were (1) whether the analyst was experienced or not in activity node identification, (2) whether the analyst performed the activity node identification task with or without DART, and (3) which of two different activity node identification problems the analyst performed. The dependent variable was the quality of the analyst's solution to the activity node identification problem.

The test setting for the empirical evaluation was created concurrently with the performance of the technical evaluation. An isolated room 12 feet × 14 feet was used for the unaided condition. A smaller room with a computer terminal and DeAnza display, both of which were linked to a VAX 11/780 system, was used for the aided condition. (Note: Operational versions of DART and the other prototypes were to be tailored for military microcomputers on subsequent procurements at the government's discretion.) Both test areas had 1:500,000 and 1:250,000 scale charts of the geographic area of interest used in the activity node identification problems.

The participant's task for each of the two problem scenarios was to identify ground components of opposing forces moving in a specified direction over the area of interest on the basis of message data. The problems differed in the number of each of 13 possible activity node types and the available message data. In the first problem there were 100 messages; in the second, 80.

Each participant had 1½ hours to perform each problem regardless of whether s/he worked with or without DART. The activity nodes identified by each participant were placed on acetate and overlaid on the large wall map representing the geographic area for which the problem scenarios were created. Since a correct solution existed for each scenario,it was possible to determine the number, location, and type of correctly identified activity nodes. Using this information and looking at the acetate overlay map, the experts then rated the quality of each participant's solution for each scenario on a 0 to 10 scale, where higher scores meant a better solution. Qualitative ratings were required because all misclassifications were not equally detrimental; the solution's quality depended on an analyst's judgment as to the importance of the type and location of the misclassifications.

We would have preferred that the experts not rate their own solutions. However, since we had to do the ratings in a group setting because of time and logistics constraints, we told the experts to rate their own solutions in order not to reveal the solution's author inadvertently. Each participant's solution was coded by letter to minimize the experts' ability to identify its author.

The empirical and subjective evaluations were conducted at PAR's corporate headquarters in New Hartford, New York, over two four-day periods in February and March 1983. The participants for the first session were RADC personnel who had no activity node identification experience; these four participants are referred to as nonexperts. The participants for the second session were U.S. Air Force analysts with considerable activity node identification experience; these three participants are referred to as experts. The participants were provided through the cooperation and courtesy of different Air Force agencies. Although the sample size was small for an empirical evaluation, it was as large as could be obtained given prior Air Force commitments. Larger sample sizes should be used whenever possible to provide the power necessary for traditional statistical tests of a prototype's effectiveness [e.g., see Adelman et al., 1982].

The session with the nonexperts resulted in three principal findings, each of which had implications for the session with the experts. First, the nonexperts did not have enough hands-on training to use DART to solve the scenario effectively. Consequently, the experts' schedule was modified to ensure that they had enough training. Second, DART was slow and cumbersome to use because it required the user to update the model manager and display manager after each message by sequentially accessing a number of menus. Consequently, DART was modified to permit the user to automatically update the model manager and display manager after each message, thereby making DART much easier and faster to use. And third, the message flow in the unaided task was found to be unrepresentative of the real environment. Consequently, the message flow was modified for the session with the experts so that it better represented their environment.

The results of the session with the nonexperts were not included in the empirical and subjective evaluations of DART. So many changes were made to the test conditions and DART user interface between sessions that, before the session with the experts, the evaluation team concluded that it was inappropriate to combine the results of the two sessions. However, it is of import to note here that the cumulative effect of the three classes of problems described above resulted in the nonexperts performing the activity node classification task worse with than without DART at a statistically significant ($p < 0.05$) level. *Integrating the feedback* from the tests with the nonexperts back into the development process *significantly improved the DART prototype.*

The schedule for the DART evaluation session with the experts proceeded as described below over the four-day evaluation period. Monday morning was dedicated to providing a technical overview of DART so that the experts would understand how DART performed activity node identification. On Monday afternoon and most of Tuesday, the experts received hands-on training in using DART. This was accomplished by providing each expert with two 1½-hour training sessions on DART. The DART test scenarios were completed by the experts on Tuesday and Wednesday. Two of the experts worked the first scenario in the unaided condition, and one used DART. In contrast, two experts worked the second scenario using DART and one worked without it. This arrangement ensured that each expert had used DART to solve one scenario, and that there were three aided and three unaided solutions in total.

On Thursday, the experts rated the quality of the solutions generated by the nonexperts and experts for each scenario. The experts' ratings were based on the number, location, and type of both correctly and incorrectly identified activity nodes. The participants also completed the evaluation questionnaires and discussed their impressions of DART's strengths and weaknesses with members of PAR's evaluation team and RADC personnel monitoring the contract.

The experts' quality ratings of the experts' solutions, and the conditions under which they were generated, are presented in Table 2.2. The higher the number, the better the quality rating. Pearson product-moment correlations (r) were calculated to determine the extent of agreement among the three experts' ratings. Correlations can vary from $+1.0$, indicating perfect agreement, to -1.0, indicating perfect disagreement; a value of 0 indicates that there is no relationship be-

TABLE 2.2   The Experts' Quality Ratings for Their Solutions With and Without DART

Scenario 1					Scenario 2				
	E1	*E2*	*E3*	*Mean*		*E1*	*E2*	*E3*	*Mean*
A (Unaided)	3	5	3	3.67	A (Aided)	6	8	7	7.0
B (Unaided)	8	8	8	8.0	B (Unaided)	9	9	9	9.0
C (Aided)	5	7	7	6.33	C (Aided)	7	8	8	7.67

tween the ratings. The correlations were computed by combining the ratings for both scenarios, thereby creating a sample size of six (instead of three) and, in turn, greater confidence in the results. The correlations between the quality ratings of experts E1 and E2, E1 and E3, and E2 and E3, were 0.94, 0.93, and 0.97, respectively. All three correlations were statistically significant at the $p < .01$ level, thus indicating that there was considerable agreement among the experts' quality ratings of the solutions.

The mean quality rating and the sample size for each of the four cells in the 2 (aid) × 2 (scenario) design for the experts' solutions are presented in Table 2.3. As can be seen, there are only three observations each in the aided-scenario I and unaided-scenario II cells. This occurred because, since only three experts participated in the evaluation, two cells of the design could only have one participant if each expert was to (1) perform each scenario only once and (2) work both with and without DART. The aided-scenario I and unaided-scenario II conditions, and the expert who worked them, were randomly selected by the evaluation team. Table 2.3 shows a sample size of three observations for these two cells because each of the three experts independently evaluated the one expert's solution. The unaided-scenario I and aided-scenario II cells have a sample size of six observations because each of the three experts independently evaluated the two experts' solutions for these two cells.

The question of interest was, of course, whether the solutions generated by the experts when they worked with DART were better than without it. The answer was no. The average quality rating for the aided solutions was 7.0; it was 6.89 for the unaided solutions. Even assuming that each rating was an independent observation would not result in this difference being statistically different with such a small number of experts.

An additional analysis was performed in an effort to better understand why there was no difference in the performance of experts working with and without DART. This aspect of the empirical demonstration illustrates but one of a number of different methods that will be considered later in this book for testing the predictive accuracy of an expert system's knowledge base. In particular, the evaluation team

TABLE 2.3   Experts' Mean Quality Ratings and Sample Size for the 2 (DSS) × 2 (Scenario) Matrix for the Experts' Solutions

	Scenario I	Scenario II	$\bar{x}$
Aided	$N = 3$	$N = 6$	$N = 9$
	6.33	7.33	7.00
Unaided	$N = 6$	$N = 3$	$N = 9$
	5.83	9.00	6.89
$\bar{x}$	$N = 9$	$N = 9$	$N = 18$
	6.00	7.89	6.95

counted the number of mistakes the experts made for the 13 different activity nodes in the two scenarios, both with and without DART. Although no statistical tests were performed because of the small size for each node, examination of the mean scores suggested that, when aided, the experts were better in identifying certain activity nodes, and worse in identifying others. This suggests that (1) DART's rule base for identifying certain activity nodes, needed improvement; and (2) that such improvement would result in experts performing the scenarios better with than without DART. There were, however, insufficient time and funds to make the necessary changes to the knowledge base and subsequently test whether these changes did, in fact, improve performance with DART.

2.3.4 Subjective Evaluation

The subjective evaluation of DART was comprised of the experts' answers to two questionnaires. The first was of a short-answer format with the questions designed to assess the expert system's performance on the subjective measures of effectiveness presented in Table 2.1. The second questionnaire had an open-ended format that gave the experts an opportunity to indicate, without any prompting from the evaluation team, what they perceived to be the strengths and weaknesses of the DART prototype and recommend improvements to it.

We will only present the results obtained from the first questionnaire for two reasons. First, there was general agreement between the answers to the two questionnaires; consequently, it is unnecessary to present the results to both of them here. Second, the short-answer questionnaire had been standardized so that, except for substantive changes unique to DART, the same questionnaire could be used to assess participants' impressions of the strengths and weaknesses of each of the five prototypes developed on the contract. Consequently, the short-answer questionnaire represented the first step in developing an empirically based questionnaire that could be used by other people evaluating decision support and expert system technology. This focus, as well as the detailed analysis of the questionnaire for all five of the prototypes developed on the contract, can be found in Adelman, et al. [1985].

Before describing the questionnaire, we will briefly describe the measurement of effectiveness hierarchy to facilitate readers' consideration of how to develop ones appropriate to their development projects. In particular, the categories were designed to be as general as possible so that the same measures of effectiveness could be used to evaluate each prototype. To accomplish this, Adelman and Donnell [1986] refined and expanded the hierarchy of evaluation criteria initially developed by Sage and White [1980] to be compatible with the three-interface perspective presented in the previous section of this chapter. In doing so, they used as many of the criteria as possible that were used earlier in the contract when deciding which prototypes to develop in the first place. Other measures of effectiveness could (and would), of course, be used in an evaluation, depending on the characteristics of the system and the concerns of members of the sponsoring and development teams.

Measures of effectiveness assessing the quality of the user interface were divided into two major groups of criteria: those that assessed the match between the system and potential user's background, work style, and operational needs; and those that assessed the adequacy of the system's characteristics. This latter group was composed of general characteristics, such as its ease of use and response time, and specific characteristics, such as the adequacy of the expert system's knowledge base, graphic displays, hard-copy capabilities, and text.

Measures of effectiveness assessing the quality of the user-system–decision-making organization interface were divided into two groups of criteria: those assessing the system's efficiency from an organizational perspective, and those assessing the system's fit into the organization. Efficiency criteria included the amount of time it took to use the system to accomplish the task it was supporting (this is distinctly different than its response time), data management and setup time requirements, and, pertinent to the present application, the system's perceived reliability and supportability under battle conditions. Criteria focusing on the system's potential effect on organizational procedures, other people's work, the flow of information, and its value in performing other tasks were used to assess the system's fit into the organization for which it was being developed.

Measures of effectiveness assessing the quality of the decision-making organization–environment interface were grouped into three major criteria: the perceived quality of decisions obtained using the system; the extent to which the system's technical approach matched the technical requirements of the task; and the extent to which the system improved the quality of the decision-making process. This last group of criteria was quite broad, ranging from the extent to which the system helped the user survey a wide range of alternatives and objectives, to the degree to which it increased or decreased the user's confidence in the decision.

We now turn to describing the short-answer questionnaire. Specifically, the questionnaire had 121 questions. Most of the questions assessed the bottom-level effectiveness measures in Table 2.1; however, six questions directly assessed overall utility (node 0.0 in Table 2.1), two questions directly assessed decision process quality (node 3.3), and three questions each assessed the quality of the training sessions and the test scenarios (neither of which are measures of system effectiveness, but were of concern to the evaluation team). All questions required the participant to respond on a 11-point scale from 0 (very strongly disagree) to 10 (very strongly agree), with 5 being "neither disagree nor agree."

There were two or more questions for each bottom-level, measurement criterion in an effort to achieve greater confidence in the criterion scores. The number in the parentheses to the right of each bottom-level measure in Table 2.1 indicates the number of questions used to assess it. The actual number depended on the availability of previously written questions assessing the measurement criterion [e.g., from Sage and White, 1980], the ease in writing "different-sounding" questions for the criterion, and its depth in the hierarchy.

Half the questions for each criterion were presented in each half of the questionnaire in an effort to ensure that the obtained scores did not depend on where the questions were in the questionnaire. In most cases, a high score indicated good performance, but typically for one question measuring each criterion, a low score indicated good performance in an effort to assure that the participants paid careful attention to the questions. A prototype's score on a bottom-level criterion was the mean score of the participants' responses to the questions assessing it. The values for criteria higher in the hierarchy were determined by calculating the mean score for the criteria below them.

It is important to make three technical notes at this point. First, by averaging bottom-level criterion scores to obtain upper-level criterion scores, the relative importance weight given to the bottom-level criteria depended on the number of bottom-level criteria comprising a more general evaluation category. For example, the four bottom-level criteria measuring the general characteristics of the DSS–user interface (node 1.1) were each given a relative importance weight of 0.25. In contrast, the eight bottom-level criteria measuring the DSS–user interface's specific characteristics (node 1.2.2) were given relative importance weights of 0.125.

This measurement approach is consistent with the perspective that all the bottom-level measures are required to assess the more general evaluation category. In some cases, it will take four bottom-level criteria to measure the more general category. In other cases, it will take eight measures, or two measures, and so on. Unless the potential users and/or members of the sponsoring team, or evaluators if their technical expertise is required to combine the bottom-level measures into the more general evaluation category, decide to give the bottom-level measures different relative importance weights, all the bottom-level measures are used equally.

Second, the substantive domain experts participating in the evaluations represented the potential users of the systems. The experts participating in the evaluation of DART, as well as the experts who participated in the evaluation of the other prototypes, may have thought that certain bottom-level criteria were more important than others. However, we decided against having experts differentially weight these criteria because we wanted to use the same weights for evaluating all five prototypes in order to provide a common evaluation baseline. And, since the hierarchy of effectiveness measures in Table 2.1 was substantially larger and in many ways different from the measures used in Task II of the project to select the prototypes for development, the evaluation team considered it inappropriate to obtain relative importance weights from the sponsoring team prior to (or during) testing and evaluation for fear that certain developers might consider their prototypes adversely affected.

Third, there is an alternative approach to obtaining the scores on the upper-level

TABLE 2.4 Experts' Subjective Evaluation Scores for DART on Each Measure of Effectiveness in the MAUA Hierarchy

0.0 Utility (i.e., potential for implementation)

—Based on 6 questions   8.22
—Based on the MAUA criteria hierarchy   7.36

1.0 DSS–User Interface 7.81	2.0 User–DSS–Organization Interface 7.17	3.0 Organization–Environment Interface 7.09
1.1 Match between DSS and personnel 7.93	2.1 Efficiency factors 6.65	3.1 Decision quality 7.58
1.1.1 Match with training and technical background 8.44	2.1.1 Speed 6.54	3.2 Technical soundness (match between DSS's technical approach and analysts' technical requirements) 6.52
1.1.2 Match with work style, work load, and interest 7.08	2.1.1.1 Time required for task accomplishment 7.11	3.3 Decision process quality (based on 10 attributes) 7.18
1.1.3 Match with operational needs 8.27	2.1.1.2 Time required for data management 6.20	—Based on 2 questions (7.83)
1.2 DSS's characteristics 7.68	2.1.1.3 Setup time requirements 6.33	3.3.1 Framework incorporating judgment 6.83
1.2.1 General characteristics 8.46	2.1.2 Perceived reliability under battle conditions 6.50	3.3.2 Survey range of alternatives 7.33
1.2.1.1 Ease of use 8.56	2.1.3 Perceived supportability under battle conditions 6.91	
1.2.1.2 Transparency (i.e., user understanding) 7.78	2.1.3.1 Skill availability 7.56	

1.2.1.3 Ease of training	8.83	
1.2.1.4 Response time	8.67	
1.2.2 Specific characteristics	6.90	
1.2.2.1 User interface	7.67	
1.2.2.2 Types of data files	6.56	
1.2.2.3 Expert judgment stored in DSS	6.84	
1.2.2.4 Ability to modify judgments	6.88	
1.2.2.5 DSS's automatic calculations	7.16	
1.2.2.6 DSS's graphs	5.84	
1.2.2.7 The need for hard copy[a]	(9.33)	
1.2.2.8 DSS's text	7.33	
2.1.3.2 Hardware availability	6.25	
2.2 Match between DSS and organization	7.69	
2.2.1 Effect on organization procedures	7.0	
2.2.2 Effect on other people's positions	7.42	
2.2.2.1 Political acceptability	7.67	
2.2.2.2 Other people's work load	7.17	
2.2.3 Effect on information flow	8.17	
2.2.4 Side effects	8.17	
2.2.4.1 Value in performing other tasks	7.50	
2.2.4.2 Value to SAC[b] or other services	8.33	
2.2.4.3 Training value	8.67	
3.3.3 Survey range of objectives	6.83	
3.3.4 Weighing consequences	7.33	
3.3.5 Assessment of consequences	6.67	
3.3.6 Reexamination of decision making process	7.11	
3.3.7 Use of information	7.78	
3.3.8 Implementation	7.50	
3.3.9 Effect on group discussion	7.11	
3.3.10 Confidence	7.33	

[a]The asterisk and parentheses for hard-copy capability mean that DART did not have one at the time of the evaluation.
[b]SAC stands for Strategic Air Command.

criteria. Specifically, one could have taken the average of the scores to all the questions assessing each upper-level criterion. For example, to obtain a score for DSS characteristics (node 1.2), we could have averaged the scores for all the questions assessing general characteristics (node 1.2.1) and specific characteristics (node 1.2.2) instead of just averaging the mean scores for lower-level criteria (i.e., for 1.2.1 and 1.2.2) as we did. The alternative approach would have given greater weight to criterion 1.2.2 because there were more questions for criterion 1.2.2 than for 1.2.1. Again, because we did not want to differentially weight the criteria, we rejected this approach.

The experts' subjective evaluation scores for all the criteria in the measurement effectiveness hierarchy are presented in Table 2.4. Overall, the experts had a strong, positive opinion of DART, which they thought had good potential for field implementation. On the basis of the evaluation hierarchy, DART received a mean overall utility score (node 0.0) of 7.36 on the 11-point scale going from 0 to 10. (Note: On the basis of the six questions directly asking about its overall utility, DART received a mean score of 8.22.)

The three experts gave DART good scores on all three interfaces. Of the three, the user interface received the highest mean score (7.81). In particular, the experts thought that DART nicely matched the training and technical background of the analysts that would use it and their operational needs. In addition, they thought it was easy to use; that it was easy to understand how it performed activity node identification; that training was easy; that DART had a fast response time; and that it had a good user interface.

Although still positive, the experts were, in comparison, less pleased with DART's data files, its knowledge base, and the ability to modify the judgments in its knowledge base, and its graphics capabilities. These findings are consistent with the results of the prototype's empirical evaluation, which was that DART's knowledge base still needed work. Finally, the experts were not especially pleased with DART's graphics capabilities and strongly thought that DART needed a hard-copy capability. (Note: See footnote regarding it in Table 2.4.)

The user-system–organization interface (7.17) and organization/environment interface (7.09) received comparable scores. In terms of the former, the experts thought there was a good match between the expert system and organizational requirements. They thought it would have a positive effect on the flow of information, that it would be politically acceptable, that it would not affect other people's work load, and that it would have a number of positive side effects. Although still positive, the experts gave DART lower scores on a number of efficiency factors in the hierarchy, such as the time required for data management, setup time requirements, and perceived reliability and hardware availability under battle conditions.

Regarding the organization–environment interface, the experts gave DART good scores on decision quality and decision process quality. (Note: There are two scores for decision process quality: one based on the bottom-level attributes comprising it, and one, in parentheses, based on two questions directly assessing it.) Although still positive, the experts were, in comparison, less pleased with DART's technical soundness, which was defined as the match between the system's technical approach and what the experts considered to be the technical requirements of the task. DART's score on technical soundness was consistent with the experts' positive, but lower scores on DART's data files, knowledge base, and the limited capacity to modify the knowledge base. And, of course, it was consistent with the empirical findings demonstrating that the experts were unable to more accurately identify certain activity nodes when using DART.

This completes the discussion of the DART evaluation. The purpose in presenting this case study was to illustrate how one might implement all three facets of the evaluation approach. We want to emphasize the illustrative nature of the presentation. Although specific evaluation data was presented about the DART expert system prototype, illustration of specific evaluation methods and the more general evaluation approach and perspective is what is most important here. For that is what is emphasized throughout this text.

2.4 SUMMARY

The purpose of this chapter was to present a general perspective and approach for evaluating decision support and expert systems, and to show how both were applied in a case study. First, evaluators should have a decision-making perspective. Decision support systems and expert systems need to be evaluated from the decision makers' perspective, including their organizational context. Second, evaluators should use a multifaceted approach: a technical facet to look "inside the black box"; an empirical facet to rigorously assess the system's impact on performance; and a subjective facet to obtain users' opinions about the system's strengths and weaknesses. Finally, the case study described the procedures for, and results of, implementing the general perspective and approach for an Air Force expert system prototype to support opposing force activity node identification.

Chapter 3

Integrating Evaluation Into Development

First, we present an overview of a nine-step approach to developing decision support and expert systems. Second, we discuss the different types of subjective, technical, and empirical evaluation methods. Third, we indicate the relative importance of the different methods for the different steps.

3.1 THE DEVELOPMENT APPROACH

3.1.1 Introduction

Developers of decision support systems and expert systems have emphasized the application of rapid prototyping methods. The purpose of prototyping is to quickly develop a working model of the system and get the user's (and expert's for expert systems) reaction to it in order to find out if the development process is on track. It is a mechanism for soliciting feedback early, and routinely throughout development.

Prototyping is based on two premises. First, that "users don't know what they want or need, but they do know what they like." And, second, that "it is a lot easier to answer the question 'How do you like X?' than to answer the question 'How would you like X?'" [Hurst et al., 1983, p. 128]. These premises put the user in the explicit role of evaluating actual working representations of the decision support system or expert system, and indicating how the systems should be modified, early in the process. To quote Hopple [1988, p. 69]:

> Prototyping highlights the working premise that interactive systems of the DSS genre cannot be developed easily, quickly, or without inputs across the life cycle from prospective users. . . . *successful* systems require user inputs and sign offs. Prototypers therefore *plan for iteration.*

These premises also hold for experts, although they get reworded a little. Specifically, experts often don't know exactly what process they go through to make a judgment, but they can tell you whether one process is better than another. To quote Harmon et al. [1988, p. 166]:

> It's not that experts will not explain what they do, it's that they can't. Knowledge engineers must work patiently through a discovery process with human experts to develop and then enhance the system. No neat phases result in products that will not be reconsidered in subsequent phases. The original rules the knowledge engineers develop may later be rewritten entirely or dropped, as the experts and knowledge engineers gradually refine their understanding of the knowledge that must go into the knowledge base.

To cite Cholawsky [1988, p. 42], "The conventional wisdom about this process is that expert systems development is necessarily an experimental process." It is one that emphasizes iteration, test and evaluation, and subsequent refinement.

Figure 3.1 presents Andriole's [1989a] "prototyping design blueprint" for developing decision support and expert system technology. Like other prototyping blueprints, it emphasizes iteration, test and evaluation, and subsequent refinement. However, Andriole's also emphasizes requirements analysis, technological fit, and pragmatism. These are essential elements to developing decision support and expert systems that are used and effective. Andriole's blueprint is also consistent with recent representations by Cholawsky [1988], Rook and Croghan [1989], and Weitzel and Kerschberg [1989].

Evaluation is an explicit step in Andriole's blueprint, as is the feedback it provides for keeping the development process on track. Moreover, evaluation is an implicit activity in each step of the blueprint; it is required to deal with the various types of judgments and decisions, by users and developers alike, that are inherent in the decision support system and expert system development process. We will overview the blueprint in some detail here to illustrate these different types of judgments, and to provide a context for considering different evaluation methods.

3.1.2 Requirements Analysis

Requirements analysis has been referred to as "system targeting" by Andriole [1989a, p. 10]. Its goal is to profile the user, the tasks that s/he perform, and the organizational context within which the user and the system will operate. Its purpose is to define (1) what the decision support system or expert system has to do in order for the user to consider it to be a good system; and (2) whether develop-

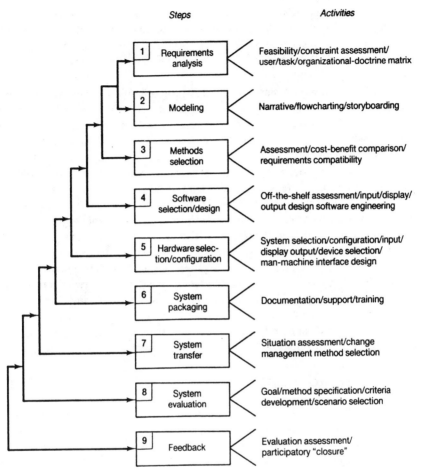

FIGURE 3.1 Andriole's nine-step prototyping design blueprint [Reprinted, with permission, from book #3240, *Handbook of Decision Support Systems* by Stephen J. Andriole. Copyright 1989 by TAB Books, a division of McGraw-Hill, Blue Ridge Summit, PA 17294 (1-800-822-8158 or 1-717-794-2191)]

ment of such a system is feasible given the financial, time, and other constraints operating in the situation. The first purpose is clearly dependent on the judgment of the decision maker(s) who will use the decision support system or expert system; the second is dependent on the judgment of the technical personnel who will build it.

The importance of requirements analysis cannot be overstated. Boar [1984] reports, for instance, that 60–80% of all system problems can be traced to inaccurate requirements definitions. Andriole [1989a, p. 9] argues that ''the [development] process itself is anchored in the quality of the requirements analysis. If the analysis is conducted poorly then the system will fail. If it is conducted well then the system has a better chance of succeeding.'' A well-performed requirements analysis should clearly identify the measures of effectiveness against which the system will be evaluated.

As important as requirements analysis is, it is often poorly performed. This is not because the development team is doing a bad job, it's because requirements analysis is a difficult task. There are many reasons for this. As we discussed above, decision makers and experts have difficulty telling us what kind of support they need. They have difficulty describing their decision process. They use a wide range of decision-making processes, and are often inconsistent in their descriptions. Salient events in the user's (and expert's) environment and memory are usually those they bring to the designer's attention. These events are typically subject to processing biases owing to the inadequacy of the feedback available to the users from the environment. Moreover, the responses that users give the designer are typically biased by the questions the designer asks, unless the latter uses multiple methods to overcome response biases. Finally, requirements analysis is compounded by the fact that designers themselves are not perfectly consistent, and two decision makers (or experts) might well use different processes to solve the same problem. And they will almost certainly have different requirements for the system. Subjective evaluation methods can help here, in terms of clarifying disagreements and establishing the criteria for defining successful development.

3.1.3 Functional Modeling

The prototyping strategy assumes that requirements cannot be accurately represented without users interacting with a functional, working model of the decision support system or expert system. There are many ways to model a system, including narratives, flowcharts, mathematical representations, storyboards, and various combinations.

Storyboarding has become increasing popular among decision support system and expert system developers with the advent of sophisticated storyboarding packages for the Apple and IBM personal computers, and their clones. Storyboarding requires developers to mock up the displays of the envisioned system in an effort to simulate human–computer interaction as it would unfold during the use of the actual system. The goal is to show decision makers exactly what the system will be capable of doing, and how it will do it. They represent what Boar [1984] has called ''hybrid prototypes'' to distinguish them from initial versions of the decision support system or expert system. (Note: Such ''hybrids'' should not be confused with decision support system hybrids using artificial intelligence and other analytical methods.)

The purpose of storyboarding and, more broadly, functional modeling is to provide users with a mechanism for evaluating the results of the requirements analysis. Thus, storyboarding represents a form of "requirements verification," to quote Andriole [1987, p. 231]. A good model, whether it is a storyboard or not, should foster discussion about what the decision support system or expert system should and should not do and, consistent with the prototyping approach, lead to revisions in both the requirements analysis and functional model such that the development process is kept on track.

3.1.4 Analytical Method Selection

It is the users' ability to apply analytical modeling methods to information in a manner that supports rather than replaces their decision-making function that is the essence of decision support technology. There are many analytical modeling methods. Andriole [1989a], for example, has classified them into the following four categories: decision analysis, operations research, management science, and computer science.

Decision analytic (DA) methods include utility/value modeling methods (e.g., multiattribute utility models, cost-benefit models, and regret models), probability modeling methods (e.g., probability trees, influence diagrams, and Bayesian models), and mixed (value–probability) models, such as decision trees and fuzzy decision analysis.

Operations research (OR) methods include descriptive and inferential statistical methods, various optimization techniques (e.g., linear, integer, and dynamic programming) and various modeling techniques (e.g., based on game theory, network theory, queuing theory, inventory methods, or simulation methods).

Management science (MS) methods consist primarily of program management methods in Andriole's categorization; for instance, milestone charts, Gantt charts, and critical path models.

Computer science (CS) includes "conventional" algorithmic methods used to collect, refine, store, route, process, and create data and information for specific problem-solving purposes, and artificial intelligence methods.

Analytical methods should be selected after the requirements analysis and functional modeling steps in the development process. This does not mean that the first two steps have to be completed or that there is no iteration with the third step. But it does mean that analytical methods need to be evaluated so that the selected method or methods are consistent with the requirements definitions for and functional model of the decision support system or expert system.

The evaluation of analytical methods is a critical and often difficult decision for the design team for three principal reasons. First, analytical methods differ in their appropriateness for different aspects of the decision problem. For example, probability models are more suitable than utility models for testing hypotheses about the state of the environment with which the decision maker is dealing, but the latter are more appropriate for choosing between alternatives for dealing with that environment. Decision makers typically want to be (and need to be) capable of addressing all aspects of the decision problem; yet, it is typically unreasonable to expect them to be capable of fully understanding many different analytical methods.

Second, there are trade-offs inherent in using one analytical method instead of another even when the methods are appropriate for a given aspect of the decision problem. Analytical methods vary in their assumptions about the sources and forms of knowledge, their ease of use, their degree of structure and flexibility, their transparency, and their evaluability.

And, third, developers are seldom experts in every analytical method, let alone in matching methods to requirements definitions. Research has, however, begun in developing taxonomies for matching analytical methods to requirements [e.g., see Adelman, 1987; Andriole, 1989a]. These technical evaluation methods will be considered in Chapter 5.

3.1.5 Software Selection and Design

There is a large amount of decision support software, typically in the form of off-the-shelf decision support system tools embodying analytical methods and expert system shells, that is available to developers. This software is available from commercial vendors and, in many cases, virtually free from the federal government. For example, Andriole [1989b] has evaluated a wide range of storyboarding software; Buede [1988] has evaluated a wide range of decision-analytic tools; Sharda [1984] has evaluated linear programming tools; Clymer [1985] has provided a sampling of artificial intelligence software; and Sage [1986] has surveyed a range of database management software, spreadsheets, and project management tools.

The development team needs to decide whether it will use off-the-shelf software or develop customized software. Clearly, there are advantages and disadvantages for each alternative, and their importance often depends on whether one's perspective is that of the user, programmer, project manager, or sponsor. Subjective evaluation methods can be used to organize these diverse judgments.

If the development team decides in favor of customized software, then it should be engineered from the requirements up, consistent with the functional model and implications of the selected analytical method(s). Since there are many excellent sources that provide extensive discussions of the guidelines and methods for effective software engineering [e.g., Fairley, 1985; Pressman, 1982; Sage, 1991; Sage and Palmer, 1990], the topic will be considered here only briefly from the perspective of decision support and expert system technology. In particular, both Andriole [1989a] and Hopple [1988] have focused on the following five components of decision support system and expert system software: dialogue, inputs, displays, language, and programming.

First, the dialogue for decision support systems and expert systems is highly interactive. Consequently, the development team needs to consider how much of the dialogue is initiated by the user versus the system, how flexible the interface will be, its complexity and power and, summarily, its potential for information (and procedural) overload of the user. Given the prototyping strategy, many of these judgments should have already been dealt with in the "living" storyboard being used to functionally model the system. The same is true for the inputs and displays. Consequently, step 4 in the approach focuses on the programming implications of the storyboard and whether it will necessitate modifications to the functional model.

The software language also should be selected based on the requirements analysis, functional model, and quality of available off-the-shelf tools embodying the selected analytical method(s). "Actually, there are relatively few decision support design situations that permit objective evaluations. Software languages are often pre-selected on the basis of biased preference, precedent, and/or the availability of programming expertise" [Andriole, 1989a, p. 148]. Such a situation may well be a constraint, and perhaps a severe one, that the development team has to live with. It is of importance to emphasize, however, that by placing language selection in step 4 the development team can make more abundantly clear to its sponsor that the selection of a language is a choice that needs to be evaluated within the context of the previously identified requirements, functional model, and analytical methods.

Finally,

> Software engineering should be conducted according to accepted programming standards. Good software, it should be emphasized, is not written—it is *engineered* by organized, systematic programmers under the management of careful analysts. Structured programming techniques, good labeling, and careful documentation are only a few hallmarks of solid code—the kind that you want in your DSS. (Hopple, 1988, 92)

Although this obviously sounds nice and right, we all also know that good programming is a difficult, creative activity. Programmers are constantly making judgments and decisions about what needs to be done and how well the software they have written does it.

There is an ever-increasing array of software-based tests and tools for helping programmers, both those working on the system and those who will have to maintain and/or test it, evaluate the quality of the written code. We will review these formal software test and verification methods in Chapter 5, which considers technical evaluation methods. In addition, that chapter will overview methods for evaluating (1) the logical adequacy and predictive accuracy of an expert system's knowledge base, and (2) projected software development costs.

3.1.6 Hardware Selection and Configuration

This step is naturally intertwined with software selection and design. And, like software language selection, the hardware is often preselected by the user, his/her sponsor, or his/her organization. When at all possible, hardware should be selected consistent with requirements, functional models, storyboards, and software design. Even when such selection is not totally up to the design team, there is often room to maneuver. For example, the team often can still evaluate alternative interfaces, memory and storage configurations, hard-copy devices, and associated peripherals that are compatible with the specific system.

The hardware, operating system, developmental tools, debugging tools, and packaged software must be considered as a whole, both in terms of the development system and the runtime system. If different development and runtime systems are used, then portability becomes an issue.

3.1.7 System Packaging

This step includes documentation, support, and training. At a minimum, good documentation includes software specification, a functional description of the software, and a user's manual. Good support includes telephone-based (although face-to-face support is preferable) and documentation-based assistance. Good training includes both on-line and conventional training. Although these activities are not glamorous, they are essential. Decision support systems and expert systems that are not supported are seldom used unless they address highly structured problems and have become part of the organization's routine.

3.1.8 System Transfer

Users are typically skeptical of decision support and expert system technologies. In many large organizations, the actual users of the decision support system or expert system may not have been part of the development team. Or, because of the changing organizational environment, the users may be new players. The more that the users that participated in the development process had been actively involved in the process and, from a sampling theory perspective, reasonably representative of the larger population of users from which they were drawn, the higher the probability that system transfer will go smoothly from the user's perspective.

However, the development team also has to consider system transfer from the perspective of other members of the organization. Implementation research [e.g., see Adelman, 1982; Ginzberg, 1977; Shycon, 1977] suggests that the transfer of a computer-based system needs to be planned just like any other significant intervention into the way an organization functions. Moreover, Adelman et al. [1985] have shown that prospective users of decision support systems and expert systems evaluate their overall utility on the basis of the system's match with organizational characteristics, as well as on the basis of its match with the characteristics of prospective users and their current problem-solving procedures. These findings suggest that [Andriole, 1989a, p. 1982]:

Change management, like the systems design and development process itself, is iterative and people-intensive. There is no way to avoid extensive personal contact with the entire user hierarchy. The amount and nature of this contact will determine how well or badly your system is received—and whether it is actually used or just displayed.

3.1.9 Evaluation and Feedback

The last steps are system evaluation and feedback, respectively. These two steps will obviously be dealt with in substantial detail throughout the remainder of the book. Two points will, however, be made here within the context of the "prototyping design blueprint." First, as Andriole [1989a, pp. 187–188] has emphasized:

> *All* decision support systems should be evaluated, and the results of the evaluation should be fed right back into the development process (which never really ends!). . . . Designers need to know if the system is—first and foremost—performing adequately. But they also need to know if the system "fits" an organization. They need to know what parts of the system need refinement, and what problems the system is not solving well.

And, second, as Andriole continues:

> Remember that the system has already been evaluated throughout its development history. Step II of the design and development process calls for the development and testing of a storyboard to validate requirements. Steps III through VII also call for assessments about the compatibility of the systems components with its users, the tasks it is intended to perform, and the methods that it uses.

As these points demonstrate, evaluation is an inherent part of the prototyping development approach. The development process is fraught with judgments and decisions because the problem and task definitions for which decision support system and expert system software is developed are typically elusive and unstructured. There are, however, formal evaluation tools for helping the team systematically address these judgments and decisions and, in turn, develop software that will have a higher probability of being used and effective.

3.2 EVALUATION METHODS

This section briefly covers subjective, technical, and empirical evaluation methods. Detailed discussions of these methods are found in Chapters 4, 5, and 6, respectively.

3.2.1 Subjective Evaluation Methods

The goal of subjective evaluations is to assess the decision support system or expert system from the perspective of potential users and members of the sponsoring team. This is accomplished by identifying the measures of effectiveness that will provide the information required by members of the sponsoring team in order to determine the system's utility. The need for the explicit identification of measures of effectiveness is particularly important at the beginning of the development process because they represent (1) reference points for the development team to use when developing the decision support system or expert system, and (2) criteria for the evaluator to monitor in order to assess whether the development process is on track.

Gaschnig et al. [1983, p. 258] have clearly addressed this point within the context of evaluating expert systems:

> It is important for system designers to be clear about the nature of their motivations for building an expert system. The long-range goals must also be outlined explicitly. *Thus stage 1 of a system's development, the initial design, should be accompanied by explicit statements of what the measures of the program's success will be and how failure or success will be evaluated.* [Itallics theirs] It is not uncommon for system designers to ignore this issue at the outset, since the initial challenges appear so great upon consideration of the decision-making task that their expert system will have to undertake. If the evaluation stages and long-range goals are explicitly stated, however, they will necessarily have an impact on the early design of the expert system.

Riedel and Pitz [1986, p. 986], as well as others [e.g., Adelman and Donnell, 1986; Sage, 1991; Ulvila et al., 1987], have pointed out that "Multiattribute Utility Technology (MAUT) provides a formal structure for conceptualizing MOE's, a mechanism for decomposing the global MOE into its component dimensions and for reintegrating them to yield one summary measure of value." This approach was used to provide the subjective evaluation of DART described in Chapter 2.

"Decomposition" was illustrated in Table 2.1. That table presented a multiattributed hierarchy that decomposed the global measure of effectiveness (i.e., the overall utility of the system) into three component dimensions: the user–system, user–organization, and organization–environment interfaces. Each of these interfaces was further decomposed into bottom-level measures of effectiveness, called "attributes" within the jargon of multiattribute utility technology.

"Reintegration" was achieved by a three-step procedure. First, the experts completed a questionnaire that essentially scored DART on each of the bottom-level attributes. Second, we assumed a positive linear utility function for each of the bottom-level attributes, thereby conceptually converting the performance score on the attribute into a utility score on that attribute. And, third, the bottom-level attributes comprising the next upper-level evaluation category were given equal weights moving up the hierarchy. This permitted us to combine the (utility) scores for lower-level attributes into more global scores at the next level of the hierarchy until we obtained an overall utility score for the DART prototype.

There are many other kinds of subjective evaluation methods. In addition to MAUT, Chapter 4 will consider cost-benefit analysis, the dollar-equivalent technique, decision analysis, and a MAUT-based cost-benefit analysis in detail. It will also mention many other subjective evaluation methods for the interested reader.

3.2.2 Technical Evaluation Methods

Formal software testing and verification methods are the ones typically thought of when one asks the question, "How well was the system built?" Obviously, the answer can affect the results of the empirical and subjective evaluations, for a poorly programmed decision support system or expert system will affect how well users can perform desired tasks with the system and, in turn, what they think of it. Moreover, poorly developed software can sour the opinion of software engineers who might be responsible for recommending whether funding of the effort should continue, even when users are positive about the design concept and initial prototype. Indeed, the author knows of at least two instances where a reasonably good decision support system concept did not proceed further than the prototyping stage because of severe inadequacies in the delivered software.

The selected analytical methods and estimated software development costs also can significantly influence the empirical and subjective evaluations. Decision support system performance and preference are particularly sensitive to the selected analytical methods because the failure to select the best method(s) means the software will not effectively support the user's decision-making process. And failure to develop a high-quality knowledge base can bring the feasibility and/or cost-effectiveness of an expert system development effort into question. Given the highly competitive nature under which many decision support system and expert system development contracts are issued, inaccurate estimation of software costs increases the probability that there will not be enough money to build a high-quality technical product and, in turn, the probability of poor performance in the empirical and subjective evaluations.

This book overviews four groups of technical evaluation methods. The first group includes two taxonomies for evaluating the adequacy of the selected analytical methods. The first taxonomy assesses the relative applicability of analytical modeling methods to different elements of the SHOR paradigm. The second taxonomy represents a requirements/methods matrix for matching analytical methods to requirements.

The second group of technical evaluation methods addresses software development costs. These methods are classified into four categories: experiential, static, dynamic, and hybrids. Experiential models rely on 'expert judgment' of key people who have the necessary experience, background, and business sense to make the estimate. Static cost estimation methods use a modeling method, such as multiple regression analysis, to relate cost factors to cost. Dynamic estimation models incorporate time as a parameter in the equation. And hybrid cost estimation models incorporate aspects of two categories.

Traditional software test and verification methods comprise the third group of technical evaluation methods. In particular, we will review both static and dynamic analysis methods. Static analysis methods may be either manual or automated approaches to analyzing the system's design and software without code execution. Dynamic methods actually execute the code by using test data to see how well the software is written.

The fourth group of technical evaluation methods are for assessing the adequacy of a knowledge base. These methods are an extension of the concepts employed in static and dynamic software testing methods. In particular, static testing can be used to assess anomalies in the logical consistency and completeness of the knowledge base. Dynamic testing uses test data to determine the knowledge base's predictive accuracy. Even if a knowledge base is logically sound, it still might not produce accurate recommendations.

3.2.3   Empirical Evaluation Methods

Even if the users like the decision support system or expert system, and even if it is a good technical product, users still may not perform better with than without it. This is true even when the predictive accuracy of an expert system's knowledge base is high. Remember, an expert system may be addressing only part of a much larger organizational decision. In addition, a user may disagree with the system's recommendation for a host of reasons. Consequently, evaluators should perform empirical evaluations to assess the system's actual effect on user performance. This book covers three types of empirical evaluations: experiments, quasi-experiments, and case studies.

When one thinks of an experiment, one typically thinks of the case where (1) one or more factors are systematically varied as independent variable(s); and (2) the dependent variable(s) are quantitative, objective measures of performance. One of the independent variables is almost always "the degree of decision support." As in the DART experiment described in Chapter 2, this independent variable typically has two levels. The first is an "unaided condition;" it is a control group that is supposed to represent the degree of support the decision maker has without the decision support system or expert system. The second level is an "aided" condition; it is the support level provided by the decision support system or expert system.

"Randomization" is essential to "true experimental designs" [Campbell and Stanley, 1966]. Randomization can be accomplished through arbitrarily assigning participants to "with system" and "without system" conditions or arbitrarily assigning the order of the conditions if participants will be repeatedly exposed to all conditions. Although the statistical tests are designed to test the null hypothesis that there is no difference between performance for the two levels, there is often the implicit, if not explicit hypothesis that the aided condition will lead to significantly better performance, otherwise the decision support system or expert system would not have been built. Consequently, as an evaluator, you must take steps to remove potential bias from the experimental test.

Five explicit steps were taken in the DART experiment with the experts to control for experimental bias. First, substantial effort was given to representing the "without system" condition accurately. Moreover, the session with the "nonexperts," that is, with the government research and development personnel from the Rome Air Development Center, was successfully directed at "pretesting" the "without system" condition in order to find ways to make it more representative of the actual military environment.

Second, performance with DART was also pretested in order to assess the adequacy of training, and to determine whether minor changes had to be made to the prototype to prepare it for a formal evaluation. As the reader will remember, substantial changes were made to the training schedule and the user interface as a result of the pretest.

Third, substantial effort was given to developing two problem scenarios. Even though DART was a prototype with limitations in the range of activity nodes that it was supposed to identify, it still had to be capable of handling the complexities representative of this real-world task. The range of these complexities had to be adequately represented in the problem scenarios.

Fourth, the order in which the experts worked the test scenarios, both with and without DART, was determined randomly. In this way, we tried to control for extraneous events that might affect the results of the experiment.

And, fifth, when the experts evaluated solution quality, they were blind as to whether the solution was produced with or without DART, or even by them or the "nonexperts" (i.e., the R&D personnel). As Gaschnig et al. [1983] point out, the early evaluations of MYCIN, an expert system for medical diagnosis, were biased against the system because the physicians knew that they were examining the output of a computer program.

The representativeness of the experimental setting and the level of the decision support system's or expert system's performance requirements should advance throughout the development cycle. And, ideally, field experimentation would be used to assess whether the decision support system or expert system significantly improved performance over that achieved in the unaided organizational setting. However, the sample size and randomization requirements of true experiments are not possible in many organizations. Quasi-experimental or case-study designs should be used in such situations.

Quasi-experiments permit the evaluator to

> . . . introduce something like experimental design into his scheduling of data collection procedures (e.g., the *when* and *to whom* of measurement), even though he lacks the full control over the scheduling of experimental stimuli (the *when* and *to whom*

of exposure and the ability to randomize exposures) which make a true experiment possible. [Campbell and Stanley, 1966, p. 34]

There are a number of different types of quasi-experimental designs. We will consider three kinds: (1) time-series designs, where the organizational unit is measured for a long period of time before and after receiving the decision support system or expert system; (2) multiple time-series designs that do not use randomization, but do use a control group that does not receive the system; and (3) nonequivalent (and nonrandomized) control group designs that rely on analysis of covariance (or gain scores) to determine whether the pretest and posttest difference for the "with system" group is significantly better than that of the "without system" control group.

Case studies are appropriate in settings where not even quasi-experimental designs are possible because there is little or no experimenter control. As Yin [1984] notes, good case studies represent high-quality detective work, where the performance level attained with the system represents the case to be solved. Case-study analyses emphasize logical deduction as a means of showing how the evidence supports one causal explanation over rival alternatives.

In all forms of empirical research, it is the logic of the research design linking the data collected, and the conclusions drawn from it, to the initial questions driving the study that determines the validity of the research. Thus, we will consider the issues of reliability and validity, and discuss how experiments, quasi-experiments, and case studies address them.

3.3 INTEGRATING EVALUATION INTO DEVELOPMENT

Table 3.1 indicates the relative applicability of each of the three classes of evaluation methods to each of the nine steps in Andriole's [1989a] prototyping design blueprint. We created the relative applicability ratings for steps 1 through 7 by (1) indicating which class of methods had the highest applicability for that step, and then (2) scoring the applicability of the remaining two methods relative to it. As can be seen, all three classes of evaluation methods are applicable throughout the development process, as well as in steps 8 and 9.

Although the assessment presented in Table 3.1 is based on the evaluation literature and my experience, it still represents only my judgment. Others may agree with various aspects of the matching to various degrees based on their experience. That's fine, for the goal is not to present a definitive assessment but, rather, to indicate the potential applicability of different evaluation methods to different steps in the development process.

The remainder of this chapter discusses the relative applicability of subjective, technical, and empirical evaluation methods to the first seven steps in the blueprint.

TABLE 3.1 The Relative Applicability of Evaluation Methods to Different Steps in The Development Process

Step in Development Process	Subjective Methods	Technical Methods	Empirical Methods
1. Requirements analysis	High	Medium	Medium
2. Modeling	Medium	High	Medium
3. Methods selection	Low	High	Low
4. Software selection/design/development	Medium	High	High
5. Hardware selection/configuration	Medium	High	Medium
6. System packaging	Low	High	Medium
7. System transfer	Low	High	Low
8. System evaluation	High	High	High
9. Feedback	High	High	High

3.3.1 Integrating Subjective Evaluation Methods

Subjective evaluation methods tend to be most applicable early in the development cycle because they represent an explicit means for defining the judgments of members of the sponsoring team and potential users of the decision support system or expert system. They can, however, also be readily used by the development team to address systematically the judgments inherent in evaluating the utility/value of the storyboards developed during functional modeling (step 2), available off-the-shelf software (step 4), various hardware configurations (step 5), or anywhere else in the development process where members of the development team need to weigh one option against another. In particular, however, we stress the value of subjective evaluation methods for linking steps 1 and 8 through the feedback provided in step 9. This provides an explicit mechanism (and audit trail) for determining whether the prototypes and operational system are consistent with the initial goals and objectives of the sponsoring team.

3.3.2 Integrating Technical Evaluation Methods

Technical evaluation methods are most applicable in software design (step 4), which includes software development. However, like subjective evaluation methods, technical evaluation methods are applicable to all steps in the development process. For example, they have considerable applicability prior to programming code, in terms of (1) verifying both requirements analysis documentation and functional models of the software, (2) developing estimates of software development costs, and (3) selecting analytical methods for the model-based management system. Additionally, software test and verification methods for evaluating the system's written code, and the knowledge base of an expert system, have much applicability once the development process is well under way during hardware configuration, system packaging, and system transfer. However, we will emphasize their application as early as possible in development because that is when errors are easiest and cheapest to remedy.

3.3.3 Integrating Empirical Evaluation Methods

Experimentation was emphasized as the principal empirical evaluation method. From an iterative, prototyping perspective, it is anticipated that experiments will be conducted throughout software development (step 4) and, to a more limited extent, during hardware configuration (step 5), as a means of objectively measuring the performance of the decision support system or expert system, and testing hypotheses for improving it. During this iterative process, experiments also can be used, although they apparently seldom are, to evaluate system documentation developed in step 6 of the process. Before software development, experimental designs can be used in evaluating alternative storyboards for the system. After the transfer of the decision support system or expert system to the test/host organization, experimental, quasi-experimental, and case-study designs can be used to evaluate performance with it in its operational setting.

3.4 SUMMARY

This chapter discussed (1) a nine-step approach to developing decision support and expert systems; (2) different types of subjective, technical, and empirical evaluation methods, and (3) the relative importance of the different methods for the different steps.

Substantially more detail about subjective, technical, and empirical evaluation methods, as well as illustrative examples, will be provided in Chapters 4 through 6, respectively. When reading these chapters, the reader is urged to keep the broader evaluation framework provided by the SHOR paradigm in mind. Remember, the initial decision to build a decision support system or expert system is really nothing more than a hypothesis that the system will improve the organization's decision making and, in turn, performance. If evaluators can help members of the sponsoring team assess the adequacy of this hypothesis early in, if not at the outset, of the development cycle, then they can potentially save substantial money and better delineate the requirements of the decision support system or expert system option. Once the development process is under way, the evaluator's job is to systematically gather, filter, and aggregate data about the system in order to test the hypothesis. The application of formal evaluation methods helps members of the sponsoring and development teams monitor the perceived utility of the system during its development and take corrective action to increase the probability of its use and effectiveness.

Chapter 4

Subjective Evaluation Methods

This chapter describes five subjective evaluation methods: multiattribute utility technology (MAUT), cost-benefit analysis, the dollar-equivalent technique, decision analysis, and a MAUT-based cost-benefit analysis. Other methods are also discussed. A case study is then presented showing how MAUT and a MAUT-based cost-benefit analysis were used to select the decision support and expert system technologies to develop on the Air Force project on which DART was developed. The next-to-last section discusses how to construct questionnaires to obtain users' opinions about the strengths and weaknesses of a decision support system or expert system. The last section presents empirical data supporting the theoretically based hypothesis that users and developers rely on different evaluation criteria when judging the overall utility of decision support system and expert system prototypes.

This chapter emphasizes using subjective evaluation methods to link steps 1 (requirements analysis) and 8 (evaluation) in the decision support system and expert system development process through step 9 (feedback). Development can be kept on track by defining the evaluation criteria at the outset of the development process, and using those criteria as guideposts throughout development. This need not imply that system requirements and, in turn, evaluation criteria cannot change during development. The sponsoring team's objectives, and particularly the trade-offs between them, can and often do change during development.

There can be many reasons for why this occurs, such as changes in the environment with which the sponsoring team is dealing, changes in the sponsoring team's membership, insights gained during development regarding what is technically feasible, and so on. Subjective evaluation methods help provide an audit trail for representing changes in the evaluation criteria and their relative importance. This audit trail can be extremely important financially, in the sense that it helps justify the need for additional system development costs. Furthermore, the audit trail can help document the changes that were made during the development process, and the reasons for them.

4.1 MULTIATTRIBUTE UTILITY TECHNOLOGY

There are numerous texts [e.g., Huber, 1980; Keeney and Raiffa, 1976; Pitz and McKillip, 1984] and papers [e.g., Edwards, 1977; Einhorn and McCoach, 1977] describing MAUT. As Huber [1980, p. 46] has pointed out:

> Multiattribute utility models (MAU models) are designed to obtain the utility of items or alternatives that have more than one valuable attribute; therefore, they must be evaluated on more than one criterion. A MAU model essentially shows a decision maker how to aggregate the utility or satisfaction derived from each of the various attributes into a single measure of the overall utility of the multiattributed item or alternative.

Decision support systems and expert systems are clearly "items" that have numerous attributes (or characteristics) of potential value to a decision maker. MAUT represents a method for combining how well a decision support system or expert system scores on these attributes (i.e., individual measures of effectiveness) into a single, overall assessment of system utility.

4.1.1 Decomposition

All the subjective evaluation methods considered in this book proceed by a "divide and conquer" or "decomposition and reintegration" approach. When using MAUT, the decision support system or expert system is conceptually decomposed into evaluation criteria against which it can be measured. These criteria need to be defined well enough so that one can obtain either subjective or objective measures of how well the system performs on each of them. This decomposition typically proceeds through the creation of a value hierarchy, such that the global criterion entitled "the overall utility (or value) of the DSS" is decomposed into major categories of criteria (e.g., the three interfaces in Table 2.1). These categories are further decomposed until one can define and obtain precise, reliable, and valid assessments (or scores) of how well the system measures up on each bottom-level criterion in the hierarchy.

(Note: According to Huber [1980], the bottom-level criteria should be called "attributes." This convention is not strictly adhered to. In fact, it is not uncommon to use the words *criteria* and *attributes* interchangeably. Moreover, it is not uncommon for the terms *multiattribute utility technology, multiattribute utility analysis* (or *assessment*), and *multicriterion decision making* to be used synonymously, even though purists within each "variation on the theme" might take issue with this. In this text, we will try to consistently use the term "attributes" to refer to the bottom-level evaluation criteria or measures of effectiveness. However, the reader should not be concerned if the terms are used synonymously.)

By precise, one means that the attribute's definition is sufficiently clear and unambiguous so that everyone knows exactly what is being measured by the attribute, and how to measure it. By reliable, one means that the system will get approximately the same score on an attribute if one uses the same measurement instrument at two different times to measure it, and there have been no changes to the system in the interim. This is referred to as "test–retest" reliability. The measurement instrument could be subjective (e.g., a person's score in answering a question) or objective (e.g., a performance score in an experiment). That does not matter. What matters, from a reliability perspective, is that one gets the same score at two different points in time. In addition, one would like to obtain "interinstrument" reliability as well, such that two measures of an attribute, whether they are subjective and/or objective, would produce approximately the same scores.

Finally, by valid, one means that the attribute contributes to the overall utility value given to the system by the key decision maker(s), users, and/or sponsoring team members. Although many people would like to think that objective, performance scores are the only valid measures of system effectiveness, the overall decision regarding the value of a decision support system or expert system is invariably a mix of subjective and objective scores. The evaluation approach needs to be capable of incorporating both types of measures.

More broadly, it is desirable that the multiattributed hierarchy have the following general features: be (1) comprehensive enough to account for all the different measures of effectiveness deemed important when evaluating the decision support system or expert system; (2) capable of differentiating between an acceptable and unacceptable (or "good" versus "bad") system; and (3) comprised of independent attributes. By "independent," we mean that the attributes represent separate evaluation criteria, not that they are uncorrelated. For instance, the system's response time and the time taken by the user to perform a task are correlated, but different criteria.

It is important to note that a hierarchy is an organizational tool. While extremely helpful, it is not absolutely essential. All that is essential is that one be able to define a comprehensive set of independent attributes that can be measured precisely, reliably, and validly so that the overall utility score can differentiate between an acceptable and unacceptable system. The hierarchy simply helps one perform this task.

The application of MAUT during, or even prior to, the requirements analysis step is typically oriented toward helping the sponsoring and development teams (1) identify the organizational requirements the system needs to satisfy, and (2) select the type of system (and/or other options) that will satisfy these requirements.

The hierarchy of effectiveness measures presented in Table 2.1 does offer a comprehensive reference point (or checklist) of the requirements a system needs to satisfy, and, therefore, provides an effective design and evaluation tool for guiding and monitoring, respectively, the development process. It does not, however, necessarily provide an effective hierarchy of effectiveness measures for initially selecting the type of system to develop, for that decision may require different information.

This point will be illuminated in the case study presented at the end of this chapter. In addition, Riedel and Pitz [1986, p. 987] illustrated it by developing a hierarchy of measures of effectiveness for answering the question, "Which of several decision aids should be funded?" In their hierarchy, the global measure of effectiveness was decomposed into ". . . two broadly defined objectives: a) maximize the importance of the aid, and b) maximize the feasibility of implementation, " each of which was further decomposed into more specific measures of effectiveness. Specifically, importance was decomposed into (1) expected frequency of use and (2) expected time and quality savings; "feasibility" was decomposed into (3) estimated costs, (4) availability of required technology, and (5) appropriateness of the decision support system for the target environment. The decision aids with the highest overall utility scores on these five measures of effectiveness were to be those initially funded by the sponsoring team.

As an evaluator, it is important to remember that the hierarchy of effectiveness measures and, more generally, the application of MAUT should be tailored to the objectives and information needs of the members of the sponsoring team with which you are working in step 1 of the development process. As will be seen later in this chapter, Rockmore et al. [1982] used a different hierarchy of effectiveness measures than Riedel and Pitz [1986] to select decision support and expert system technologies for development. An essential question is, "What techniques should I use to develop the MAUT hierarchy?"

In fact, few techniques have been proposed by decision scientists for identifying evaluation attributes and structuring them into a hierarchy of effectiveness measures. Two techniques have, however, been routinely used by analysts applying MAUT: a top-down (or hierarchical) approach [Keeney and Raiffa, 1976], and a bottom-up (or attribute listing) approach [Kelly, 1979]. The top-down approach to structuring the hierarchy proceeds as follows. The upper level nodes are listed first; then each node, in turn, is subdivided into its component attributes. The process continues until it identifies the lowest-level attributes.

In contrast, the bottom-up approach proceeds by first obtaining a list of all of the possible attributes (i.e., lower-level nodes of the hierarchy) without any concern for the hierarchical nature of the problem. An effective procedure for doing this that is consistent with the SHOR paradigm is to ask the participant (e.g., a decision maker considering alternative solutions) to describe how the alternatives are different (e.g., better or worse) from one another. The differences typically represent the bottom-level attributes. The list of attributes are subsequently clustered together to form the criteria representing the branches of the hierarchy.

In general, there has been minimal research evaluating the relative effectiveness of MAUT structuring techniques, and only one study [Adelman et al., 1986a] doing so under conditions where there existed an accepted multiattributed hierarchy as a criterion for measuring effectiveness. With regard to the latter, Adelman et al. found no significant difference in the accuracy of top-down and bottom-up structuring techniques. Although equivocal, their results indicated that the top-down technique results in deeper hierarchies than the bottom-up technique. Since the deeper hierarchies did not result in more accurate ones, these results suggest that greater depth is merely a byproduct of the top-down approach and not a function of a more comprehensive problem decomposition. Their "post hoc" analysis strongly suggested that combining the two approaches would result in more accurate hierarchies; consequently, that is how we recommend that you proceed.

4.1.2 Reintegration

Reintegration typically occurs within MAUT through the application of utility functions and relative importance weights. Remember, the decision support system or expert system is being evaluated on many different attributes. The natural measurement scale for an attribute depends on the attribute. For example, an attribute's scale could be in objective units (e.g., minutes for time) or subjective units (e.g., the 11-point questionnaire scale used in the DART evaluation). A common scale is, however, required in order to compare scores on one attribute with scores on another, that is, "apples with oranges," and, by so doing, obtain an overall score for the decision support system or expert system being evaluated by users and sponsoring team members.

A "utility" scale, which conceptually measures psychological value or worth or satisfaction, meets this requirement. Utility (or value) functions are used to translate the performance on an attribute into a utility score on that attribute. Then, relative importance weights (or other forms of decision rules) are used to assess the relative value of a utility score on one attribute with the utility score on another. These utility scales and relative importance weights should be elicited from the user(s) on the development team and, depending on the attributes, members of the sponsoring team.

Utility functions and relative importance weights represent subjective judgments that can be used to measure the system's value to users and sponsors. Unless these judgments require technical expertise, which they seldom do, they should not be made by evaluators or other technical members of the development team, for such personnel are rarely given the formal responsibility to make these valuative judgments. The overriding principle is that valuative and technical judgments should be kept separate. The former are the responsibility of the sponsoring team; the latter the responsibility of the development team, which includes evaluators.

Utility functions for individual attributes tend to be linear increasing or decreasing in form, as we used in the case study shown in Chapter 2. But as Hammond et al. [1975] point out, there is no reason why they cannot be U-shaped or inverted U-shaped or even a step function such that the utility score on an attribute is zero until a certain level of performance is achieved on the attribute. These functions can be represented pictorially by utility curves, such as the hypothetical ones in Figure 4.1.

The specific range for the utility scale is arbitrary. For instance, Huber [1980] uses a 0 to 100 range throughout his book; Keeney and Raiffa [1976] use a 0 to 1.0 range throughout theirs. What is critical, however, is the relative utility (or value) of the scores on the scale, and the relationship between differences on the scale. A utility score of 50 on a 0 to 100 utility scale (or 0.5 on a 0 to 1.0 utility scale) indicates that it is midway in value between the lowest and highest values on that scale. The difference between 25 and 50 on a utility scale is equivalent to the difference between 50 and 75 on that scale.

Huber [1980] and Keeney and Raiffa [1976] describe a number of different methods for obtaining utility functions and curves. Graphical techniques represent one general, straightforward approach. In this technique, the attribute's natural scale is on the horizontal axis, and the utility scale is on the vertical axis. One begins by assigning a utility value of 100 to the best value on the attribute's natural scale; a 0 to the worst value. The intermediate points are then sketched in so that the height of the utility curve reflects the relative satisfactoriness of the corresponding point on the natural scale. (Note: Although development of utility curves and functions sounds exceedingly simple, it requires care to ensure that the utility numbers convey a person's subjective feelings. Practitioners often use multiple methods to obtain these curves in an effort to make the representation as accurate as possible.)

An attribute's natural and utility values often do not conform to a straight-line function. Consider the hypothetical utility function in Figure 4.2, which transforms "setup time" (in minutes) onto a 0 to 100 point utility scale for evaluating an Army expert system prototype. A utility score of 100 is obtained for a setup

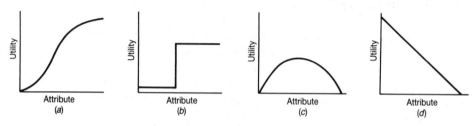

FIGURE 4.1 Possible shapes for utility functions

time of 0 minutes; a utility score of 0 is obtained for a setup time of 60 minutes. One obtains half (or more) of the utility if the system is setup in 5 minutes (or less). An increase from 5 to 15 minutes, which has a utility scale value of 25, was considered as serious as an increase from 15 to 60 minutes. This utility scale clearly tells the developer the importance of a fast, versus slow, setup time to the user.

But how important is system setup time versus system performance versus available graphics capabilities, and so on? The relative importance of a utility score on a bottom-level attribute is reflected typically by (1) its relative weight compared to the other bottom-level attributes comprising a global criterion, and (2) the relative weight of these criteria moving up the hierarchy. These relative weights scale the "100" points on the attributes' utility scales so that one knows the overall utility of a score on one attribute versus another.

For example, Figure 4.3 considers the relative importance of five attributes, which we'll assume are bottom-level attributes to the same upper-level criterion. Specifically, each of the five rectangles in the top half of Figure 4.3 represents the utility scales for five attributes. The rank order of the rectangles (going from left to right) represents the rank order of the attributes in terms of their relative importance; that is, attribute A is more important than attribute B, and so forth. The relative height of the rectangles indicates their relative importance weights. For instance, attribute B is about 60% as tall as attribute A; hence, a utility score of 100 on attribute B is equivalent to a utility score of 60 on attribute A. Likewise, attribute C is half as tall as attribute B; thus, a utility score of 100 on attribute C is equivalent to a utility score of 50 on attribute B and a utility score of 30 on attribute A.

The bottom half of Figure 4.3 illustrates the "paired comparison" weighting technique, which uses the (utility) scaling concepts shown in the top half of the figure. Specifically, it shows that a utility score of 100 on attribute B plus a utility score of 100 on attribute C results in a (combined) utility score of only 90 on

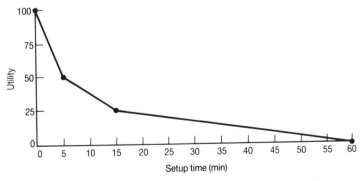

FIGURE 4.2 Hypothetical utility function for DSS setup time

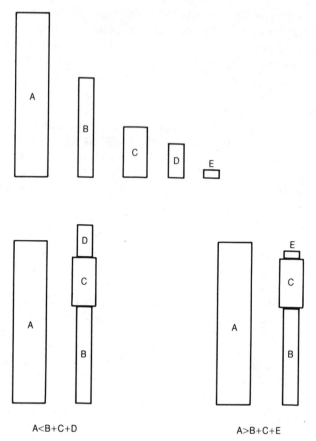

FIGURE 4.3 A pictorial representation of the relative importance of different utility scales [Buede and Adelman, 1987, p. 143]

attribute A; consequently, the combined relative importance weights for attributes B and C must be less than the weight for attribute A. In the example shown, the added importance weights for attributes B, C, and D are greater than that for attribute A, but the added weights for attributes B, C, and E are not. By comparing the overall value of a utility score of 100 on each of the attributes, one is able to assess the relative importance of the attributes.

The same procedures can be used to assign relative weights to the attributes at the next level of the hierarchy, and so on up the hierarchy until all the attributes at each level of the hierarchy have been assigned relative importance weights. The weights at each level of the hierarchy should be proportional such that the sum of the weights at each level is the same. We recommend weights that sum to 1.0 at each level so that the overall utility scale is the same as that for each attribute. If one then multiplies the weights along each branch from the top to the bottom of the hierarchy, one will obtain a cumulative weight on each bottom-level attribute that indicates the overall importance of one bottom-level attribute versus another. That is how one uses MAUT to answer the question, "How important is the relative importance of system setup time versus system performance versus available graphics capabilities, and so forth?" The same principles as those illustrated in Figure 4.3 still hold. For example, if system performance is five times as important as system setup time, then its cumulative weight should be five times as large as the latter's.

There are many different techniques for obtaining relative importance weights across attributes. Although differences have been observed in the relative accuracy and/or agreement among the methods, one is struck by how similar the results tend to be for different methods. For instance, Adelman et al. [1984] evaluated the relative accuracy of six different techniques, including the paired-comparison technique described above, for four tasks that varied in the number of attributes and the peakedness of the distribution of correct attribute weights. They found that, on average, the six techniques led to essentially equivalent and high levels of accuracy across the four tasks. More importantly, there was a significant main effect for the number of attributes; all techniques were more accurate the smaller the number of attributes that had to be weighted. The results strongly suggest that, if possible, one should limit the number of attributes at nodes of the hierarchy by partitioning the larger set of attributes into smaller subsets.

As has been discussed thus far, reintegration of the bottom-level scores for a decision support system or expert system into the global measure of effectiveness is typically achieved in MAUT by the weighted sum of all the utility scores. This can be represented algebraically by equation 1:

$$U(i) = w_1 u(x_{i1}) + \cdots + w_j u(x_{ij}) \tag{1}$$

where

$U(i)$ is the overall utility for alternative i;

there are j attributes;

w_j is the "cumulative" relative weight on attribute j; and

$u(x_{ij})$ is the utility scale value for alternative i on attribute j.

Equation 1 focuses on the bottom-level attributes in a hierarchy, for the relative weights (w_j) in equation 1 represent the "cumulative weights" on the bottom-level attributes. They are obtained by multiplying the weights along each branch of the hierarchy from the top to the bottom.

As Hogarth [1987] has pointed out, the additive decision rule shown in equation 1 is a compensatory combination rule because high utility values on certain attributes can compensate for low values on other attributes and still result in a good score on the global measure of effectiveness. However, as Riedel and Pitz [1986] note, it might be more appropriate to use a noncompensatory rule to ensure that the decision support system or expert system gets a low score on the global measure of effectiveness if it fails to achieve the necessary performance level on a critical bottom-level attribute. This perspective can be readily handled arithmetically in MAUT by using (1) a 0 to indicate that the decision support system or expert system failed to pass the threshold on the critical dimension(s), and a 1 (or the utility scale) if it did; and (2) a multiplicative combination rule instead of the additive one in equation 1 to obtain the global measure of effectiveness score. By multiplying the scores, a 0 on a critical bottom-level attribute would result in an overall score of 0 for the system.

The MAUT hierarchy, utility functions, and relative weights (or other combination rule) represent an analytical model for users and sponsoring team members to use to combine test scores on different effectiveness measures into an overall assessment of the value of the decision support system or expert system. Moreover, the model permits sensitivity analyses. That is, one can use the MAUT model to analyze whether the overall utility assessment is sensitive to changes in the scores the system receives for certain criteria, and the relative importance of these criteria. One routinely finds that the overall assessment is sensitive to certain scores and weights, but not others. This information can help direct the development effort.

4.2 COST-BENEFIT ANALYSIS AND THE DOLLAR-EQUIVALENT TECHNIQUE

With MAUT, cost is simply considered as one of the (higher-level) measures of effectiveness of the decision support system or expert system. Its impact on the evaluation is determined by its impact on the overall utility score, which is achieved by (1) the utility function translating dollar costs into a utility score, and (2) the relative importance given to the cost measure of effectiveness. As Huber [1980, pp. 79–83] points out, in traditional cost-benefit analysis and the dollar-equivalent methods, however, all the benefits, as well as costs, are translated into dollar values instead of utilities. In the former, standard economic or accounting practices, such as employing the rate of return or time value of money concept, are used to create monetary equivalents. In the latter, ". . . the monetary equivalents are developed judgmentally when the standard economic techniques are stretched beyond their limits."

The conceptual similarity between cost-benefit analysis and MAUT can be illustrated by listing the following five principal steps for implementing the former, as identified by Keim and Janaro [1982]:

1. Identification of pertinent measures of effectiveness, that is, benefits.

2. The description of alternatives.
3. The "expression" of performance and cost as functions of the characteristics of each alternative.
4. Estimation of appropriate (dollar) values for the (performance) equation parameters.
5. Computation, sensitivity analysis, and presentation of results.

This sounds remarkably like the MAUT procedures described above, where one

1. Decomposed the global measure of effectiveness into a hierarchy of effectiveness measures (i.e., attributes);
2. Defined the alternatives (i.e., the decision support system or expert system and/or other options for potentially improving the organization's effectiveness);
3. Identified the natural scale value for each bottom-level attribute, and scored the alternatives on them;
4. Constructed utility functions for each bottom-level attribute, and relative weights for all the attributes, in order to convert the natural scale values into utility scale values; and
5. Computationally used a weighted, additive decision rule (or some other combination rule) to convert an alternative's scores on each of the bottom-level attributes into an overall utility score on the global measure of effectiveness. Sensitivity analysis is also routinely performed in MAUT.

The big differences between cost-benefit analysis and MAUT are that the former relies as much as possible on tangible (i.e., objective) benefits, and uses dollars instead of utilities to measure value. From a MAUT perspective, the omission of intangible benefits (and costs) is equivalent to the omission of attributes from the hierarchy. Whether this is acceptable or not depends on the nature of the "item(s)" being evaluated by a cost-benefit analysis.

Lay [1985, p. 32] has discussed this point with consideration to decision support systems:

> Most capital investments decisions in the business field can be evaluated in terms of return on investment (ROI). This is because the asset that is being evaluated will create tangible benefits (such as the manufacture of a product for subsequent sale). An information system (particularly Decision Support Systems), may only produce intangible benefits [e.g., information and decision process support] and therefore the ROI criteria can no longer be applied. Intangibles, although not quantifiable, should be included in the process since their impact on the organization may be significant.

We disagree with Lay's statement that intangibles are not quantifiable, for MAUT provides explicit procedures for quantifying the perceived value of intangibles. We do, however, agree with his focus on the significance of including intangibles when evaluating decision support systems and expert systems. However, their inclusion or omission should depend on what factors the sponsoring and development teams consider to be important requirements for the system. If intangibles are not important enough to include in the analysis, especially after discussions on the advantages and disadvantages to including them, then it might be more appropriate to perform cost-benefit analysis than MAUT because of its greater familiarity and use as common business practice.

As Huber [1980, p. 83] indicates, traditional cost-benefit analysis is a special case of the dollar-equivalent method, which is ". . . a special case of the more general . . . MAU model technique." The appropriateness of the two methods versus MAUT depends on the defensibility of converting a decision support system or expert system's score on the attributes to monetary equivalents. If standard economic practices are clear and defensible, then the traditional cost-benefit analysis approach is often preferred because its conversions are more explicit and agreed upon. If the practices are not defensible, but scores on the attributes can be readily converted to dollar equivalents through the judgments of users and members of the sponsoring team, then the dollar-equivalent technique is preferred because a single aggregate figure derived in dollars can be more easily understood than one in utilities. If this is not the case, then MAUT should be used. As always, the needs and preferences of members of the sponsoring and development teams should be factored into the decision regarding which subjective evaluation method to use.

In closing this section, we note that Keim and Janaro [1982] have argued for a phased cost-benefit analysis, where the nature of the analysis changes through the development cycle. Specifically, at the beginning of the effort, they argue for a relative cost-benefit analysis, where the focus is on identifying the relative costs and benefits of a range of alternative system configurations in order to select an alternative (or limited range of alternatives) for further specification. Their reasoning is that ". . . due to the evolutionary nature of the final system configuration the original estimates are often grossly distorted. The only way to make evaluations reasonable is to compare relative cost-benefit scenarios for the range of alternatives under consideration" (p. 25). As one moves through the different development steps, the system design becomes more specific; consequently, one can drop the "relative analysis" focus because increasingly specific and quantifiable information is available for the system evaluation.

Such a "phased" orientation is, of course, consistent with our perspective of integrating evaluation into development. A relative MAUT and cost-benefit analysis was used in the case study described later in this chapter.

4.3 DECISION ANALYSIS

Decision analysis is a formal method for combining uncertainties with utilities (or monetary equivalents) when evaluating alternative decision options. There are numerous texts on the subject [e.g., see Brown et al., 1974; von Winterfeldt and Edwards, 1986; Watson and Buede, 1987]. We will not discuss it in great detail because, at least to our knowledge, it has not yet been applied to evaluating decision support systems or expert systems. The interested reader is, however, referred to Cohen and Freeling [1981], who provide a detailed theoretical presentation of its potential applicability for evaluating information systems, and to O'Connor [1989], who discusses its applicability in developing and evaluating alternative architectures for the Strategic Defense Initiative.

Decision analysis is particularly appealing for evaluating decision support systems and expert systems because it uses scenarios to represent the uncertainties in the decision-making situation facing members of the sponsoring team. Within decision analysis, these scenarios represent the members' hypotheses regarding alternative states of the world, a perspective that is consistent with the SHOR paradigm. Remember, at the broadest level, and especially if the situation permits it during step 1 of the development process, the evaluator's job is to help the sponsoring team decide whether developing a decision support system or expert system is an effective option for dealing with the organization's current and/or future problems.

From a decision-analytic perspective, the overall utility, or more appropriately, expected utility of different options depends on (1) the probabilities assigned to the scenarios, and (2) the utility of each option for each scenario. This situation can be illustrated by the concept of a payoff matrix, an example of which is presented in Table 4.1. The rows of the matrix represent the alternative options. The columns represent the different scenarios that could significantly affect the attractiveness of the options. The $p_1 \ldots p_k$ values represent the probabilities for each scenario, with their sum being 1.0. The cell entries indicate the utility (or value) of the outcome or "payoff" of each combination of options and scenarios. The "best" option is the one with the highest expected utility, which is calculated for each option by first multiplying the utilities for the outcomes and probabilities for the scenarios, and then summing the products. (Note: For monetary equivalents, the outcomes are expressed in terms of dollars instead of utilities and, as a result, one calculates "expected values" instead of "expected utilities.")

Substantial care must be given to defining the scenarios and obtaining the probability assessments. O'Connor and Edwards [1976] point out that not only do the scenarios have to be realistic, they have to be representative of a wide range of possible futures states of nature without being a long, tedious list of uncertainties. Further, they must be capable of discriminating among the options in order to have any decision-making value. In short, they need to be, conceptually, an appropriate sample from the larger population of possible scenarios.

With respect to probability assessments, "[t]he credibility of a scenario to a subject seems to depend more on the coherence with which its author has spun the tale than on its intrinsically 'logical' probability of occurrence" [Spetzler and Stael von Holstein, 1975, p. 347]. Kahneman et al. [1982] have compiled an anthology

TABLE 4.1   A Simple Payoff Matrix

Alternatives	States of Nature			
	$(p_1)S_1$	$(p_2)S_2$	$\cdots\cdots$	$(p_k)S_k$
A	a_1	a_2	$\cdots\cdots$	a_k
B	b_1	b_2	$\cdots\cdots$	b_k
.	.	.	$\cdots\cdots$	.
.	.	.	$\cdots\cdots$	.
.	.	.	$\cdots\cdots$	.
N	n_1	n_2	$\cdots\cdots$	n_k

of research studies demonstrating that, when compared to the tenets of probability and statistical theory, humans have limited appreciation for the concepts of randomness, statistical independence, sampling variability, data reliability and validity, and other concepts essential to estimating probabilities. Moreover, the way that information is presented can often mask the problem's logical structure.

It is essential that evaluators using decision analysis describe key statistical concepts to participants. In addition, they should use multiple methods to elicit the probability estimates to ensure their consistency. Finally, they need to give substantial care to presenting the scenarios so that their logical probabilistic structure and, hence, the probabilities can be more easily estimated by members of the sponsoring team. This often requires using a probability tree to decompose the scenario into its critical, uncertain events.

This point can be illustrated by considering an uncertainty dear to the heart of members of the development team, which is whether or not the sponsoring agency can provide the necessary funding level for a decision support system or expert system throughout its development cycle. Figure 4.4 presents a highly simplified hypothetical probability tree representing only two uncertain events: whether or not the funding environment is stable and, conditional upon it, whether or not the requested funding level is satisfied.

As you can see, we are assuming a good state of affairs. A stable funding environment is considered twice as likely as an unstable one. If the environment is stable, we are assuming that it is four times as likely as not that the development team will receive the necessary funding. If it is not stable, then we are assuming the opposite. If one multiples out the probabilities for each branch of the tree, and then sums the probabilities for the two "request satisfied" branches, one finds, however, that the probability that the development team will have the necessary funding is actually only 0.62.

The situation gets somewhat more discouraging if one now considers the probability that the development team will develop an effective system. Figure 4.5 shows the probabilities for developing an "effective" decision support system (or expert system) for each of the four branches of the tree in Figure 4.4. Again, we

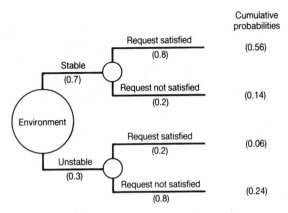

FIGURE 4.4 A highly simplified probability tree for illustrating the uncertainty in funding for a DSS throughout the duration of the development process

have assumed a good state of affairs; two to one odds for developing a successful system if provided with the necessary funding. But after multiplying out all the probabilities in the tree and summing them for the appropriate branches, one finds that the probability of developing an "effective" decision support system is 0.548, only a little better than the odds involved in flipping a coin.

The purpose in presenting what one might consider to be a reasonable, if not realistic, scenario was threefold. The first purpose was to illustrate the importance of considering the structure of a scenario, not just its content. Substantial care must be given to eliciting probability estimates when using decision analysis, particularly the greater the ambiguity and the longer the time horizon for the uncertainties of interest. This is typically the case in step 1 of the development process.

The second purpose was to provide an alternative perspective on the sad fact that many decision support systems and expert systems are not successfully implemented. From a statistical perspective, a large number of things have to go right for successful implementation. And the third purpose was to emphasize again the importance of considering the uncertainties inherent in decision-making situations. As the example illustrates, it may be just as important for the development team to consider these uncertainties as the sponsoring team. Decision analysis can alert members of the development team to the uncertainties in the situation within which they will be working and, thereby, help further clarify the general requirements that the decision support system or expert system will have to satisfy under various future conditions.

In closing this brief discussion of decision analysis, it is worth reiterating that decision analysis combines both probability and utility assessment. As was illustrated with the payoff matrix shown in Table 4.1, the "best" option is the one with the highest expected utility, which is calculated for each option by first multiplying the overall values (i.e., utilities) for the outcomes and the probabilities for

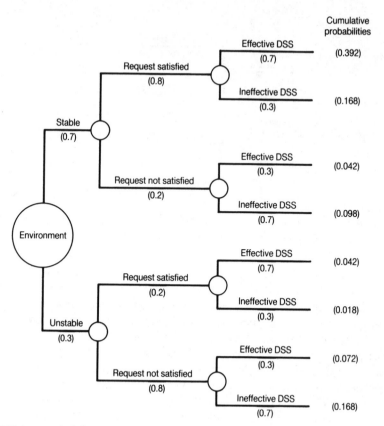

FIGURE 4.5 A slightly expanded probability tree for the hypothetical funding illustration

the scenarios, and then summing the products. The payoff matrix can be expanded [e.g., see Pitz and McKillip, 1984, p. 111] by using (1) a decision tree to represent scenarios pictorially and, thereby, reflect the uncertainty in obtaining the outcomes for the options under consideration; and (2) a MAUT hierarchy to illustrate that the overall utility for an option, independent of the probability of obtaining it, is a composite score on multiple attributes. The expected utility for each option under consideration is the sum of the products for the probabilities for the scenarios and the utilities for the attributes.

The process of performing a decision analysis is typically slow and difficult, for the decision-analytic representation of the problem can be quite large and the judgments quite extensive. Consequently, decision analysis is most viable if there is sufficient time (and resources) for the evaluator to work with the sponsoring team when (1) it is still considering a range of options, that is, prior to step 1 in the development cycle; and (2) preliminary discussions suggest that uncertainties about the future environment may play a significant role in assessing the viability of developing a decision support system or expert system. Once the development process is under way, however, the utility component is of most concern to evaluation, since the probability of alternative future states is typically not under the sponsoring or development team's control.

4.4 MAUT-BASED COST-BENEFIT ANALYSIS

MAUT-based cost-benefit analysis uses multiattribute utility technology judgment elicitation procedures and the benefit-to-cost ratio concept to identify the best option for various levels of dollar cost. Although this method is not widely known, it has been used to help develop advanced helicopter designs [Adelman, 1984], the U.S. Marine Corps' annual budget [Watson and Buede, 1987], health and hospital service plans [Weiss and Zwahlen, 1982], and the training curriculum for a federal government agency [Medlin and Adelman, 1989]. Section 4.7 illustrates how Rockmore et al. [1982] used the method to select DART and the four other decision support system and expert system prototypes developed for the Rome Air Development Center (RADC). This section will provide a general outline of the procedural steps of the method, and indicate its general applicability to selecting a set (or suite) of decision support and expert system technologies that meets the sponsoring team's requirements.

MAUT-based cost-benefit analysis has six basic steps:

1. Divide the problem into areas (or "variables") over which benefits and costs can vary almost independently.
2. Identify distinctly different actions (or "levels") on each variable that increase in benefit and cost.
3. Assess the relative benefit and cost of each level on each variable.
4. Assess the relative benefit of one variable against another by assigning relative weights to the variables.
5. Calculate the delta benefit to delta cost ratio for each level of each variable as one moves from the lowest to the highest level of each variable.
6. Use an optimization algorithm to calculate the efficient frontier defining the most beneficial package (i.e., one level on each variable) for varying degrees of (total) cost.

When selecting a suite of decision support and expert systems, the different variables represent the different areas for which systems are being considered by the sponsoring team. For example, assume that an organization is considering the development of decision support and expert systems for each of three divisions

(A, B, and C) within the organization. The three divisions represent the variables. The first level on each variable is either the status quo, which may be "no system," or the cheapest, most "bare bones" system concept for that division. In the case study, the status quo of "no system" is represented by level 0; the "bare bones" concept is represented by level 1. The last level on a variable represents the most expensive, "gold-plated" (yet realistic) conceptualization of the decision support system or expert system. The intermediate levels on a variable represent intermediate conceptualizations of the system as one moves from the "bare bones" to more "gold-plated" concepts.

A relative benefit scale is established for each variable such that the initial level is given a value of 0 and the "gold-plated" level is given a value of 100. Paired comparisons are typically used to determine the relative benefit of the intermediate levels on a variable. In particular, the focus is on how much benefit an intermediate level provides between the two endpoints of the variable's scale; that is, between the 0 and the 100.

For instance, let's assume that the first level for variable A (for division A) is the status quo, which is "no system." Level 2 is a minimal, "bare bones" decision support system concept. Now, from a relative benefit perspective, the first question is whether level 2 on variable A (i.e., the "bare bones" system concept for division A) provides less than, more than, or exactly half the additional value of the "gold-plated" concept when compared to "no system" status quo. Its benefit value would be a 50 if its additional value was exactly halfway between the two extremes, and greater than 50 if it provided more than half the value, and less than 50 if it provided less than half the value. For discussion purposes, let's assume that the level 2 system concept provided less than half the additional value of the "gold-plated" concept. Now the questioning focuses on how much less than 50 the benefit value for level 2 should be.

Let's assume, for example, that the relative benefit value for level 2 was 10. That would mean that the level 2 system concept provided 10% of the benefit between the "no system" status quo (level 1) and the "gold-plated" system concept for division A. If the benefit value was 20, then it would be 20% of the benefit between the two extremes, and so on. Once a relative benefit score is obtained for level 2, the focus shifts to level 3 on the variable. Level 3 must have a relative benefit score between that for level 2 and the "gold-plated" system concept. The process would continue in this manner until a relative benefit value was assigned to all the intermediate levels of the variable. By specifying the relative values for each of the intermediate levels on a variable, one develops a subjective benefit scale for the variable that is analogous to a utility function that converts natural scale points on an attribute into utilities.

Relative importance weights are then used to indicate the relative benefit of improving from the initial level to the "gold-plated" on each variable; that is, from 0 to 100 for variable A (i.e., division A in our example) versus 0 to 100 for variable B versus 0 to 100 for variable C in our example. For instance, let's assume that going from the status quo of "no system" to "gold-plated" on variable *A* was thought to be twice as beneficial as doing so on both variables *B* and *C*, which are equally important. If the relative importance weights sum to 100, then the relative weight on variable *A* would be 50 and the relative weights on variables *B* and *C* would be 25.

The overall benefit given to any level on any variable is calculated by multiplying (1) the relative weight for the variable and (2) the benefit value for the level within the variable. For instance, let's assume that level 3 for variable *A* had a within-variable benefit value of 50. Since, in our example, variable *A* has a relative weight of 50 and variable *B* a relative weight of 25, level 3 on variable *A* has the same overall benefit as the gold-plated concept on variable *B* because 50 × 50 equals 100 × 25. (Note: The overall benefit of each level for each variable in the design could be assessed directly using paired-comparison techniques. However, experience suggests that participants find the above procedure easier, especially when there are many levels and variables.)

In addition, a cost estimate also needs to be obtained for each level of each variable. The cost estimate for the first level on each variable is only important in providing a reference point, for the analysis assumes that the starting point (or first set or solution) is represented by the initial level on each variable. This would be the "status quo" in our example if the first level of each of the three variables (i.e., divisions) was "status quo." Of course, the first level for one or more of the variables could be a "bare bones" system concept. In that case, the starting point would include a "bare bones" system concept for one or more of the divisions. Again, the starting point is represented by the initial level on each variable.

The cost estimates could be in absolute dollars or in "relative costs," depending on which one the participants (or more likely, the personnel responsible for software cost estimation) feel more confident in using in the analysis. In almost all cases, higher levels on a variable will cost more. That is, level 3 on variable *A* would be expected to cost more than level 2 because the former is a more enhanced system concept than the latter. There is, however, no basis for assuming that a level on one variable will cost the same as the same level on another variable. For example, there is no reason to assume that level 3 on variable *A* will cost the same as level 3 on variable *B*. Even if essentially the same system is being proposed in both cases, the personnel and organizational structure of the divisions may be so different that the software development costs could, in fact, differ. One would, however, expect the costs to be comparable in the two cases.

One can now calculate the overall incremental benefits and costs of moving from one level to another on each variable. The goal is to maximize the incremental benefits to incremental costs (i.e., the delta benefit to delta cost ratio) every time one increases the outlayed costs. For instance, if the "no system" status quo defines the initial level on all the variables, then the first system concept purchased should be the one that provides the most benefit to the organization for the money spent. Again, considering our example, that might be selecting level 2 on variable

A, level 2 on variable *B*, level 3 on variable *C*, or whatever increase provides the most benefit per unit cost to the organization. The second purchase should be the next system concept, regardless of which division, that provides the most benefit per unit cost given that the organization has already made the first purchase. The third purchase should be the remaining system concept that provides the most benefit per unit cost given the second purchase, and so forth.

Figure 4.6 pictorially represents what is being done. The horizontal axis represents increasing costs as one moves from left to right. The vertical axis represents the percentage of increased overall benefit to the organization, going from 0% to 100%. The asterisks represent the progression of system concepts (i.e., purchases) that provides the greatest incremental benefits, per unit costs, and their total benefit percentage and dollar costs. The first asterisk represents the initial level on all the variables. The last point represents the "gold-plated" system concept on all the variables and, in turn, a 100% increase in incremental benefit. If one were to draw a curve connecting all the asterisks, this would represent an efficient frontier. The efficient frontier presented in Figure 4.6 is a hypothetical one for illustrative purposes.

The procedure for generating the points shown in Figure 4.6 has three principal steps. First, we calculate the incremental delta benefit to delta cost ratio for each level of each variable as one moves from the lowest to the highest level of each variable. Second, we order the levels on the basis of their delta benefit to delta cost ratio. Third, we sequentially select the level with the highest delta benefit to

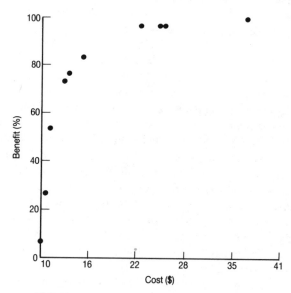

FIGURE 4.6   A hypothetical efficient frontier

delta cost ratio. Thus, each incremental point on the efficient frontier represents a set of decision support and expert systems that was identical to the one that preceded it except for one change, that remaining level with the highest delta benefit to delta cost level at that time.

(Note: Although this algorithm may not derive all the points on the efficient frontier, it is guaranteed to derive the frontier's convex hull; that is, its smooth outline. Moreover, experience has shown that this algorithm is easier than other approaches for decision makers to understand, and to follow its implications. Finally, it can be readily programmed for, and will operate quickly on, personal computers.)

MAUT-based cost-benefit analysis can also be used to identify the most beneficial configuration of components of a particular decision support system or expert system at different levels of cost. For example, Sprague and Carlson [1982] and Sage [1986, 1991] have conceptualized decision support systems as being comprised of three principal components: the database management system, the model-base management system containing the system's analytic method(s), and the user interface. In the terms of a MAUT-based cost-benefit analysis, these three components can represent the different variables. The different potential levels of sophistication for each of the three components represent the different levels on the three variables. Relative benefit values are obtained from representative users and sponsoring team members for the levels within each variable, as are relative weights for indicating the perceived relative importance of the three variables. Software costs are estimated for each level by appropriate personnel. Then, the procedure described above is used to generate points on the efficient frontier indicating the set of component parts providing the most incremental benefit per unit cost at different levels of total cost.

4.5 OTHER SUBJECTIVE EVALUATION METHODS

The subjective evaluation methods discussed above represent different approaches to modeling and, thereby, supporting the judgments inherent in the decision support system and expert system development process. There are, of course, other subjective evaluation methods, as well as variations on the above themes.

Two examples are feature-based criteria lists and value of information analysis. According to Riedel and Pitz [1986, p. 992]:

A number of feature-based criteria lists have been developed. The Sixth Army data base evaluation form includes the following criteria: material and organization, packaging, menus, help, data entry, training, installation, multitasking/multiuser/LAN, security, data protection, program protection, sorting/indexing, reports, specific DBMS requirements, and general options. Within these are 149 subcriteria.

It would be unfortunate if these features merely represented a checklist, for they appear to correspond to the attributes in a MAUT. That is, one would like to know how a system's score on these attributes is converted into a value score on a global measure of effectiveness. Are utility functions (and relative weights) used? Are dollar equivalent functions used? The fact that these attributes are very different than those used in the subjective evaluation of DART or in the analyses presented below should not bother one. Remember, the purpose of the attributes is to reflect the information and decision needs of the relevant decision makers accurately.

Similarly, value of information has been used to evaluate information systems. Although there have been numerous definitions of the construct, the bottom line is that information only has value if it can affect decision making. This concept is explicitly captured in decision analysis. Specifically, "The value of information is equal to the difference between the net expected payoff from the decision made without the information and the net expected payoff from the decision made with the information" [Huber, 1980, p. 127].

From an organizational perspective, it doesn't matter whether the information was captured with or without decision support or expert system technologies. From an evaluation perspective, however, attempting to capture the value of information provided by a decision support system or expert system within a decision-analytic framework can be quite complex. The interested reader is referred to Cohen and Freeling [1981] for an extended discussion of the concept from the perspective of evaluating information systems, as well as Brown et al. [1974] and Watson and Buede [1987] for an introduction to decision analysis in general and value of information in particular.

Although not described here, other subjective evaluation methods have been used to evaluate expert systems. For example, Liebowitz [1986] has used the analytical hierarchy process developed by Saaty [1980], Tong et al. [1987] have proposed a frame-based approach, and Klein and Brezovic [1988] and Slagle and Wick [1988] have used subjective test and evaluation approaches analogous to multiattribute utility technology. The interested reader is urged to consider them.

4.6 DISCUSSION

We have emphasized five subjective evaluation methods: multiattribute utility technology (MAUT), cost-benefit analysis, the dollar-equivalent technique, decision analysis, and a MAUT-based cost-benefit analysis. All five are oriented to evaluating the overall value (or effectiveness) of a decision support system or expert system. With MAUT, utility functions and a weighted, additive decision rule are typically used to convert scores on multiple attributes (or evaluation criteria) into a single, global measure of effectiveness. With cost-benefit analysis and the dollar-equivalent technique, dollars are used instead of utilities to represent overall effectiveness. Cost-benefit analysis uses standard accounting practices, such as rate of return and time value of money, to create monetary equivalents. The dollar-equivalent technique develops the equivalents judgmentally when the standard practices are stretched beyond their limit. Decision analysis provides a formal method for combining uncertainties with utilities or dollar equivalents. Finally, the MAUT-based cost-benefit analysis uses cost-benefit ratios, where benefit is defined in terms of a utility scale, to evaluate options. Conceptually, it could also be done for dollar equivalents.

All five subjective evaluation methods are applicable throughout development. The appropriateness of a method depends on the information and decision needs of members of the sponsoring and/or development team, available time and resources, and the comfort that participants have with the method. These factors represent three attributes for evaluating the appropriateness (or utility) of the methods; there are, obviously, additional attributes depending on one's situation. "Information need" and "comfort" are conceptually independent. For example, decision makers typically feel more comfortable with "objective, quantitative" measures of effectiveness. However, they need to consider more qualitative, subjective measures of effectiveness. All five subjective evaluation methods are capable of handling both objective and subjective effectiveness measures.

The measures of effectiveness, and subjective evaluation methods used to convert performance measures into them, should be used early in development, and throughout it, to evaluate the system. All that changes with time is the basis for these judgments, both in terms of the specificity of the decision support system or expert system and, for certain measures of effectiveness, the availability of empirical and technical performance data. Accordingly, it is important to obtain consensus among the sponsoring team, which should include representative users, about the measures of effectiveness (and their relative importance) early in (if not prior to) development. To quote O'Connor [1989, p. 103], "These attribute trade-offs are not after-the-fact evaluation issues. Rather, they are decision issues relevant to the design problem and should be resolved before detailed system design and testing take place."

All five methods develop an analytical model to represent the judgments of the participating decision makers. One of the principal advantages of a "model" is that it permits sensitivity analysis; members of the sponsoring team can change their judgments and see if the changes have any effect on the results. For example, does changing the relative importance placed on an attribute (e.g., response time) in a MAUT suggest that a different system design be implemented? Sensitivity analysis is an important capability early in development because there may exist considerable disagreement among the sponsoring team owing to both information input uncertainty regarding the hypotheses and consequence-of-action uncertainty regarding options. The ability to perform "what if" analysis helps sponsoring team members deal with this disagreement.

There is a long line of research [for a review, see Delbecq et al., 1975] demonstrating that, more often than not, structured facilitation procedures can focus a group's discussion, thereby increasing the probability not only of a more accurate final position, but one that is more strongly supported by the group. The subjective methods described above further improve discussion by letting members of the sponsoring team focus on a quantitative model instead of each other. Eils and John [1980], for instance, found that groups using multiattribute utility assessment procedures in conjunction with group facilitation procedures tended to make more accurate decisions than groups using only facilitation procedures.

Better discussion occurs because group members have to define their thought processes in order to provide the numerical inputs required by the model. At the same time, however, the model permits group members to retreat from their original position, or more strongly voice it, on the basis of the numerical outputs and sensitivity analyses. Directing the discussion toward aspects of the model helps remove some of the "personal" focus of group decision making.

The presentation has focused on the applicability of subjective evaluation methods during requirements analysis (step 1), the purpose of which is to define (1) what the decision support system or expert system has to be capable of doing in order for the decision maker who is using it to consider it to be a good system, and (2) whether development of such a system is feasible given the financial, time, personnel, and other constraints operating in the situation. As mentioned earlier, explicit identification of measures of effectiveness, and procedures for converting performance scores into a global MOE, represent reference points for the development team to use when developing the decision support system or expert system, and criteria for the evaluator to monitor in order to determine whether the development process is on track.

MAUT, cost-benefit analysis, decision analysis, and the different variations on these methods were developed to help decision makers systematically evaluate decision options, regardless of what they might be. Consequently, they are potentially applicable anywhere in the development process where members of the development team need to evaluate one option against another. In particular, they are applicable to evaluating the storyboards developed during functional modeling (step 2); balancing the trade-offs inherent in selecting one (or more) analytical methods (step 3); evaluating off-the-shelf software (step 4); selecting a hardware configuration (step 5); or evaluating alternative users' manuals (step 6), or management approaches for system transfer (step 7).

We now present the case study, which showcases MAUT and the MAUT-based cost-benefit analysis.

4.7   CASE STUDY

This section summarizes the analysis presented in a report by Rockmore et al. [1982]. The purpose for doing so is to illustrate how subjective evaluation methods can be used to (1) identify the requirements that decision support systems and expert systems need to satisfy in a particular situation, and (2) select systems for satisfying them. The presentation of data from the report is for purely illustrative purposes.

The report by Rockmore et al. represents the results of Task II on the Decision Aids for Target Aggregation (DATA) contract from the Rome Air Development Center (RADC) to PAR Technology Corporation; the subcontractors were Decisions and Designs, Inc. and Systems Control Technology, Inc. The contract represented the first major "decision aiding" development efforts funded by RADC. Its objective was to demonstrate the feasibility, and evaluate the utility, of decision aids highlighting the analytical methods of decision analysis, artificial intelligence, or operations research for decisions made above the single-unit level but below the battle staff (i.e., general officer) level of the Tactical Air Control System. DART was one of the five systems selected, designed, developed, and evaluated on the project. The term *decision aid* is used below to refer to both decision support and expert system technology:

> Task I of the D.A.T.A. effort concentrated on the characterization of Tactical Air Force Command, Control, Communications, and Intelligence (TAF C^3I) decision situations. The elements of the TAF C^3I process that have been identified indicate a high potential for being aided using such technologies as decision analysis, artificial intelligence, and operations research. This task resulted in the specification of nineteen descriptions of C^3I activities in context, denoted "aid frames." Task II . . . was primarily concerned with the [conceptual] design of candidate decision aids for each aid frame and the selection of the aids to be built. . . . In particular, one or more decision aids were proposed for each aid frame of Task I, leading to an initial total of 28 aids. . . . Then a multi-attribute utility analysis [MAUA] was performed on the performance and risk of these aids. . . . After this analysis, the fourteen highest scoring aids were subsequently evaluated using a cost/benefit analysis. [Rockmore et al., 1982, pp. 1–2]

The remainder of this section describes the MAUT and MAUT-based cost-benefit analyses. These analyses were performed in a conference setting composed of the RADC program monitors who sponsored the development effort and the contract personnel.

Figure 4.7 presents a pictorial representation of the multiattributed hierarchy developed to evaluate candidate decision aids. As can be seen, overall utility was decomposed into two principal attributes: performance and risk. Performance was decomposed into task performance, which received almost all of the weight, and other uses. Task performance was further decomposed into output quality, speed, ease of use, transparency, robustness, and combat supportability. Two of the task performance attributes were further decomposed to obtain bottom-level attributes. Specifically, speed was decomposed into time for accomplishment and time for data management; combat supportability was decomposed into skill availability, hardware necessary, and setup time.

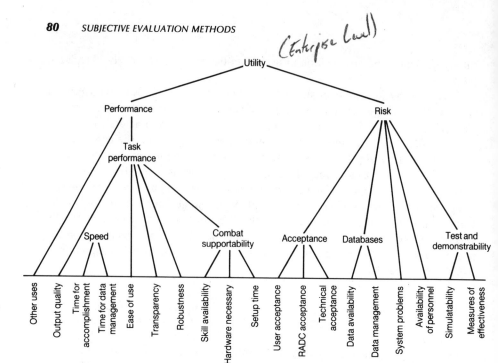

FIGURE 4.7 A pictorial representation of the MAUA (multiattribute utility analysis) hierarchy used to evaluate candidate decision support systems

Risk was decomposed into five principal attributes: acceptance, databases, system problems, personnel availability, and test and demonstrability. Acceptance, databases, and test and demonstrability were further decomposed to obtain bottom-level attributes. Specifically, acceptance was decomposed into user, RADC, and technical acceptance to represent the different perspectives of members of the sponsoring and development teams; databases was decomposed into data availability and data management; and test and demonstrability was decomposed into simulatability and measures of effectiveness.

Definitions and scales were developed for each of the bottom-level attributes. Table 4.2 presents the definitions and scales for the first three bottom-level attributes listed in the hierarchy: other military uses, quality of task output, and time for task accomplishment. As these attributes illustrate, the bottom-level attributes were a mix of subjective and objective measures of effectiveness. In all cases, however, the scale values for the attribute was converted to a utility scale going from 0 to 100.

Figure 4.8 presents the hierarchy, but now with the relative weights assigned to the attributes. The weights at each node of the hierarchy sum to 100. For example, at the top level of the hierarchy, performance has a weight of 70 and risk

TABLE 4.2 The Definitions and Utility Scales for the First Three Bottom-Level Attributes

Attribute Scale Definitions

A. *Other Military Uses.* Includes use of aid in training, combat use by other levels and components in TACS[a], and potential value to SAC[b] or other services.

> 100 = Greatly improves training for this task and also substantially improves other combat tasks at any level.
> 50 = Improves training or other combat tasks, but not both.
> 0 = No significant improvement, training, or other tasks.

B. *Quality of Task Output* using the aid under "average" battle conditions. Consider accuracy, completeness, and relevance in judging output quality.

> 100 = Optimal. Quality of output is the best that could be expected, given the available information, if the best experts had all the time they needed to perform the task and the most advanced computer assistance possible.
> 0 = Status quo (SQ).

C. *Time for Accomplishment* of task.

> 100 = Instantaneous.
> 0 = 100 minutes (for NRT[c] aids).
> 0 = 10 hours (for HOURS[d] aids).

[a]TACS stands for Tactical Air Control System.
[b]SAC stands for Strategic Air Command.
[c]NRT stands for Near Real Time.
[d]HOURS stands for an aid that takes hours to perform its task.

has a weight of 30; this means that, in general, performance was $2\frac{1}{3}$ times more important than acceptance. Within the performance node, task performance has a weight of 95 and other uses has a weight of 5. In contrast to this sharp differentiation, the attributes comprising the risk node have more similar weights. Even so, test and demonstrability is considered, in general, to be three times more important than system problems.

The weights on the bottom-level attributes represent their cumulative weights, which is obtained by multiplying the relative weights from the top to the bottom of the hierarchy. As can be see, output quality and robustness were clearly considered to be the two most important bottom-level attributes by the sponsoring and development teams. These two attributes account for 33% of the total weight (or value) of all the bottom-level attributes in the hierarchy.

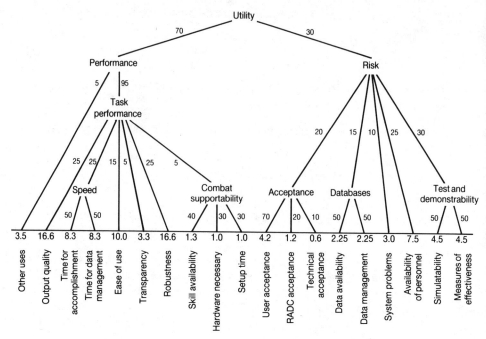

FIGURE 4.8 The MAUA hierarchy with relative weights

Each of the candidate decision support systems and expert systems was scored on the bottom-level attributes, and these scores were converted into an *initial* overall utility value for each system using equation 1, which was presented earlier in this chapter. Table 4.3 shows the results for the system candidates that were not proposed as real-time aids; they were referred to as "hours" aids. The columns indicate the score for each system at each level of the hierarchy, which is represented by the rows. The higher the number, the better the utility score. In case you're curious, the heading "DAR" refers to the DART expert system. DART had a total utility score of 56, just one point less than two other systems; it had the best assessment on risk. (Note: Cost was given a weight of 0 because (1) all of the proposed systems could be produced to a demonstrable stage with available project resources, and (2) it was decided that cost could be better incorporated into the selection process using the MAUT-based cost-benefit analysis.)

The *final* utility score for each decision support system and expert system candidate was actually obtained using equation 2:

$$U_i = \underset{\substack{\text{risk}\\\text{attributes}}}{\text{SUM}} \; W_j A_{ij} + \text{MILVAL}_i * \underset{\substack{\text{performance}\\\text{attributes}}}{\text{SUM}} \; W_j A_{ij} \qquad (2)$$

where

U_i = the utility of system i;

W_j = the weight of attribute j;

A_{ij} = the utility score of system i on attribute j; and

MILVAL$_i$ = the military value of the aid frame system i is proposed to support.

The MILVAL parameter was an important addition to the basic MAUT additive decision rule in this situation because it

> . . . reflects the fact that some aids are potentially more valuable than other aids by virtue of the aid frame, not the aid. Thus the overall performance should reflect both the aid quality and the aid frame importance. . . . Notice that the weights are independent of the aid evaluated, as they should be. Also notice that the inclusion of MILVAL does not alter the linearity of the analysis; it merely rescales (in a consistent manner) the weights of the performance attributes. [Rockmore et al., 1982, p. 13]

MILVAL increased the relative importance of the performance versus risk attributes. The increase depended on the problem the candidate system was to address. This not a typical MAUT application where relative weights are independent of the options being evaluated, such as in the initial assessment presented in Table 4.3. Nevertheless, it did permit the sponsoring and development teams to incorporate the importance of the area being supported by the decision support system or expert system into the utility assessment. This is consistent with the "organizational effectiveness" focus stressed throughout the book.

The MAUT-based cost-benefit analysis was performed on the 14 decision support systems and expert systems (out of an initial set of 28) that passed the multiattribute utility analysis (MAUA) described above. The 14 systems represented 14 variables in the MAUT-based cost-benefit analysis. The first step was to define levels of sophistication for each of the 14 systems.

The levels were developed by those members of the development team that would actually develop the decision support system or expert system prototype, who in this case were the representatives of the three participating contractors. Level 0 for each system was "status quo," which meant "no system," so that the analysis could incrementally indicate which levels of which variables (i.e., systems) provided the best benefit-to-cost ratio. Level 1 indicated the basic, "bare bones" level of development for the decision support system or expert system. The highest level on each variable indicated the highest level of sophistication that could be developed for that system given available financial resources to the development contractor. Intermediate levels on a variable indicated intermediate levels of sophistication between level 1 and the highest development level for the system. Table 4.4 shows the levels for each of the 14 variables (i.e., systems).

Overall benefit (or utility) was decomposed into two attributes: (1) the military value of the decision support system or expert system, assuming it had been trans-

TABLE 4.3 The Initial Utility Scores Based on Performance and Risk for the "Hours" Decision Support Systems

—HOURS TOTAL

FACTOR	WT	GTA	ICM	OAS	TCO	REM	ESA	TPA	CTA	DAR	DAG	GSP	C3P	TLD	DYS	IWA
1. Performance	(70)	21	16	9	30	17	29	28	37	44	47	34	52	38	47	29
2. Risk	(30)	76	76	58	80	79	62	78	73	83	80	77	69	75	65	75
3. Cost	(0)	0	0	0	0	0	0	0	0	0	10	9	18	9	12	9
TOTAL		*38*	*34*	*23*	*45*	*35*	*39*	*43*	*48*	*56*	*57*	*47*	*57*	*49*	*52*	*43*

—HOURS TOTAL—PERFORMANCE

FACTOR	WT	GTA	ICM	OAS	TCO	REM	ESA	TPA	CTA	DAR	DAG	GSP	C3P	TLD	DYS	IWA
1. Task perf	(90)	16	7	4	28	14	21	26	33	40	46	29	48	33	41	23
2. Other uses	*(10)	70	100	50	50	40	100	50	70	82	55	80	90	80	100	85
TOTAL		*21*	*16*	*9*	*30*	*17*	*29*	*28*	*37*	*44*	*47*	*34*	*52*	*38*	*47*	*29*

—HOURS TASK PERF

FACTOR	WT	GTA	ICM	OAS	TCO	REM	ESA	TPA	CTA	DAR	DAG	GSP	C3P	TLD	DYS	IWA
1. Outpt qual	*(35)	70	90	50	90	70	70	95	50	60	93	75	70	90	90	80
2. Speed	(10)	30	75	15	85	20	83	73	43	58	83	55	53	85	90	68
3. User ease	*(10)	0	25	0	-3	20	-13	0	16	16	50	50	50	50	50	30
4. Transparen	*(15)	-10	15	0	-25	-30	-30	-20	10	19	15	10	34	10	10	-10
5. Robustness	*(25)	0	25	0	0	0	-15	0	21	31	40	40	21	5	15	15
6. Combat sup	(5)	-6	-15	-3	-18	-18	-15	-19	-19	-9	-5	15	25	-19	-18	-12
TOTAL		*26*	*49*	*19*	*35*	*23*	*26*	*37*	*31*	*38*	*58*	*49*	*46*	*47*	*50*	*39*

—HOURS TASK—SPEED

FACTOR	WT	GTA	ICM	OAS	TCO	REM	ESA	TPA	CTA	DAR	DAG	GSP	C3P	TLD	DYS	IWA
1. Time accmp	*(50)	60	75	30	80	40	65	45	35	55	90	80	55	70	80	75
2. Time D/M	*(50)	0	75	0	90	0	100	100	50	60	75	30	50	100	100	60
TOTAL		*30*	*75*	*15*	*85*	*20*	*83*	*73*	*43*	*58*	*83*	*55*	*53*	*85*	*90*	*68*

—HOURS TASK—COMBAT SUPPORT

FACTOR	WT	GTA	ICM	OAS	TCO	REM	ESA	TPA	CTA	DAR	DAG	GSP	C3P	TLD	DYS	IWA
1. Skill avail	*(40)	0	0	0	0	0	0	0	39	14	25	50	64	0	10	25
2. Log sup	*(30)	-20	-25	-10	-35	-20	-25	-40	5	-33	-25	-15	-8	-40	-50	-65
3. Setup time	*(30)	0	-25	0	-25	-40	-25	-25	5	-17	-25	0	5	-25	-25	-10
TOTAL		*-6*	*-15*	*-3*	*-18*	*-18*	*-15*	*-19*	*19*	*-9*	*-5*	*15*	*25*	*-19*	*-18*	*-12*

—HOURS TOTAL—RISK

FACTOR	WT	GTA	ICM	OAS	TCO	REM	ESA	TPA	CTA	DAR	DAG	GSP	C3P	TLD	DYS	IWA
1. Acceptance	(22)	69	95	30	69	75	61	83	82	88	94	87	79	83	89	76
2. Data bases	(16)	65	60	60	68	65	50	50	67	69	68	65	65	50	50	65
3. Sys problm	*(5)	90	75	90	75	90	75	75	80	72	70	85	75	70	70	85
4. Pers avail	*(26)	100	85	70	95	100	70	85	71	85	85	90	61	75	60	90
5. Test/demo	(31)	65	63	60	83	70	60	83	71	88	75	65	71	83	60	65
6. Relat cur	*(0)	100	75	50	75	50	75	75	70	82	0	0	0	0	0	0
TOTAL		*76*	*76*	*58*	*80*	*79*	*62*	*78*	*73*	*83*	*80*	*77*	*69*	*75*	*65*	*75*

(*continued*)

TABLE 4.3 (Continued)

—HOURS TOTAL—RISK—ACCEPTANCE

FACTOR	WT	GTA	ICM	OAS	TCO	REM	ESA	TPA	CTA	DAR	DAG	GSP	C3P	TLD	DYS	IWA
1. User accep	*(70)	65	100	25	65	70	50	80	78	85	100	90	75	80	90	75
2. Radc accep	*(20)	80	90	25	75	90	95	90	95	95	75	80	95	90	95	80
3. Tech accept	*(10)	80	75	80	90	80	75	90	84	92	90	80	78	90	75	80
TOTAL		*69*	*95*	*30*	*69*	*75*	*61*	*83*	*82*	*88*	*94*	*87*	*79*	*83*	*89*	*76*

—HOURS TOTAL—RISK—DATA BASES

FACTOR	WT	GTA	ICM	OAS	TCO	REM	ESA	TPA	CTA	DAR	DAG	GSP	C3P	TLD	DYS	IWA
1. Data avail	*(50)	70	60	50	60	50	50	50	63	70	60	70	63	50	50	70
2. Data mgmt	*(50)	60	60	70	75	80	50	50	71	67	75	60	67	50	50	60
TOTAL		*65*	*60*	*60*	*68*	*65*	*50*	*50*	*67*	*69*	*68*	*65*	*65*	*50*	*50*	*65*

—HOURS TOTAL—RISK—TEST/DEMONSTRABILITY

FACTOR	WT	GTA	ICM	OAS	TCO	REM	ESA	TPA	CTA	DAR	DAG	GSP	C3P	TLD	DYS	IWA
1. Simultblty	*(50)	70	75	70	75	90	70	90	74	95	60	70	74	90	70	70
2. Meas effec	*(50)	60	50	50	90	50	50	75	68	80	90	60	68	75	50	60
TOTAL		*65*	*63*	*60*	*83*	*70*	*60*	*83*	*71*	*88*	*75*	*65*	*71*	*83*	*60*	*65*

TABLE 4.4 The Problem Representation for the MAUT-Based Cost-Benefit Analysis

Decision Support System (DSS)	Level 0[a]	Level 1	Level 2	Level 3
ADRA	SQ	Plan detailer	Plan refiner	
ADW	SQ	Air defense allocator	+ Maps	
C3P	SQ	Feasibility study	Plan criticizer	+ More plans
CART	SQ	Rule-based correlation		
CTA	SQ	Total planner		
DAGR	SQ	Limited fusion	+ More targets	
DART	SQ	Map and minimal rule base	Usable rule-based system	
DYSA	SQ	I.D. of low-level goals	I.D. of midlevel goals	
ESA	SQ	BHI[b] and MAU		
ICM	SQ	Collection validator		
RPA	SQ	Optimization and explanation	+ Comparison	
TCOR	SQ	Easier data handling	Piecewise correlator	Complete model
TLD	SQ	Single-goal prioritizer	Multiple goals	
TPA	SQ	N-goal prioritizer	+ Maps	

[a]SQ stands for Status Quo.
[b]BHI stands for Bayesian Hierarchical Inference.

ferred to an operational environment; and (2) its ability to demonstrate this potential value. "This is an important distinction, because an aid developed under the current effort may be very useful in demonstrating the potential military value of the aid while still requiring considerable development before implementation" [Rockmore et al., 1982, p. 34].

The actual benefit value for each level of each variable depended on "within variable" and "across variable" parameters. There were three "within variable" parameters. First, the team assessed the (1) relative military value (MVL_{ij}) and (2) relative demonstration value (DVL_{ij}) of each of the levels within each variable. This was accomplished by creating two relative benefit scales (MVL and DVL), with an arbitrary range of 0 to 100, for each variable. Specifically, level 0 (i.e., the status quo) for each system was assigned a MVL of 0 and a DVL of 0. The highest level for each system was assigned a MVL of 100 and a DVL of 100. Intermediate levels were assigned values between 0 and 100, depending on the team's assessment of the system's relative value to the Air Force in an operational environment (MVL) and its capability to demonstrate this potential military value (DVL) on the project. Although the intermediate MVL and DVL values were global judgments, they were affected by the systems' scores on the performance attributes in the MAUT.

The third "within variable" parameter was D_{ij}, which was the expected percentage of degradation in the military value of each level, for each system, that

TABLE 4.5 The Military Value (MVL$_{ij}$), Demonstration Value (DVL$_{ij}$), and Degradation Value (D$_{ij}$) for Each Decision Support System Level Beyond Status Quo

Aid	Level 1	Level 2	Level 3
ADRA	57/60/75	100/100/60	
ADW	80/60/35	100/100/25	
C3P	5/0/99	20/40/60	100/100/50
CART	100/100/65		
CTA	100/100/40		
DAGR	50/67/90	100/100/80	
DART	40/60/80	100/100/70	
DYSA	50/75/85	100/100/70	
ESA	90/95/60	100/100/60	
RPA	78/85/90	100/100/80	
TCOR	40/1/80	65/40/70	100/100/60
TLD	40/67/75	100/100/75	
TPA	80/60/95	100/100/85	

was likely to result from risk factors, such as its degree of acceptance, system and/ or database problems, personnel availability, and so on. There was no D_{ij} value for level 0 (i.e., no system). The highest degradation value for a level 1 on a variable was 65% degradation; the lowest value was 1%. The variation in the level-1 D_{ij} values reflected the team's thinking regarding the variation in risks posed by the different basic, "bare bones" system concepts. The degradation value increased for each level of the variable in an effort to represent the increased risk associated with the increased sophistication of the system concept. The MVL$_{ij}$, DVL$_{ij}$, and D_{ij} values for each level of each variable are shown in Table 4.5. The D_{ij} values were coded so that higher values meant less degradation.

The two "across variable" benefit parameters were the relative military value (MV$_i$) and relative demonstration value (DV$_i$) of one system versus another. The MV$_i$ values were relative weights representing the relative military importance of the 14 decision support system and expert systems; the DV$_i$ values were relative weights representing the relative demonstration value of the 14 systems. Although they were holistic judgments, the MV$_i$ and DV$_i$ values were based on the MIL-VAL$_i$ assessments in the MAUT.

The MV$_i$ and DV$_i$ values for the 14 systems are presented in Table 4.6. Examination of the table shows that the highest MV$_i$ value was 100 and the highest DV$_i$ value was 120. This indicates that demonstration value was slightly more important than military value in calculating the overall benefit for each level of each decision support system and expert system.

The overall benefit for a level of a variable was calculated using equation 3 to combine the estimates for the above parameters:

TABLE 4.6 The Military Value (MV$_j$) and Demonstration Value (DV$_i$) for Each Decision Support System

Aid	Military Value (MV$_i$)	Demonstration Value (DV$_i$)
ADRA	70	40
ADW	90	24
C3P	100	70
CART	85	100
CTA	100	96
DAGR	100	90
DART	100	120
DYSA	80	80
ESA	100	66
RPA	90	120
TCOR	80	48
TLD	100	60
TPA	80	120

$$B_{ij} = (W) \text{ MVL }_{ij}D_{ij}\text{MV}_i + (1 - W) \text{ DVL}_{ij}\text{DV}_i \qquad (3)$$

where

B_{ij} = the benefit of system i at level of sophistication j;

W = percentage of benefit given to military value;

MVL_{ij} = relative military value of system i at level j;

D_{ij} = percent degradation risks contribute to system i and level j;

MV_i = relative military value of system i relative to the other decision support and expert systems;

DVL_{ij} = relative demonstration value of system i at level j; and

DV_i = relative demonstration value of system i relative to other decision support systems and expert systems.

The W and $(1 - W)$ values were the consensus judgment of participating members of the sponsoring and development teams:

The consensus judgment was that 40% of the benefit is derived from military value, while 60% is from demonstration value. . . . A sensitivity analysis on these evaluations was done wherein the military value contributed 60% and the demonstration value contributed 40%; the results were not materially changed. [Rockmore et al., 1982]

Table 4.7 shows the overall, *incremental* benefit value for each level of each variable, beginning with level 1 of the variable, rescaled to a 0 to 100 scale. By incremental benefit, we mean that the benefit values shown in Table 4.7 for higher levels of sophistication do not include the benefits for the lower levels of the decision support or expert system.

The last estimate required for the MAUT-based cost-benefit analysis was the cost assessment for each level of sophistication for each variable. The three participating contractors independently generated the cost estimates for the different system concepts that, on the basis of the MAUT analysis, they proposed to develop on the project. The estimate for each level of the variable represented the cost, in person-months, of (1) building and testing the system prototype, (2) building any necessary input data generators, and (3) transferring and evaluating the prototype at the RADC C^2 Simulation Facility that was under development at the time of the project. To the best of our knowledge, no software cost estimation models were used to generate the cost estimates.

Table 4.8 presents the *incremental* cost estimates for each level of each variable. By incremental costs, we mean that the cost estimates shown in Table 4.8 for higher levels of sophistication do not include the cost of building the lower-level system concepts.

The incremental benefits (Table 4.7) and incremental costs (Table 4.8) were presented because the optimization procedure for calculating the efficient frontier used the incremental (or delta) cost-to-benefit ratios for the levels. (Note: The terms *lowest delta cost to delta benefit ratio* and *highest delta benefit to delta cost ratio* are used synonymously throughout this chapter, for one is the inverse of the other.) The efficient frontier incrementally defines the most beneficial system concept per unit cost for increasing amounts of total cost. The first package on the

TABLE 4.7   The Overall Incremental Benefit Value for Each Level Above Status Quo for Each Decision Support System Variable

Air	Level 1	Level 2	Level 3
ADRA	26	15	
ADW	18	5	
C3P	2	20	40
CART	82		
CTA	74		
DAGR	54	32	
DART	56	44	
DYSA	50	20	
ESA	60	4	
RPA	86	15	
TCOR	10	17	21
TLD	36	30	
TPA	68	31	

TABLE 4.8 The Overall Incremental Cost Value for Each Level Above Status Quo for Each Decision Support System Variable

Aid	Level 1	Level 2	Level 3
ADRA	13	15	
ADW	12	5	
C3P	2	10	48
CART	22		
CTA	17		
DAGR	13	12	
DART	20	7	
DYSA	13	12	
ESA	12	2	
RPA	7	6	
TCOR	8	6	17
TLD	10	9	
TPA	15	5	

frontier begins with level 0 on each variable; that is, the status quo. The second package is identical to the first package except that it now includes the level on the variable with the lowest delta cost to delta benefit ratio. The third package is identical to the second package except it now includes the level on the variable that now has the lowest delta cost to delta benefit ratio; and so forth.

Table 4.9 identifies the decision support system and expert system concepts that were on the efficient frontier, and gives their rank order, incremental cost-benefit ratio, cumulative costs, and benefits. Specifically, the first package on the efficient frontier would be level 1 for the RPA system and level 0 for all the other systems. Building only level 1 of the RPA prototype was estimated to have a cumulative cost of seven person-months and a cumulative benefit of 86 utility points. The second package would be level 1 for the ESA system, level 1 for the RPA, and level 0 on all other variables. The third package would add level 2 for the TPA system to the second package; notice that it was more cost-beneficial to skip over level 1 for the TPA system. Thus, the system selection process continued along the efficient frontier. The last package on the frontier is defined by the highest levels on the variables listed in Table 4.9; that is, the "gold-plated" system concepts. This package has a cumulative cost of 318 person-months and a cumulative benefit of 916 utility points.

In case you're curious, level 2 for DART was tied for the #7 (and #8) rank order overall with level 1 for the CART system. DART was developed before the latter because ". . . it posed less risk and the CART aid was originally planned to evolve from the DART design" [Rockmore et al., 1982, p. 47].

**TABLE 4.9   The Rank Order and Incremental Cost-Benefit Ratio for the Most
Cost-Beneficial Decision Support System Levels as One Moves Along the Efficient
Frontier**

Rank	Cost-Benefit Ratio	Aid and Level	Cumulative Cost	Cumulative Benefit
1	0.08	RPA-L1	7	86
2	0.20	ESA-L1	19	146
3	0.20	TPA-L2	39	245
4	0.23	CTA-L1	56	319
5	0.24	DAGR-L1	69	373
6	0.26	DYSA-L1	82	423
7	0.27	CART-L1	104	505
8	0.27	DART-L2	131	605
9	0.28	TLD-L1	141	641
10	0.30	TLD-L2	150	671
11	0.38	DAGR-L2	162	703
12	0.40	RPA-L2	168	718
13	0.50	ADRA-L1	181	744
14	0.50	ESA-L2	183	748
15	0.55	C3P-L2	195	770
16	0.36	DYSA-L2	207	790
17	0.65	TCOR-L3	238	838
18	0.67	ADW-L1	250	856
19	1.00	ADW-L2	255	861
20	1.00	ADRA-L2	270	876
21	1.20	C3P-L3	318	916

4.8   CONSTRUCTING QUESTIONNAIRES

This section discusses how to construct questionnaires to obtain users' opinions
about a decision support system or expert system. Throughout, we will assume
that the users' responses to the questionnaire are used to score the system on subjective criteria in the evaluation hierarchy, as was done in the subjective evaluation
of the DART expert system discussed in Chapter 2.

   We begin this section by reviewing two critical measurement concepts, reliability and validity. Reliability means that the measurement instrument (e.g., questionnaire) gives the same results when it is used on two different occasions. The
key idea here is *replication*; one can repeat the measurement process with the same
result. A basic assumption is that there have been no changes in the object being
measured (e.g., the system) in between the two measurement periods. By validity,
we mean that the instrument is measuring what it is supposed to measure. An
instrument can be reliable (i.e., it produces the same results upon replication), but
invalid (i.e., it reliably measures the wrong thing). However, an instrument cannot

be valid if it is totally unreliable because the latter implies that it will give very different answers when used to measure the same thing on two or more occasions. We will consider how these two concepts were assessed for the DART questionnaire. First, though, we will review the characteristics of the questionnaire.

4.8.1 Characteristics of the DART Questionnaire

As you may remember, the DART questionnaire was designed to obtain users' opinions about DART with respect to the evaluation criteria (also called "attributes" and "measures of effectiveness"), identified in Table 2.1. The questionnaire had 121 questions. Most of the questions assessed the bottom-level attributes in Table 2.1. However, six questions directly assessed overall utility (node 0.0 in Table 2.1), two questions directly assessed decision process quality (node 3.3 in Table 2.1), and three questions assessed the quality of the training sessions and test scenarios (neither of which were evaluation criteria in Table 2.1, although important to the test and evaluation team).

Two questions from the DART questionnaire are presented below to give you a feeling for the kinds of questions in the questionnaire. The first question measures response time (attribute 1.2.1.4 in the hierarchy); the second question measures acceptability of time for task accomplishment (attribute 2.1.1.1):

I had to wait too long for the DART aid to respond to my inputs.

Very Strongly Disagree				Neither Disagree nor Agree				Very Strongly Agree	
0	1	2	3	4	5	6	7	8	9	10

Use of the DART aid will not slow down the identification process now used in the Tactical Air Control System.

Very Strongly Disagree				Neither Disagree nor Agree				Very Strongly Agree	
0	1	2	3	4	5	6	7	8	9	10

As can be seen, all questions required the participant to respond on an 11-point scale from 0 (very strongly disagree) to 10 (very strongly agree), with 5 being "neither disagree nor agree." This type of scale is referred to as a Likert scale, after the man who first developed it. The length of the scale (i.e., 11 points) and the endpoints (i.e., 0 and 10) are arbitrary. We could have used a 3-, 5-, 7-, or whatever point scale we wanted. We chose an 11-point scale in order to give the users plenty of room to express the extent to which they agreed or disagreed with each question/statement. The use of only positive numbers is also arbitrary. We could have used negative numbers to represent disagreement and the 0 point to represent "neither disagree nor agree." We chose to use positive numbers because, as was illustrated by the first question above, sometimes we wanted the user to disagree with the statement in order to score DART highly. Therefore, we were concerned that the use of negative numbers might be confusing.

There were two or more questions for each measure of effectiveness (i.e., bottom-level attribute in Table 2.1) in an effort to achieve greater confidence in the criterion scores. In addition, this permitted us to calculate a split-half reliability measure, which is described in the next subsection. The number in the parentheses to the right of each bottom-level attribute in Table 2.1 indicates the number of questions assessing it. The actual number depended on the availability of previously written questions assessing the criterion, the ease in writing "different-sounding" questions for the criterion, and its depth in the hierarchy. We tended to use more questions when we were measuring bottom-level attributes high in the hierarchy; for example, decision accuracy (attribute 3.1).

Half the questions for each criterion were presented in each half of the questionnaire in an effort to prevent the questions' order in the questionnaire from affecting the attributes' scores. And, as will be seen, this is also appropriate for calculating a split-half reliability measure. In most cases, a high score indicated good performance, but typically for one question measuring each criterion, a low score indicated good performance. The questionnaire was varied in this way to ensure that the participants paid careful attention to the questions. DART's score on a bottom-level attribute was the mean score of the participants' responses to the questions assessing it. Values for criteria moving up the hierarchy were the mean score for the criteria below it.

As we noted in Chapter 2, by averaging lower-level attributes' scores to obtain upper-level criterion scores, one is giving equal weight to each attribute comprising the criterion. For instance, by averaging the mean scores for training (attribute 1.1.1), work style (attribute 1.1.2), and operational needs (attribute 1.1.3), each of three attributes received a relative weight of 0.333 in determining the score on match with personnel (attribute 1.1). Although participating experts may have thought that certain attributes were more important than others, members of the test and evaluation team thought it inappropriate to have them differentially weight the attributes for two reasons. First, we wanted to use the same weights to evaluate all five prototypes being developed on the contract in order to provide a common evaluation baseline. And, second, there was no reason to believe that the experts for the different prototypes or members of the sponsoring team would agree on the weights.

Keep the following points in mind when developing the questions for your questionnaire. First, people do not like completing questionnaires. Some people complete them as quickly as possible, often not reading the questions carefully. Other people seem to scrutinize every word and nuance in the question, just trying to find something wrong with it. Consequently, try to keep the questions short and to the point. Do not use qualifying phrases in a question if you can help it because respondents may inadvertently respond to the qualifying phrase instead of the principal one. In a similar vein, minimize the use of the word "not," because respondents sometimes misinterpret it or fail to recognize it when they are rushing through a questionnaire.

Second, have a colleague critically review your questions. Ask that colleague to suggest better ways of asking any questions they are having trouble answering. Third, pilot-test your questionnaire with representative users before you actually use it to obtain users' opinions. Ask the pilot participants to think aloud when they answer the questions so you can determine whether others are interpreting the questions in the way that you intended. If they have no objections, tape-record the session so that you don't have to rely on your memory. Revise questions that are being misinterpreted during the session to see if you can reword them in a way that removes the ambiguities. Continue pilot-testing the questionnaire until most (if not all) questions are interpreted in the way you intended by most of the participants.

We now turn to consider how we assessed the reliability and validity of the above questionnaire. Only four technical representatives (i.e., the nonexperts) and three experts participated in the DART evaluation; this is too small a sample size to calculate the questionnaire's reliability and validity. Accordingly, we used the responses from all technical representatives and experts who participated in evaluating the five decision support system and expert system prototypes developed on the contract. Remember, there were two evaluation sessions for each system. In all cases, technical personnel (i.e., engineers and computer scientists) from RADC participated in the first session, and Air Force experts in the decision task for which the system was designed participated in the second session. In general, each session followed the same format: the first day was dedicated to providing a detailed overview of the system, the second day provided "hands-on" training in using the system; on the third day the participants worked test problems with and without the system; and on the fourth day the participants completed the questionnaires and discussed the prototype with members of the evaluation, development, and sponsoring teams.

In total, 15 Air Force substantive domain experts and 20 RADC technical personnel participated in the evaluation sessions for the five prototypes. However, we only used the data for 13 technical personnel in the reliability and validity analysis reviewed below for two reasons. First, in three cases, the same technical representatives participated in more than one evaluation. To ensure that the results were not skewed by these participants, we only used the questionnaire responses from their first evaluation session. And, second, the responses for four technical representatives were not included in the analyses because the prototype they were supposed to evaluate was not functioning well enough to permit an accurate

assessment of its strengths and weaknesses. The system problems for this prototype were corrected, primarily by moving the evaluation from the designated host
site back to the contractor's development site, for the session with the domain
experts.

4.8.2   Reliability of the DART Questionnaire

Split-half reliability and test–retest reliability measures were calculated. A split-
half reliability is a measure that relates the halves of the questionnaire. A split-
half reliability measure was possible because two or more questions were used to
assess the participants' response for each attribute in the evaluation hierarchy, and
the questions were divided between the two halves of the questionnaire. If the
questionnaire was a reliable measurement instrument, then there should be a high
correlation between the two halves of the questionnaire, for the questions were
presumed to be measuring the same attributes.

The following formula from Gulliksen [1950] was used to calculate the split-
half reliability of the questionnaire:

$$r_{xx} = 2 * [1 - [(s_{x1}^2 + s_{x2}^2)/s_x^2]] \tag{4}$$

where

r_{xx} = the split-half reliability of the questionnaire;
s_{x1}^2 = the variance of the first half of the questionnaire;
s_{x2}^2 = the variance of the second half of the questionnaire; and
s_x^2 = the variance of the sum of the scores on the two halves of the questionnaire ($x = x_1 + x_2$).

The split-half reliability measure was 0.74 for the experts and 0.71 for the technical representatives. Both reliability measures were significantly different than
zero at the $p < 0.01$ level (df = $x_1 - 2 = 58 - 2 = 56$).

The most conservative measure of a questionnaire's reliability is obtained by
readministering the questionnaire after a month or more has passed, and then cor-
relating the participants' responses to the questions. Three of the technical representatives, each for different prototypes, agreed to complete the questionnaire a
second time. Six to eight weeks separated the second completion of the questionnaire, in an effort to ensure that the participants remembered the prototype's general characteristics but not their responses to specific questions. The three test–
retest correlations were 0.44, 0.61, and 0.56.

Although these correlations may seem low to the reader, it must be remembered
that, unlike questionnaires assessing personality or attitude traits which are presumed to be stable and unchanging, we were assessing the participants' memory
of the system's many characteristics, which is presumed to be more unstable and

subject to change. All three correlations were significantly different than zero at the $p < 0.01$ significance level (df = $x_1 + x_2 - 2 = 114$). These results indicate that if this questionnaire is used to determine respondents' opinions about a decision support system or expert system at two different times, and there is no difference in the system in the interim, then the evaluator will obtain similar opinions from the respondents.

4.8.3 Validity of the DART Questionnaire

There are three different forms of validity. First, face (or content) validity implies that, at least on the surface, a questionnaire appears to be measuring what it is supposed to be measuring. Face validity was assured in our questionnaire by having a retired Air Force lieutenant colonel, who was an expert in the tactical decision-making problems that the prototypes were developed to support, write the questions.

Second, predictive (or external) validity implies that the instrument is consistent and agrees with another established measure of the same attribute. To measure the questionnaire's predictive validity, we used the same basic approach as that used by Bailey and Pearson [1983]; we correlated the participants' global evaluations of the prototype with the results of the questionnaire. Specifically, we correlated the participants' mean responses to the six questions directly asking about the prototype's overall utility with the participants' scores for the prototypes based on the MAUT evaluation hierarchy (i.e., node 0.0 in Table 2.1). The correlation for the 15 experts was 0.85 ($p < 0.01$, df = 13), and the correlation for the 13 technical representatives was 0.60 ($p < 0.05$, df = 11).

Third, construct validity examines the theoretical adequacy of the construct being measured, typically by comparing the scores obtained from two separate instruments that are supposed to be measuring it. We reasoned that if the questionnaire had construct validity, then it should be possible to relate aspects of the prototypes that the participants indicated they liked and disliked in the open-ended questionnaire to the attributes in the MAUT hierarchy that were scored high and low, respectively. Two specific steps were required to calculate a measure of construct validity. First, for each prototype, we matched those aspects that experts indicated they liked or disliked in the open-ended questionnaire to specific attributes in the hierarchy. Second, for each prototype, we rank-ordered the attributes according to their mean score on the 11-point scale. We found that 78% of the matched attributes fell into either the top 30% or the bottom 30% of the distribution of rank-ordered attributes, thereby indicating a relationship between both of our questionnaires and construct validity.

4.8.4 Other Types of Questionnaires

In this subsection, we will consider two other types of questionnaires. The first is the traditional open-ended questionnaire; the second is designed to directly score the system on the bottom-level attributes in a MAUT hierarchy. Although additional analysis is not provided here, the reader should remember that reliability and validity are also important concepts for these questionnaires.

An open-ended questionnaire is analogous to an interview in that it gives respondents an opportunity to say what they want. In fact, an open-ended questionnaire should be given in conjunction with an interview or roundtable discussion. The use of open-ended questionnaires, interviews, and discussions is important because we don't want to lose critical information simply because we didn't ask the right question. More importantly, we want to give the users an opportunity to elaborate on their numeric answers. For example, we want them to tell us why they gave the system a 0 on usability or confidence or whatever. Moreover, we want them to tell us what change they think would improve the system's scores on those criteria for which it is scoring poorly. Although the numbers may tell us that a system is scoring poorly in the users' eyes, it doesn't tell us why. That's where the open-ended questionnaire or interview comes in.

The 10 questions used in the DART open-ended questionnaire are presented below. We provided space after each question for the users' responses, although it is omitted below. In examining the questions, you will notice that, while we wanted the users to tell us (1) what they considered the system's strengths and weaknesses, and (2) how to improve them, we still gave them some direction in order to focus their responses. In addition, we used the questionnaire as a means to document the users' experience and background.

1. What did you like and/or find most useful about the DART aid?

2. What did you dislike and/or find to be a hindrance about the DART aid?

3. What specific changes and/or modifications would you suggest regarding the following characteristics of the DART aid? Write NONE if you have no suggestions for improving the particular characteristics.

   a) Regarding the aid's general technical approach to identification, and its degrees of belief.

   b) Regarding the different types of expert knowledge stored in the aid.

   c) Regarding the value of the explanation mechanism in the DART aid.

   d) Regarding the user interface with the DART aid.

   e) Regarding the DART's graphic displays.

4. What would you envision to be the future potential of this aid in your present or most recent operational environment. Why?

5. Were the instructions sufficient to enable you to use this aid efficiently? Comments?

6. Where do you feel a second-generation, operational version of the aid would receive good acceptance?. Why?

7. What would you envision to be the future training potential of the DART aid? Why?

8. Please state your experience in performing the task you performed here today. Also, please state relevant duty assignments, and the number of years you performed them.

9. Please state your level of experience and training with computers and decision aids.

10. Please give any other comments that you feel are relevant to this questionnaire.

The second type of questionnaire is designed to generate utility scores for the decision support system or expert system on the bottom-level attributes in MAUT evaluation hierarchy. That is, the user scores the system on a 0 to 100 (or 0 to 1.0 or 10 or whatever) value scale for each of the bottom-level attributes. For instance, instead of answering a series of questions about the system's response time, the user would score the acceptability of the system's response time on a 0 to 100 acceptability scale.

This type of questionnaire was not used to assess DART, but it could have been. It is important to note at the outset that this type of questionnaire is difficult for users to complete, for it represents the utility scoring part of multiattribute utility assessment, but without access to an analyst or computer program. By utility scoring, we mean that it not only involves scoring the expert system on a subjective scale (e.g., for "ease of use"), but then translating that performance score into a utility score (e.g., the acceptability of the system's "ease of use").

Figure 4.9 presents an example from Adelman et al. [1990] of a questionnaire for obtaining utility scores; it is based on the approach in Ulvila et al. [1987]. In particular, the figure is requesting that the user indicate the adequacy of the system's response time performance. The 50 point means that the system fully meets the user's performance expectations for the system on the attribute. The 0 indicates the system fails the performance expectations. The 100 means that the system not only fully meets the performance expectations, but greatly exceeds them. These scores represent utilities in MAUT.

More generally, scores below 50 indicate that, in the user's judgment, the system was in some fashion deficient on the attribute; scores above 50 mean that the system was providing added value on the criterion. The scale permits the user to score the level of deficiency or the level of added value numerically. For example, let's consider evaluating a system on response time. If the system met the user's performance expectations for an acceptable waiting period between inputs and outputs, then the user would give it a score of 50. Let's assume that the user considered the system's response time deficient (i.e., less than 50), but not a complete failure (i.e., greater than 0). Then the question is, "What is its numerical level of deficiency between 0 and 50?"

If the deficiency is very minor in the user's mind, then the score would be close to 50 (e.g., greater than or equal to 45). On the other hand, if the deficiency was

1. RESPONSE TIME PERFORMANCE

```
100 ┬   Greatly Exceeds Performance Expectations
 90 ┤
 80 ┤
 70 ┤
 60 ┤
 50 ┤   Fully Meets Performance Expectations
 40 ┤
 30 ┤
 20 ┤
 10 ┤
  0 ┴   Fails to Meet Performance Expectations
```

- Have you previously expressed performance expectations for this criterion?
  (Circle "yes" or "no.")

                                                        Yes   No

- Have you previously heard anyone else express performance expectations?
  If yes, please comment.

                                                        Yes   No

  _____

  _____

  _____

  _____

- WHAT ARE YOUR PERFORMANCE EXPECTATIONS?

  _____

  _____

  _____

  _____

- NUMERICAL SCORE: _____

- REASONS FOR SCORE:

  _____

  _____

  _____

  _____

FIGURE 4.9 An example of a questionnaire for obtaining utility scores

very great, but still not 0, then the score would be close to 0 (e.g., less than or equal to 5). If the user thought the level of deficiency was about halfway between meeting the expectation and failing it, the user would give the system a score of 25; if it was a quarter of the way, s/he would score it 12.5, and so forth. In short, the user would use the bottom half of the scale to specify the system's level of deficiency on the attribute numerically. In addition, one needs to know the reason(s) for the user's score. Consequently, space is provided for users to specify their expectations, assuming they had ones, and the reasons for the score on the attribute.

In a similar fashion, users can use the scale between 50 and 100 to specify the level of "added value" numerically. For instance, if the system barely exceeded the user's performance expectations for response time, then it would receive a score slightly above 50. If it considerably exceeded the performance expectations but was not a 100, it might receive an 85, 90, 95, and so on. If the degree of added value was about halfway between meeting the user's performance expectations and greatly exceeding them, it would score 75. If the benefit was a quarter of the way, the system would receive a score of 62.5; if it was three-quarters of the way, it would receive a score of 87.5, and so forth. Again, it is important to know the reasons for these utility scores.

The questionnaire would contain such a scoring sheet, or some derivative of the above approach, for each bottom-level attribute in the MAUT evaluation hierarchy requiring the user's opinion about the decision support system or expert system. These are not easy judgments to make. As a means of helping users, we first ask them to think about their performance expectations for the system on the attribute. What level of performance do they consider acceptable (i.e., a 50)? We give them room to write their performance expectations on the scoring sheet. They are also given an opportunity to indicate (1) whether they have previously expressed performance expectations on the attribute, and (2) whether they have heard anyone else express performance expectations. Then we ask that they provide a numerical score, and the reasons for it. If they cannot (or do not want to) score the system on an attribute, we do not force them to do so. A number of omissions would indicate the inadequacy of this type of questionnaire, and we would subsequently use the Likert type with open-ended questionnaires and/or interviews.

4.8.5 Discussion

The questionnaires considered here attempt to capture users' opinions about a decision support system or expert system, although, more generally, these types of questionnaires can be used to obtain opinions about any system. Open-ended questionnaires, interviews, and roundtable discussions are important because they give users an opportunity to indicate what they liked and disliked about the system, and how they would improve it. The short-answer, Likert-type questionnaires are important because they attempt to quantify the users' opinions. By building it around a MAUT evaluation hierarchy, this familiar type of questionnaire provides a means for scoring the system on the more "subjective" attributes in the hierarchy. Finally, the "utility" questionnaire goes one step further and translates the scores on these attributes into utility values.

The Likert-type questionnaire used in the DART evaluation assumed a linear scale for converting the users' responses (i.e., "scores") into utility values on the attributes. For example, we assumed that a 5 on the 0 to 10 Likert scale was interpreted as essentially a 50 on a 0 to 100 utility scale; a 2.5 as 25, and so on. However, we cannot confirm the accuracy of that assumption. For all we know, a respondent may have been thinking that a 2 or a 3 or a 7 (or whatever) represented the 50 point on the utility scale. After correcting for all negatively oriented questions, all we can confidently assume is that the larger numbers represented greater utility than the smaller ones. That is, that a 8 had greater utility than a 5 or 3, and less utility than a 9 or 10. As a result, the 0 to 10 Likert scale we used to evaluate DART represents an ordinal scale. We cannot be sure of the shape of the curve relating the numbers on the Likert scale to the numbers on a utility scale.

The utility questionnaire is an attempt to obtain the utility numbers ideally desired for MAUT directly. Instead of using a 0 to 10 ordinal scale, we attempted to create a 0 to 100 ratio scale. The latter scale is a ratio scale because we tried to define the 0 point to be the natural origin; that point where the system provided no value on an attribute. For the attribute shown in Figure 4.9, the 0 point meant that the system failed to meet the user's expectations for response time in any way and, therefore, had no value on that attribute. The 50 point represented the point where the user's expectations for response time had been fully met; a 25 was halfway between the 0 and 50 points both conceptually and numerically. The 100 represented that point where the "added value" the system provided on response time was, theoretically, twice as valuable as meeting the expectations (i.e., the 50).

We could have increased the scale to 150 utility points to indicate that point where a system's "added value" on an attribute was worth three times the value as "meeting expectations" or, alternatively, made 33 (and not 50) the "meeting expectations" utility point. As these latter considerations suggest, a "utility" questionnaire is difficult for users to complete without the clarification and guidance provided by the evaluator. It is a difficult process because it conceptually involves two steps: first, scoring the system on a performance score defined by one's expectations and, second, translating that performance score into a utility score representing degree of value. Because of this difficulty, and the need for a written questionnaire requiring minimal interactions with members of the evaluation team during its completion, we chose to use a Likert scale to obtain respondents' opinions for DART and the four other decision support and expert system prototypes developed for the Air Force.

The type of responses being elicited with a "utility" questionnaire, although difficult, are at the heart of quantifying the value that users place on a decision support system's or expert system's performance for all the evaluation attributes, not just the more subjective ones. "Scoring" and "weighting" are separate steps in MAUT. The utility scale converts the system's scores on the different scales being used to measure the different attributes into a common value scale. The relative weights indicate the attributes' relative importance. How far one wants to go in the process is a critical issue for the evaluation team. Some subjective evaluation methods, such as feature-based criteria lists, stop with just a listing of the attributes. We went a few steps further. Implementing the entire MAUT process, although difficult and time-consuming, more effectively focuses development on the user's objectives and, thereby, better integrates evaluation into the development process.

We now turn to consider the different types of attributes that potential users and system developers deem most important when evaluating decision support system and expert system prototypes.

4.9 USERS VERSUS DEVELOPERS

There is little empirical research regarding how users and developers evaluate the utility of decision support systems and expert systems. Such research is vital because it will help span ". . . the semantic gap between the user and the specialist . . ." [DeBrabander and Theirs, 1984, p. 142]. The purpose in spanning this gap is to help ensure that the system will be tailored to the user's preferences and needs, as represented within their organizational context, and not the developers' perceptions of what is important or necessary. The empirical findings of a study performed by Adelman et al. [1985] are reviewed here because the study represents an initial step toward generating the necessary knowledge, and it utilized the short-answer questionnaire used to evaluate DART, with which the reader is now familiar.

The theoretical position guiding the research was that people use themselves (i.e., their knowledge, skills, needs, etc.) as a reference point when evaluating the potential utility of decision support and expert system prototypes. This position is consistent with the judgment theory developed by Sherif and Hovland [1961]. That theory states that people judge the acceptability of stimuli by comparing them to an internal frame of reference based on their past experience and immediate surroundings. Since users and developers have different professional experiences and surroundings, it seemed reasonable to propose that they would have different frames of reference for evaluating system prototypes. Furthermore, these differences should be exhibited by the different importance weights the two groups intuitively assign to evaluation criteria when evaluating the overall utility of the prototypes.

In particular, we predicted that, in general, potential users would most heavily weight those factors assessing how well the decision support system or expert system prototype matched user and organizational characteristics. We also

predicted that developers, in contrast, would most heavily weight those characteristics assessing the system interface and technical underpinnings. Although these
predictions had not been tested empirically, they were consistent with a long line
of research [e.g., see Adelman, 1982; Ginzberg, 1977; Shycon, 1977] demonstrating the positive relationship between user participation in computer system development and its subsequent implementation, for it is argued that user involvement
is required to overcome the semantic gap between users and developers.

We were able to test these predictions using the experts' and nonexperts' responses to the short-answer questionnaire used to subjectively evaluate DART and
the other four decision support system and expert system prototypes developed on
that project. Specifically, the Air Force substantive experts who participated in
evaluating the five system prototypes represented potential users; the RADC engineers and computer scientists who participated represented system developers.
As was the case for the reliability and validity analysis described in Section 4.8,
we used the data for 15 Air Force substantive experts and 13 RADC technical
personnel in the analysis reported below.

To test our predictions, we examined the correlations between the participants'
mean responses to the six questions directly asking about the prototype's overall
utility and the mean scores calculated for the five upper-level nodes in the MAUT
evaluation hierarchy (Table 2.1) that we thought would best discriminate between
the substantive experts' and technical personnel's utility judgments. Specifically,
if our predictions were correct, we expected the substantive experts' judgments of
the prototypes' overall utility to be more highly correlated with their judgments of
the prototypes' match with personnel (node 1.1), match with organizational factors
(node 2.2), and match with problem requirements (node 3.2) than with their assessment of the DSS–user interface characteristics (node 1.2) and efficiency factors
(node 2.1). In contrast, we predicted just the opposite for the technical personnel.
That is, we predicted that their overall utility judgments would correlate more
highly with their judgments of the prototypes' DSS–user interface characteristics
and efficiency factors than with their assessment of its match with personnel, match
with organizational factors, or match with problem requirements.

We did not expect the correlation between the overall utility judgments and
other two upper-level nodes, decision accuracy (node 3.1) and decision process
quality (node 3.3), to discriminate between the two participant groups. Moreover,
we expected decision accuracy to have a higher correlation with the overall utility
judgments than decision process quality for both participant groups. Finally, we
expected the correlations between the utility judgments and all seven upper-level
nodes to be significantly larger than zero for both groups.

Three points must be emphasized before presenting the results. First, remember, we are referring to the responses to the six questions asking the participants
about the prototype's overall utility, and not the overall utility score calculated
from the responses to all 121 questions by all participants. We averaged the six
answers for each participant to obtain a mean overall utility judgment for each

person. Therefore, we had 15 mean overall utility judgments for the group of substantive domain experts, and 13 such judgments for the group of technical personnel.

Second, we calculated a score for each participant on each of the seven upper-level nodes using the same, general procedure we described in Chapter 2. That is, for each participant, a prototype's score on a bottom-level attribute was the mean score of the participant's responses to the questions assessing it. Values for criteria moving up the hierarchy were the mean score for the criteria below it.

And, third, the correlational analysis had 15 data points for the substantive domain experts because there were 15 experts. The analysis for the technical personnel had only 13 data points because we only used the data for 13 "technical" participants.

The correlation matrices showing the intercorrelations between the judgments for overall utility and the scores for the seven upper-level nodes are shown, for both the substantive experts and technical personnel, in Table 4.10. For both participant groups, there are large intercorrelations among the utility judgments and scores for the upper-level nodes, thereby indicating strong relationships among the evaluation criteria. To statistically control for these relationships and, in so doing, test our hypotheses, we used the following equation from Cohen and Cohen [1975, p. 53]:

$$t = \frac{(r_{xy} - r_{vy})[(n - 3)(1 + r_{xv})]^{1/2}}{[2(1 - r_{xy}^2 - r_{vy}^2 - r_{xv}^2 + 2r_{xy}r_{xv}r_{vy})]^{1/2}} \tag{5}$$

where

r_{xy} and r_{vy} are correlations between utility (Y) and two upper-level nodes (X and V);

r_{xv} is the correlation between two upper-level nodes; and

n is the number of participants.

Table 4.11 presents the predictions, correlations, and t-values for the substantive experts and technical personnel. One-tailed t-tests were used because we had directional hypotheses. As can be seen, all of the predictions were confirmed for the substantive experts. The correlations between their overall utility judgments and their judgments regarding the prototypes' match with personnel (node 1.1), match with organizational factors (node 2.2), and match with problem requirements (node 3.2) were all significantly higher than the correlations between their utility judgments and those pertaining to DSS–user interface characteristics (node 1.2) and efficiency factors (node 2.1). In contrast, none of the hypotheses for the technical personnel were confirmed at a statistically significant level. Table 4.11 does indicate, however, that except for the correlation between the utility

TABLE 4.10 Correlational Matrices Between the Judgments for Overall Utility and the Scores for the Seven Upper-Level Nodes, for Both the Substantive Experts and the Technical Personnel

	1 (0.0)	2 (1.1)	3 (1.2)	4 (2.1)	5 (2.2)	6 (3.1)	7 (3.2)	8 (3.3)
Substantive Experts								
1 (0.0)	1.00	0.93	0.63	0.65	0.90	0.87	0.86	0.73
2 (1.1)	0.93	1.00	0.71	0.67	0.91	0.90	0.87	0.81
3 (1.2)	0.63	0.73	1.00	0.77	0.67	0.86	0.71	0.90
4 (2.1)	0.65	0.67	0.77	1.00	0.75	0.82	0.73	0.82
5 (2.2)	0.90	0.91	0.67	0.75	1.00	0.83	0.88	0.77
6 (3.1)	0.87	0.90	0.86	0.82	0.83	1.00	0.84	0.88
7 (3.2)	0.86	0.87	0.71	0.73	0.88	0.84	1.00	0.83
8 (3.3)	0.73	0.81	0.90	0.82	0.77	0.88	0.83	1.00

Mean Intercorrelation = 0.80

	1 (0.0)	2 (1.1)	3 (1.2)	4 (2.1)	5 (2.2)	6 (3.1)	7 (3.2)	8 (3.3)
Technical Representatives								
1 (0.0)	1.00	0.70	0.66	0.69	0.57	0.63	0.31	0.54
2 (1.1)	0.70	1.00	0.83	0.63	0.80	0.82	0.62	0.54
3 (1.2)	0.66	0.83	1.00	0.51	0.70	0.64	0.64	0.75
4 (2.1)	0.69	0.63	0.51	1.00	0.55	0.80	0.34	0.22
5 (2.2)	0.57	0.80	0.70	0.55	1.00	0.85	0.83	0.74
6 (3.1)	0.63	0.82	0.64	0.80	0.85	1.00	0.69	0.46
7 (3.2)	0.31	0.62	0.64	0.34	0.83	0.69	1.00	0.67
8 (3.3)	0.54	0.54	0.75	0.22	0.74	0.46	0.67	1.00

Mean Intercorrelation = 0.63

TABLE 4.11 The Predictions, Correlations, and *t*-Values for the Substantive Experts and Technical Personnel[a]

Substantive Experts				Technical Representatives			
Predictions	r_1	r_2	t-Value (df = 12)	Predictions	r_1	r_2	t-Value (df = 10)
$r_{1.1} > r_{1.2}$	0.93	0.63	3.92^c	$r_{1.1} < r_{1.2}$	0.70	0.66	0.339
$r_{1.1} > r_{2.1}$	0.93	0.65	3.26^c	$r_{1.1} < r_{2.1}$	0.70	0.69	0.063
$r_{2.2} > r_{1.2}$	0.90	0.63	2.65^c	$r_{2.2} < r_{1.2}$	0.57	0.66	0.546
$r_{2.2} > r_{2.1}$	0.90	0.65	2.82^c	$r_{2.2} < r_{2.1}$	0.57	0.69	0.58
$r_{3.2} > r_{1.2}$	0.86	0.63	2.05^b	$r_{3.2} < r_{1.2}$	0.31	0.66	1.77
$r_{3.2} > r_{2.1}$	0.86	0.65	1.94^b	$r_{3.2} < r_{2.1}$	0.32	0.69	1.45
$r_{3.1} > r_{3.3}$	0.87	0.73	2.03^b	$r_{3.1} < r_{3.3}$	0.63	0.54	0.414

[a] r_i means correlation between $node_i$ and utility (node 0.0).
[b] $p < 0.05$, one-tailed test.
[c] $p < 0.01$, one-tailed test.

judgments and match with personnel, all the correlations were in the predicted direction.

In addition, as predicted, the correlation between the utility judgments and decision accuracy judgments was higher than the correlation between the utility judgments and the decision process quality judgments for both groups. We were, however, surprised to find that the difference in the correlations was statistically significant for the substantive experts. Finally, except between the utility judgments and match with problem requirements for the technical personnel, all the correlations between the overall utility judgments and the upper-level nodes were, as predicted, significantly greater than zero for both participant groups. Taken together, these findings provide initial support for the theoretical position that people use themselves as a reference point when evaluating the potential utility of decision support and expert system technologies.

A small sample size, and its corresponding decrease in statistical power, is one hypothesis for explaining why none of the predictions were confirmed statistically for the technical personnel. While possible, this explanation is unlikely, for there were only two less technical personnel ($n = 13$) than substantive experts ($n = 15$). Moreover, it fails to explain why match with personnel had the highest correlation with the overall utility judgments of the technical personnel.

A more likely explanation for the above results is that the technical personnel were more representative of the user community than originally anticipated by the evaluation team. As it turned out, 11 of the 13 technical participants were in the Air Force. Perhaps they were, conceptually speaking, in the middle of a continuum with substantive experts on one end and nonmilitary technical personnel on the other end.

To test this hypothesis, future research will have to include civilian technical personnel with graduate training and/or decision support system or expert system development experience as well as substantive experts and military technical personnel. If the theoretical position that people use themselves as a reference point when evaluating the utility of decision support system and expert systems prototypes is correct, then one should find that (1) as in the present study, substantive experts most heavily weight factors assessing how well the system matches characteristics of the user and their organizational and problem context; (2) civilian technical personnel most heavily weight characteristics regarding the system's user interface and technical underpinnings; and (3) as suggested by the present study, military technical personnel fall in between the two extremes.

4.10 SUMMARY

This chapter offered an overview of five subjective evaluation methods: multiattribute utility technology (MAUT), cost-benefit analysis, the dollar-equivalent technique, decision analysis, and a MAUT-based cost-benefit analysis. A case study was presented to show how MAUT and the MAUT-based cost-benefit analysis could be used to select decision support and expert system technologies for development. This was followed by a discussion on how to develop different types of questionnaires for measuring users' opinions about a decision support system or expert system. Finally, empirical results were presented demonstrating that potential users and system developers differentially weight evaluation criteria when assessing the overall utility of decision support and expert system prototypes.

Chapter 5

Technical Evaluation Methods

This chapter considers four classes of technical evaluation methods: those for evaluating the appropriateness of the analytical methods chosen for decision support and expert systems; those for estimating software development costs; those for formal software testing and verification methods; and those for evaluating the logical adequacy and predictive accuracy of a knowledge base.

5.1 EVALUATING ANALYTICAL METHODS

The evaluation of analytical methods for decision support and expert system technologies is a critical and often difficult decision for the design team for three reasons. First, analytical methods differ in their appropriateness for different stages in the decision-making process. Second, there are trade-offs inherent in using one analytical method over another even when the methods are suitable for a given stage in the decision-making process. Third, developers are seldom experts in every analytical method, let alone in matching methods to requirements definitions.

Researchers have, however, begun developing taxonomies for matching analytical methods to requirements. These taxonomies can be used in step 8 to look inside the "black box" and evaluate the selected method embodied in the transferred system prototype, as was illustrated in the DART case study. However, they also represent methods for evaluators (and developers) to use early in the development process to determine the general appropriateness of the analytical method(s) being proposed for the system.

It must be stressed at the outset that the taxonomies are only designed to provide general guidance; consequently, there are numerous exceptions to the rule. Nevertheless, they provide a evaluation method for addressing the potential value of the system's analytical method(s) for those decision-making processes the system is being developed to support. Furthermore, taxonomies provides an early checkpoint regarding whether or not the developers are focusing on the stages of the decision-making process considered most important by the members of the sponsoring team. Finally, when combined with multiattribute utility technology (MAUT) concepts, the taxonomies can help clarify the trade-off judgments inherent in the selection of analytical methods.

Two taxonomies for selecting and evaluating analytical methods are discussed below. The first uses the SHOR paradigm to evaluate the appropriateness of analytical methods; the second uses the task, user, and organizational profile developed during requirements analysis. Both taxonomies have their strengths and weaknesses. Therefore, consistent with the multimethod perspective advocated throughout this book, the application of both taxonomies is recommended when evaluating (and selecting) analytical methods.

5.1.1 The SHOR-Based Taxonomy

The SHOR paradigm can be used to guide the general specification of analytical methods for decision support and expert system technology, as well as to identify those aspects of the decision-making process the methods are best suited to support. In particular, Table 5.1 presents the author's assessment of the relative applicability of different classes of methods for the four components of the SHOR paradigm. Although this assessment is based on a review of the applications literature, it still represents only the author's judgment; thus, others may well disagree with various aspects of the assessment to various degrees. The goal is not to present a definitive assessment but, rather, to demonstrate the potential applicability of different analytical methods to the different components of the SHOR paradigm as a means of supporting the selection and evaluation of analytical modeling methods for decision support technology. Once evaluators know the components of the SHOR paradigm the system is supposed to support, they should be able to use the taxonomy to initiate a discussion regarding whether the developers have selected the best analytical method (or combination of methods) for inclusion in the system. The interested reader is referred to Adelman [1987] for more details.

Table 5.1 shows that there is a wide range of analytical modeling methods. Andriole [1989a] classified them into four categories: decision analysis, operations research, management science, and computer science. Moreover, as noted in Chapter 3, each category contains a host of methods. Decision analysis, for example, includes utility/value modeling methods, probability modeling methods, and mixed (value–probability) modeling methods. Operations research is comprised of descriptive and inferential statistical methods, and various modeling and optimization techniques. Management science includes various scheduling and program management methods, such as milestone charts, Gantt charts, and critical

TABLE 5.1 The Relative Applicability of Different Methods of the SHOR Paradigm[a]

Methods	ST	C	E	SE				
Database management system	H	L	L	L				
Decision analysis								
Probability models	L	–	H	H				
Utility models	–	–	L	L				
Operations research								
Inferential statistics	L	–	H	H	–	L	L	L
Optimization methods	–	L	L	L	H	H	H	L
Computer science								
Simulation models	–	–	H	H	–	H	H	L
Artificial intelligence	L	L	H	H	L	L	L	L
Management science								
Scheduling	–	–	L	L	–	L	L	H
Management	–	–	L	L	–	L	L	H
Brainstorming	–	H	L	L	H	L	L	L
Graphics	L	H	L	L	H	L	L	L

[a]Legend: ST = stimulus; H = hypothesis; O = option; R = response; C = create; E = evaluate; SE = select; H = high applicability; L = low applicability; and – = no applicability.

path models. And computer science encompasses "conventional" algorithmic methods for collecting, refining, storing, routing, processing, and creating data for specific problem-solving purposes, and artificial intelligence methods.

Four points should be made in the context of Andriole's categorization of analytical methods. First, as was emphasized throughout this book, expert systems are a type of decision support technology. Second, the appropriateness of artificial intelligence, or any other analytical method providing decision support, depends on the problem. "It is dangerous to approach any decision support problem with preconceived notions about which method or methods will work the best. It is impossible to make that decision until after the requirements definition is fully developed" [Andriole, 1989a, p. 88]. Third, many decision support systems use combinations of analytical methods and therefore, actually represent "hybrids" [Andriole, 1989a; Hopple, 1988]. For example, Andriole et al. [1986] and Lehner et al. [1985c] developed decision support systems combining artificial intelligence and decision-analytic methods; Riemenschneider et al. [1983] developed a system integrating operations research and artificial intelligence methods; Buede et al. [1985] developed a concept design for a program manager's decision support system incorporating management science and decision-analytic methods; and so on. Fourth, a formal evaluation approach must be capable of evaluating decision support technology regardless of the latter's analytical method.

Before further considering the above four categories of methods, it should be

.t that Table 5.1 also includes three other analytical methods, all of which
. decision-making components represented in the SHOR paradigm. First,
.-based management systems are principally oriented toward the aggregate/dis-
play and store/recall functions comprising the stimulus component of the SHOR
paradigm. Second, graphics are listed because they can play a critical role in supporting all four components of decision making. And, third, brainstorming methods are included because they are often considered in the literature as the principal,
if not only means for supporting the option generation process. Examination of
Table 5.1 illustrates that they actually represent but one means for supporting option generation. Also, as demonstrated by the multiattribute-based cost-benefit
analysis, brainstorming methods can be enhanced by combining them with more
analytical methods.

As shown in Table 5.1, probability models are most applicable in supporting
hypothesis evaluation and selection. In contrast, utility models have their greatest
applicability in supporting option evaluation and selection. The distinction is,
however, not a hard and fast one. As Wohl [1981] points out, probability models
(and artificial intelligence and statistically based pattern recognition techniques)
can be used to filter data; that is, support the stimulus component in the SHOR
paradigm. In addition, traditional decision-analytic models combining probabilities and utilities are routinely used in option evaluation. However, utility-based
models can be used for hypothesis evaluation. For instance, Lehner et al. [1985b]
and Phelps [1986] used multiattribute utility models to evaluate enemy courses of
action; that is, to assess the utility of various enemy actions as perceived from the
enemy commander's perspective. Nevertheless, most of the time probability models
will be more applicable than utility models for hypothesis evaluation and selection,
and utility models more applicable than probability models for option evaluation
and selection.

This matter of "degree" is also true for inferential statistics and optimization
methods. When one thinks of inferential statistics, one naturally thinks of hypothesis evaluation and selection. And, by and large, inferential statistics and optimization methods are used to support this decision process. But, care must again be
used in assessing appropriateness. For example, there is no reason why options
cannot be thought of as hypotheses during the "evaluation" function, particularly
during "feasibility testing." Similarly, one naturally thinks of optimization methods being used for option creation, evaluation, and selection. However, BETAC
[1985] used optimization methods to delineate a range of enemy aircraft sortie
capabilities, that is, the hypothesis component in the SHOR paradigm. Additionally, optimization methods are used for data fusion and hypothesis evaluation in
military, situation assessment contexts [e.g., see Wohl et al., 1987]. And the
MAUT-based cost-benefit analysis illustrates how optimization methods can be
used to support option creation, as well as evaluation.

Both simulation modeling and artificial intelligence methods can facilitate the
evaluation of hypotheses and options, although they are typically used for the

former. Also, artificial intelligence methods can support hypothesis and option creation, as well as evaluation. This can be seen from the perspective of a nonexpert working with an expert system; many of the hypotheses and/or options being tested by the system will, in essence, be creative ones from the perspective of the naive decision maker. Further, expert systems can more quickly focus decision makers on hypothesis and option creation by quickly testing and eliminating the routine hypotheses and options that might be initially proposed. Artificial intelligence methods can also facilitate the creation function by, for instance, (1) being embedded in computer-based map displays for testing the feasibility of certain actions [e.g., see Andriole et al., 1986], (2) by providing advice on how to broaden one's cognitive model of the problem [e.g., see Hopple, 1988], and (3) by guiding the on-line use of brainstorming and its integration with other model-based methods. Nevertheless, at present, artificial intelligence methods primarily support hypothesis evaluation and selection.

Finally, scheduling methods (e.g., Gantt charts and critical path modeling) and management methods (e.g., precedent diagramming and time scale charts) principally focus on the response (R) component of the SHOR paradigm. However, as Table 5.1 indicates, these management science methods (as well as database management methods) can also play a role in hypothesis and option evaluation. For example, within a military context, one can easily imagine the use of scheduling methods to assess whether enemy and friendly forces can implement various courses of actions under various time constraints and, by so doing, support hypothesis and option evaluation, respectively.

It needs to be emphasized that the applicability ratings in Table 5.1 are ones of degree. That is, we are saying that, in general, one analytical method is more appropriate than another for supporting certain stages in decision making. The key evaluation question being addressed by the taxonomy is, "Did the development team select the most appropriate analytical method(s) for supporting the specified decision processes?" The ratings do not address how well developers implemented a particular analytical method. That assessment requires an expert and/or experts in a particular analytical method to evaluate how well that specific method has been implemented by the development team. Furthermore, the latter evaluation also needs to use formal software testing and verification methods to determine how well the software implementing the analytical method is written. This assessment should include an empirical demonstration that the method provides the correct answer for a range of test data representative of the data that would exist in the actual setting in which the system would be used. In the case of expert systems, as will be discussed later in this chapter, one needs to use methods for assessing the logical consistency and predictive accuracy of the knowledge base.

Given that (1) different analytical methods may be appropriate for supporting the same stage in the decision-making process, and (2) that even less suitable methods still may be applicable depending on the problem context and skills of the users and development team, how should one evaluate the appropriateness of the selected analytical method(s)? The answer is twofold. First, the selected analytical method needs to be evaluated against the requirements analysis document. The results of the requirements analysis represents the reference point against which all components of a system must be verified. If the selected analytical method does not match the stated support needs of the users, they will not use the system unless they are forced to.

The assumption is that the requirements analysis accurately portrays what the users need to have in order to improve performance in their environment. This assumption may, of course, be false; even a system that is verified against the requirements document may still fail to improve performance when evaluated in a realistic environment. Therefore, the second part of the answer is that the appropriateness of the analytical method(s) also must be evaluated within the context of an empirical evaluation. However, the requirements document will be the only available (external) referent early in the development effort; consequently, it is the one that must be relied upon at that time by the evaluator.

5.1.2 Andriole's Requirements/Methods Matrix

Andriole [1989a] presents a ''requirements/methods matrix'' for matching analytical methods to the requirements analysis. The matrix implicitly addresses four general characteristics inherent in the different methods. They are the method's epistemological basis, its ease of use, its degree of structure and flexibility, and its degree of transparency versus safety. The characteristics help clarify trade-offs between methods when considered against the task, user, and organizational requirements guiding a decision support system or expert system development effort. Accordingly, they will be discussed in some detail before presenting the requirements/methods matrix. We note at the outset, however, that just like the SHOR-based taxonomy, the matrix only provides general guidance for the selection and evaluation of analytical methods; it does not represent a hard and fast criterion.

An analytical method's epistemological basis addresses the assumptions made about the data and, perhaps most critically, the rule used to combine data to reach a conclusion. For instance, decision-analytic and artificial intelligence methods typically use subjective data (i.e., judgments), whereas simulation and optimization methods typically use objective, empirical data. Decision-analytic methods use axiomatically based calculations, such as expected value, to combine probability and utility judgments, which themselves are presumed (and elicited) to be consistent with the axioms of rational choice. In contrast, artificial intelligence methods, such as those to be found in most expert systems, use heuristics (e.g., if–then rules) to represent how experts supposedly combine subjective data to reach a conclusion. And most simulations and optimization methods use mathematical formulas to represent the relationships between data and perform calculations necessary to reach a solution on the basis of verifiable proofs.

There are, of course, exceptions to these rules. The probabilities used in a decision-analytic representation or artificial intelligence heuristics can be based on empirical data; certain multiattribute utility assessment techniques use mathematical programming to calculate the solution [e.g., see Sage and White, 1984]. However, in general:

> When large amounts of verifiable quantitative-empirical data exists, and when the problem at hand lends itself to its application, then analytical methods that best exploit this combination—like OR methods—should be preferred. . . . On the other hand, when the problem is unstructured and very little verifiable data has been quantified, then you should turn to AI and decision analytic techniques. One-of-a-kind problems, problems that occur only once every few years, and problems that involve value-based prescription are amenable to the methods that rely upon "softer" data. [Andriole, 1989a, p. 103]

From the perspective of the requirements analysis, task characteristics tend to determine the appropriateness of the epistemological basis of an analytical method. In contrast, user (and organizational) characteristics tend to determine how easy an analytical method is to use and understand. To quote Andriole [1989a, p. 104]:

> Decision analytic methods are intuitively more appealing than OR methods because their models are more compatible with the way many humans solve problems. It is relatively easy to understand the general divide-and-conquer decision analytic strategy; it is not so easy to understand the mathematics that drives dynamic programming tools. Some methods are simply harder to comprehend than others. In order to apply many OR methods well, it is necessary to have a solid background in mathematics. Many of the methods anchored in inferential statistics require a statistical background. Many AI methods, while computationally complicated, are conceptually quite simple. The idea of developing simple "if . . . then" rules and then stringing them all together in a computer program is inherently easier to understand than the simultaneous equations in a linear programming model.

Ease of understanding does not always nicely translate into ease of use. For instance, the general principles of decision analysis are relatively easy to understand. However, as Andriole points out, the use of Bayes' theorem to elicit necessary conditional probabilities may be anything but easy for even the most "understanding" user.

All analytical methods impose a structure on the decision problem, for they create a model (or representation) of it. One should examine the suitability of a decision support system's or expert system's structural model(s) from the perspective of both the task and the user (and organization). For, as Hogarth [1987, p. 223] noted:

> . . . by definition the model is an abstraction, and thus a simplification of reality.
> . . . it must—by necessity—fail to be a complete representation of the task. . . .
> Considering the complexity of decision tasks relative to the capabilities of the human information processing system, it must also be the case that people's models (i.e., mental representations) of tasks are incomplete.

As a result, one often has two incomplete representations of the task: the analytical method's and the user's. These two representations need to complement one another for decision support and expert system technologies to be both effective for solving the problem it is supporting and used by the decision maker.

All analytical methods do not provide the same degree of flexibility. Decision-analytic and operations research methods, for example, typically provide considerable flexibility because they rely on sensitivity analysis; that is, the modification of input values (not algorithms) in order to assess the sensitivity of the solution to these values. In contrast, the artificial intelligence methods represented in expert systems can be relatively inflexible unless their knowledge base and/or inference engine can be accessed in real time. Consequently, one needs to consider the required degree of methodological flexibility when selecting and evaluating analytical methods.

Similarly, evaluators must assess the implications of the structure imposed on the problem when evaluating the appropriateness of the analytical method. The author knows of one case where a highly flexible decision support system was dismissed out of hand because its structural representation of the problem was completely at odds with that of potential users and the larger organization of which they were a part. More generally, and as discussed in Section 4.9, users' judgments of the utility of decision support system and expert system prototypes have a positive linear relation with how well the system's structure matches their own problem representation and technical approach; the higher the match, the higher the perceived utility.

The fourth issue that evaluators need to consider when assessing the suitability of analytical methods is what Andriole [1989a, pp. 106–107] has called the transparency versus safety issue:

> The issue of transparency vs. safety is related to the ease of use issue, but is different because it suggests that perhaps complicated methods made *too* easy to use will betray their users. It is possible that we have taken too seriously the challenge of "user friendliness," and excessively reduced the amount of problem-solving logic presented to the user in an effort to unburden him from the messy details that comprise all analytical methodologies. Is this dangerous? There is a balance that must be struck among ease of use, methodological transparency, and the development of clear "audit trails" of the interactive problem-solving process.

Clearly, this balance must be specified as a result of the requirements analysis. The appropriateness of the selected analytical method should be evaluated (in part) against this specification.

Table 5.2 presents Andriole's requirements/methods matrix. The requirements are defined generically according to three global categories: task, user, and organization-doctrine. The latter category is not explicitly considered in the matrix because it is implicitly considered in the task and user categories.

The task categories are based on those of Berliner et al. [1964]. There are four: perceptual, mediational, communicative, and motor. To quote Andriole [1989a, pp. 110 and 112]:

> . . . perceptual tasks are those that involve searching for and receiving information. Tasks like "read," "scan," and "inspect" are typical perceptual tasks. Mediational tasks include information processing, problem solving, and decision-making. Some typical mediational tasks include "calculation," "estimation," and "analysis." Communication tasks include "advise," "answer," and "direct," while motor tasks include "activate," "align," and "disconnect."

There are three user categories: users who are experienced with analytical computing, those who are inexperienced with it, and the infrequent user. It is important to distinguish between a user who is experienced with analytical methods and those experienced in analytical computing, which is the application of such methods in a interactive computer system. The user who is inexperienced in a analytical method needs to understand enough about it to feel comfortable using it. Such users tend to focus on how well the system meets their personal, organizational, and technical needs, not the analytical method the system contains. In contrast, users who are experienced in the analytical method, but not analytical computing, tend to focus their attention on the procedural characteristics of the application of the method, and not on how it is programmed or even the user interface.

Users who are experienced in both analytical methods and computing often focus on all aspects of the implementation. The research by Ramsey and Atwood [1979] suggests that this group may be the most difficult to please. Finally, irrespective of the above differentiations, infrequent users are going to require the decision support system or expert system to have more computer-initiated dialogue and tutorial features than the frequent users in order to maintain their understanding of what the system can do and how it does it.

The entries in the matrix will now be considered from the perspective of these four issues. First, task characteristics are the primary determinant of the method rankings for motor tasks; the same rank order is found regardless of user category. Motor tasks are, in general, best served by conventional computer science (CCS) and artificial intelligence (AI) methods. The reason lies in the epistemological nature of motor tasks, for they tend to be highly structured and deterministic (some would say mechanical), with a reliance on objective data. While a "user-friendly" interface is desirable, it is not necessary. Moreover, ease of understanding, structural flexibility, and safety versus transparency do not tend to be issues.

The procedural characteristics of communicative tasks also tend to be rather straightforward and deterministic; accordingly, they are well served by CCS methods. Although the content is highly qualitative, it is not as well served by decision analysis (DA) or AI methods as by management science (MS), especially

TABLE 5.2 Andriole's Requirements/Methods Matrix[a]

Legend

DA = decision analysis
OR = operations research
CCS = conventional computer science
AI = artificial intelligence
MS = management science

Organizations—Doctrine (Held constant for methods assessment): Fixed military, Flexible military, Open industry, Closed industry

Tasks		Users			
		Inexperienced (I)	Experienced (E)	I/E infrequent (I)	I/E infrequent (E)
"Motor"	Activate, Close, Adjust, Synchronize . . .	CCS, AI, I, OR, MS, DA	CCS, AI, I, OR, MS, DA	CCS, AI, I, OR, MS, DA	CCS, AI, I, OR, MS, DA
Communicative	Advise, Inform, Instruct, Request . . .	MS, CCS, DA, AI, OR	CSS, MS, OR, AI, DA	MS, CCS, AI, DA, OR	CCS, MS, AI, OR, DA
Mediational	Information processing, Problem-solving and, Decision making . . .	DA, AI, OR, MS, CCS	OR, AI, DA, CCS, MS	DA, AI, MS, OR, CCS	AI, OR, DA, MS, CCS
Perceptual	Search for/receive information, Identify objects, actions, events . . .	CCS, MS, OR, AI, DA	CCS, MS, AI, OR, DA	MS, CCS, AI, OR, DA	AI, OR, CCS, MS, DA

[a]Reprinted, with permission, from book #3240 *Handbook of Decision Support Systems* by Stephen J. Andriole. Copyright 1989 by TAB Books, a division of McGraw-Hill, Blue Ridge Summit, PA 17294 (1-800-822-8158 or 1-717-794-2191).

scheduling techniques. Further, Table 5.2 shows a difference in ranking for user type. For example, CCS and operations research (OR) methods have higher rankings for experienced users than for inexperienced users. This reflects the former's preference for mathematical and formal modeling methods, as well as the fact that ease of understanding and transparency are not as big issues to users experienced in analytical computing.

Distinct user preferences are depicted for mediational tasks. According to Andriole [1989a], inexperienced users prefer DA (and AI) methods for mediational tasks; experienced users prefer OR (and AI and DA) methods. From the perspective of users who are inexperienced in analytical computing, DA and AI methods are easier to understand, provide more structural flexibility (particularly DA methods), and are more transparent than OR methods. This is not necessarily true for experienced users, who tend to have as good (if not better) familiarity with OR methods than with AI and DA methods.

However, one should not lose sight of the fact that epistemological issues have a (if not the) major impact on the rankings in Table 5.2. To quote Andriole [1989a, p. 112]:

> Mediational tasks . . . tend to be ill-structured and unbounded. There often exist few analytical precedents for solving such problems, and they tend to be non-routine and non-repetitive. The method selected to solve these problems must be flexible. Decision analytic methods are tailor-made for unstructured problems, and many AI methods can also be applied to these problems.

Of course, mediational problems that repeat themselves in a consistent fashion and, thereby, permit the collection of empirical data, lend themselves to the application of mathematical modeling techniques found in the "operations research methods" category.

Finally, epistemological issues are the major determinant of the ranking for perceptual tasks. Conventional computer science methods, as represented by database management systems, are obvious methods for searching for and receiving information. Personally, we would have thought that artificial intelligence methods would have been given a higher ranking because of their value in identifying objects, actions, and events. However, Andriole only ranks AI methods first for the infrequent, experienced user. Perhaps this reflects the fact that, relatively speaking, the structural inflexibility of expert systems is not a big issue to experienced users who will only be using the system occasionally, and therefore, want ease of use.

In closing this section, it is important to emphasize again that the entries represent guidelines for method selection and evaluation. To quote Andriole [1989a, p. 110]:

. . . the search for task, user, organizational-doctrinal, and method compatibility is not trouble-free, nor are the results ever exact. Good decision support systems designers are adaptive, flexible, and creative. They are also pragmatic. There may be times when one method is only marginally "better" than another, but its implementation costs may be orders of magnitude greater. There may be times when one method is clearly preferred over another, but the data necessary to implement it is unavailable. The matrix can provide guidelines for the selection of methods but it cannot make adaptive choices for you.

Evaluators not only have to keep such pragmatism in mind, they must test its adequacy in the development setting.

5.2 EVALUATING ESTIMATED SOFTWARE COSTS

Software cost estimation methods are typically classified as software metrics. But what is a software metric, and why is it important for evaluation? The first issue of *The Deadline Newsletter* [1988, pgs. 5 & 6] provides the answer echoed throughout this text in a review of a book by Grady and Caswell [1987] describing the company-wide software metrics program at Hewlett-Packard:

> A software metric is simply a standard way of *measuring* some attribute of the software development process or of the product delivered, such as *size, cost, or number of defects*. You use metrics to gather a quantitative history of a software project as it goes along. You use the data gathered in a metrics program to help estimate project milestones, monitor progress, and predict problems. . . . A metrics program is NOT a software *project*—it is part of the *process of management* of every project. . . .[it] is the starting point for instituting . . . quality improvement.

In short, software metrics represent a form of evaluation, for they quantitatively estimate how things should go at the start of a development effort, and subsequently provide feedback regarding how well they are actually going. As has been emphasized throughout this text, feedback is essential if evaluation activities are to represent the control mechanism in the development process. "Metrics" represent a way of measuring whether progress is on track and, if it is not, taking corrective action as quickly and cost effectively as possible.

It is important to emphasize at the start that a focus on software cost estimation is directly related to verification concerns regarding software reliability. Many of the reliability parameters used for estimating the number of faults in a program, and hence its failure rate, are determined by the program's size and complexity. These considerations are also essential to cost estimation. To quote Rushby [1988, p. 19]:

Whereas measurements of the static properties of completed programs (e.g., size and complexity) may help in predicting some aspects of their behavior in execution (e.g. reliability), similar measurements of "requirements" or "designs" may help to predict the "effort" or cost required to develop the finished program.

Estimation and evaluation concerns should go hand in hand prior to and throughout the development effort.

Software cost estimation metrics should play an especially important role early in the decision support system and expert system development process because such systems are usually funded incrementally. That is, an initial allocation of funds is made to develop an initial prototype, which is then subjected to evaluation by members of the sponsoring team; additional development funds are contingent on the outcome of the evaluation. Given the highly competitive environment in which many decision support system and expert system development contracts are issued, inaccurate estimation of software costs early in the development process increases the probability that there will not be enough money to build a high-quality prototype and, in turn, that subsequent development efforts will cease. Although there are many reasons for this state of affairs, it is safe to say that the majority of decision support system and expert system development efforts never proceed past the prototyping stage.

The dependent variable for software cost estimation metrics (or, more broadly, models) is some quantification of effort. Effort is typically expressed as the number of person-months required to develop the system in order to generate a metric that is not subject to organizational variations in salary structures. (An actual dollar cost can, of course, be generated by multiplying the effort estimate by the average "fully loaded" cost of a member of the development team [i.e., salary, fringe benefits, overhead, etc.] or by estimating the percentage involvement of different categories of development personnel to determine the person-months for each category, and then using the average [or actual] category costs to estimate the cumulative costs.) Models differ, however, in both the cost factors used as the independent variables to predict effort, and the presumed relationship between these factors and effort. However, as Fairley [1985] points out, the major factors that influence software costs are programmer ability, product complexity, product size, available time, required reliability, and level of required technology. All software cost estimation models take these factors into account in different ways, including assuming them away in some cases.

Pfleeger [1988, 1989] classifies software cost estimation models into three general categories: experiential, static, and dynamic. Each category will be overviewed, in turn. We use the word *overview* purposely because (1) there are many more cost estimation models than the ones included here, and (2) the amount of discussion given to each model has been limited due to space considerations. The goal here, as throughout this book, is to introduce the evaluation methods under consideration. The interested reader is urged to consult the provided references.

We want to make two introductory points. First, as Conte et al. [1986], Kemerer [1987], and Pfleeger [1988, 1989] have emphasized, no cost estimation model has been shown to be superior to another. Consequently, evaluators need to use two or more methods in an effort to arrive at a more accurate cost estimate. This is consistent with the multimethod evaluation approach espoused in this text. Second, Kemerer [1987] has provided empirical data demonstrating that the applications environment significantly affects the accuracy of the model. Therefore, evaluators should try to select estimation models developed in environments similar to theirs or attempt to (re)calibrate the model to their environment. To quote Conte et al. [1986, p. 27], "Most software models cannot be transported directly from one environment to another without re-calibrating. The price paid for violating this standard is erroneous or misleading predictions."

The tone of these points is nicely summarized by Pressman [1982, p. 68], who pointed out that ". . . no estimation model is appropriate for all classes of software and in all development environments. The empirical data that support most models are derived from relatively limited samples of projects. Therefore, estimation models must be used judiciously." Nevertheless, their (judicious) use can be extremely beneficial to the development team. To quote Pressman [pp. 65–66] again, "Large cost estimation errors can make the difference between profit and loss. . . . software costing can be transformed from a black art to a series of systematic steps that estimate dollar costs with acceptable risk."

5.2.1 Experiential Cost Estimation Models

Four types of experiential cost estimation models will be considered, in turn: straight estimation, Fairley's work breakdown structures, Wolverton's cost matrix, and Albrecht's function points. Straight estimation, means that the expert(s) arrives at a cost estimation relying totally on his or her own experience and not the models or metrics developed by researchers, such as Fairley, Wolverton, or Albrecht. As Sage and Palmer [1990, p. 451] point out, these estimates represent "educated guesses." These "guesses" may be derived from either a top-down or bottom-up analysis of the system. However, the primary input to the cost estimation is "expert-wholistic-based judgment."

A good example of this approach is provided by Fairley [1985, p. 73]:

An expert might arrive at a cost estimate in the following manner: The system to be developed is a process control system similar to one that was developed last year in 10 months at a cost of $1 million. . . . The new system has similar control functions, but has 25 percent more activities to control; thus, we will increase our time and cost estimates by 25 percent. . . . however, we will use the same computer and external sensing/controlling devices, and many of the same people are available to develop the new system, so we can reduce our estimate by 20 percent. Furthermore, we can reuse much of the low-level code from the previous product. . . . The net effect of these considerations is a time and cost reduction of 20 percent . . .

The example illustrates how experts use a judgmental strategy or "heuristic" called anchoring and adjustment [Tversky and Kahneman, 1974]. In using this strategy, one first anchors on the value for a previous, related event and then adjusts either upward or downward depending on the circumstances for the present case. This strategy has the advantage of using previous efforts as analogies, a mode of reasoning that research [e.g., Klein and Weitzenfeld, 1982] indicates people frequently use. It also has two potentially serious flaws.

First, the adequacy of the analogy depends on the total similarity between the previous and current case (e.g., development effort). If subtle, yet critical aspects of the environment have changed, or simply been forgotten over time, the prediction can be greatly in err. Second, people tend to be overconfident in their predictions of uncertain events in general, and in their time predictions in particular. Many of us have heard the phrase, "In order to be more realistic, double your time estimate," as a means of dealing with overconfidence.

Groups are often used to deal with the uncertain validity of individual predictions. Groups, including those comprised of experts making cost estimation predictions, typically proceed by face-to-face discussion. However, substantial research [see Delbecq et al., 1975, for a review] suggests that techniques that channel the interaction process among group members can overcome some of the negative aspects of freely interacting groups, such as the tendency of certain individuals to dominate the discussion. Two such techniques are the Delphi technique, developed by Dalkey and Helmer [1963], and the nominal group technique (NGT), developed by Delbecq and Van de Ven [1971].

Group members in a Delphi group are anonymous and the interaction process is structured via questionnaires designed to obtain specific predictions from the respondents. Group estimates are determined arithmetically (e.g., by calculating the mean and standard deviation of the individual estimates) and are sent back to the experts as feedback with accompanying rationale, especially for extreme estimates. The experts are then asked to generate new estimates, and the process continues until there are minimal revisions in the estimates. In contrast, there is a face-to-face group for the NGT, but the interaction is structured according to the following steps: (1) silent generation of ideas, estimates, and rationale; (2) presentation of each expert's information to the group via a round-robin procedure; (3) controlled discussion of all information for clarification and evaluation; (4) anonymous voting on the estimates; and (5) subsequent discussion and voting, with the group decision being derived mathematically.

Sage and Palmer [1990, p. 451] point out that experts are often asked to make three predictions in a Delphi approach to forecasting: an optimistic prediction, a pessimistic prediction, and a most likely prediction:

If A represents the optimistic cost estimate, B the pessimistic one, and C the most likely cost estimate, the final estimate of cost or effort is presumed to be

$$\text{Cost} = \frac{A + 4C + B}{6}$$

This is simply a weighted average in which it is assumed that the weight of the most likely estimate has a worth of four times that of either the most optimistic or most pessimistic estimate. Alternately, the resulting estimate can be said to follow what is called a beta probability distribution.

As Sage and Palmer note, there is no scientific basis to support the use of this cost relation. One could, for example, assume that A and B are equally spaced around the most likely cost estimate C, such that A and B really served only as reference points to help make the most likely estimate C, which is then used by the development team. In either case, however, the Delphi technique is used to generate A, B, and C by taking the average of many individuals' judgments of these predictions. In the nominal group technique, A, B, and C are the product of a structured group interaction process.

Individual or group judgments also can be used to implement the second type of experiential cost estimation approach considered here, which is Fairley's [1985] application of work breakdown structures. A work breakdown structure is a hierarchical representation that breaks the system development effort down into its component activities, such that the nodes at the bottom of the hierarchy represent the work packages that need to be produced in order to complete the task processes (or products) at higher levels of the tree. Expert judgment is used to estimate the time duration (D) and number (and type) of personnel (P) required to produce each work package.

Assuming that the effort required to complete a work package is normally distributed, one uses expert judgment to generate a personnel by time effort distribution table for each work package. In this way, one can estimate the cumulative probability of completing each work package within the specified duration for different numbers of personnel. The effort distribution for higher-level nodes is calculated by fixing the duration for each lower-level node (subtasks or tasks) and summing the means and standard deviations of the effort distributions for the subtasks. According to Fairley [1985, p. 75], "The primary advantages of the WBS [Work Breakdown Structure] technique are in identifying and accounting for various process and product factors, and in making explicit exactly which costs are included in the estimate."

The third experiential cost estimation approach considered here is Wolverton's [1974] software cost matrix. The matrix is based on the type and difficulty in building different types of software modules. Table 5.3 illustrates such a matrix. The rows represent the six different types of software modules. The columns represent development difficulty. Difficulty is based on two judgments: (1) whether the problem is old (O) or new (N); and (2) whether it is easy (E), moderate (M), or hard (H). The matrix elements are costs per line of developed uncommented code, as calibrated from historical data. To use the matrix, one must (1) estimate the number of lines of code for each cell in the matrix, that is, rely on straight estimation; (2) multiply that number by the historical "cost per line of code" entry in the matrix; and then (3) sum the total in order to obtain an overall system cost estimate.

This global procedure is best performed by first partitioning the system development effort into distinct modules such that one can relate the different modules to different cells in the matrix. For example, assume that modules 1, 3, and 5 are the only "control" modules in the decision support system. Further assume that all three control modules are addressing an old and easy problem (OE). To estimate the cost of developing the control modules, one would (1) estimate the size of each module, as measured in the number of lines of developed uncommented code; (2) sum the estimates for the three modules to obtain the total number of lines of code for the control modules; and (3) multiply this sum by the cost per line of code for that particular type of code (i.e., $21/line of code for the OE control code in Table 5.3). The same procedure is performed for the remainder of the system's software modules throughout the matrix; that is, for I/O OE modules, algorithm OE modules, and so forth. Some matrix categories (i.e., control NE in our hypothetical discussion) will have a total cost of $0 because there are no modules in that category. The total estimated cost for the system is the sum of the total costs of the modules for categories in the entire matrix.

The reader is, of course, cautioned against using the cost estimates presented in Table 5.3, for they were calibrated from historical data at TRW in the early 1970s. In order to use Wolverton's approach, you would have to develop your own cost database for his categories from more recent development efforts relevant to your project, or use one developed by others. The latter option may be difficult because developers routinely consider cost data to be proprietary. However, Wolverton's procedure is straightforward and represents a good example of experiential cost estimation.

TABLE 5.3 Illustration of Wolverton's Software Cost Matrix[a]

Type	Difficulty	OE	OM	OH	NE	NM	NH
Control		21	27	30	33	40	49
I/O		17	24	27	28	35	43
Pre/post processor		16	23	26	28	34	42
Algorithm		15	20	22	25	30	35
Data management		24	31	35	37	46	57
Time critical		75	75	75	75	75	75

[a]From Pfleeger [1989].

The last experiential model considered here is Albrecht's [1979; Albrecht and Gaffney, 1983] function point model. Like Wolverton's matrix, the function point model also relies on estimates of the characteristics of the different software modules and their difficulty. However, unlike Wolverton's approach, the function point model does not rely on estimates of lines of code. Instead, it attempts to capture the number of times the software will have to perform various functional activities. This functional count is then adjusted for the complexity of writing code to perform the required functions.

There are two general steps in using Albrecht's function point model to predict software cost. The first is to estimate (and weight) the number of instantiations of the five functional categories, as seen from the user's perspective and as specified in the requirements document. The second is to adjust the resulting "function count" for processing complexity. Each of the two steps is considered in turn.

Table 5.4 illustrates how to complete the first step. First, after completion of the requirements definition document, members of the development team count the number of instantiations for the five functional domain areas listed in Table 5.4. These counts are entered into column 2 of the table. Second, the development team estimates the complexity level for each of the five functional areas. For instance, considering the first row of Table 5.4, are the input data items, on the average, simple, average, or complex in nature? Complex functions get a larger weight than simple ones. Notice, however, that the weights depend on the type of functional domain item. In fact, simple domain items of one type can get a larger weight than complex domain items of another type. For example, simple files get a larger weight than complex input data items. Third, the count and weight for each domain item are multiplied to obtain the entries for the last column in the table. And, fourth, the five products are added to obtain a total function count (FC).

Table 5.5 demonstrates how to complete the second step, called complexity adjustment. Members of the development team (or outside experts) rate each of the 14 questions listed in the table on a functionality scale ranging from 0 (no influence) to 5 (essential). The ratings are summed and multiplied by 0.01, and

TABLE 5.4   Function Point Computation Chart[a]

Domain Item	Count	Weight			F_i
		Simple	Average	Complex	
Number of distinct input data items	_____	3	4	6	_____
Number of output screens or reports	_____	4	5	7	_____
Number of types of on-line queries	_____	3	4	6	_____
Number of files	_____	7	10	15	_____
Number of interfaces to other systems	_____	5	7	10	_____
				Total:	_____

[a]From Pfleeger [1989].

then added to 0.65 to calculate the process complexity adjustment (PCA) value. (Albrecht calibrated the values 0.01 and 0.65 from a database of previous projects.) The function count (FC) obtained at the end of step 1 is multiplied by the PCA to determine the function point (FP) estimate. Once the function point is calculated for a current project, it can be compared with the function point estimates for completed projects in order to estimate project size and, in turn, cost.

There have been very few independent empirical efforts to estimate the predictive accuracy of different software cost estimation models in general, let alone for decision support system and expert system development efforts in particular. However, in a recent empirical effort, Kemerer [1987] found Albrecht's function point model to be a good predictor for 15 large business data-processing projects. Therefore, readers should certainly consider the application of Albrecht's function point model for cost estimation if they access to completed projects for calibration purposes. (Note: Readers also are referred to Symons's [1988] efforts to improve the function point model.)

Caution is, however, warranted because of the potentially profound difference

TABLE 5.5   Complexity Adjustment for the Function Point Model[a]

Each factor is rated on a scale from 0 to 5:

    0—no influence
    1—incidental
    2—moderate
    3—average
    4—significant
    5—essential

1. Does the system require reliable backup and recovery?
2. Are data communications required?
3. Are there disturbed processing functions?
4. Is performance critical?
5. Will the system run in an existing, heavily utilized operational environment?
6. Does the system require on-line data entry?
7. Does the on-line data entry require the input transaction to be built over multiple screens or operations?
8. Are the master files updated on-line?
9. Are the inputs, outputs, files or inquiries complex?
10. Is the internal processing complex?
11. Is the code designed to be reusable?
12. Are conversion and installation included in the design?
13. Is the system designed for multiple installations in different organizations?
14. Is the application designed to facilitate change and ease of use by the user?

[a]From Pfleeger [1989].

between data-processing systems and decision support system and expert systems. In addition to the function point model's potentially strong dependency on the application domain, Sage and Palmer [1990] have identified a number of other issues that need to be considered before blindly using the model. In particular, they point out that it does not include information concerning either the development language or software development tools to be used, or user or developer experience in producing software. Moreover, a system's internal processing requirements are reflected only in the logical file types and in the answer to question 10 for complexity adjustment in Table 5.5: "For programs involving highly complex algorithms, often occurring in autopilot and other physical system areas, neither program size nor complexity will be adequately captured by this model" (p. 458). In short, although the empirical results for the function point model appear promising, it and all the other software cost estimation models need to be used with caution.

5.2.2 Static Cost Estimation Models

In contrast to relying on expert judgment, static models typically use regression analysis to generate equations relating cost factors to effort. The basic idea is that one can develop a "best fit" equation to predict effort (the dependent variable) by using a database of previous projects for which one has data on cost-relevant factors (the independent variables). Expert judgment only comes in identifying the independent variables for which to collect data, and in selecting the general form of the equation to use for prediction.

Both linear and nonlinear regression analyses (and, thus, equations) have been used to represent the relationship between effort and cost factors. The linear analyses tended to be performed in the mid-1960s [e.g., Nelson, 1966; Farr and Zagorski, 1965]. Their independent variables are not always appropriate for the modern software and hardware environment. In addition, a recent empirical study by Conte et al. [1986] found large prediction errors for the linear models ". . . doubtlessly because the costs do not really increase linearly with the factors influencing cost" [Sage and Palmer, 1990, p. 460]. Consequently, we will only consider the more recent, nonlinear analyses in the overview presented here.

Two nonlinear static cost modeling approaches are reviewed here: Halstead's [1977] and Bailey and Basili's [1981]. Both approaches begin with predicting the project size (S), which is defined as the number of lines of code (in thousands). In particular, Halstead's approach assumes that the effort required to develop a system is based on its total number of operators and operands (N). The basic assumption is that the amount of effort is directly related to the number of mental discriminations (N).

Halstead begins by predicting S so that he has a reference point for predicting N according to the equation $N = k(S)$, where k is a constant signifying the average number of operators and operands per line of code for a particular language. For example, k is approximately 7 for FORTRAN and 5 for PL/1. Then, the total number of operators and operands (N) is calculated according to the following formula, where n is the number of unique operators and operands in a module:

$$N = n \, (\log_2 [n/2])$$

Finally, effort (E) is predicted according to the formula

$$E = (1/4) \, (N^2) \, (\log_2 n)$$

According to Pfleeger [1989, p. 37]:

The Purdue Software Metrics Research Group [Conte et al. (1986)] reports that E can be approximated by

$$E = (1/4) \, (N^{2.28})$$

In general, because the exponent is so large, the Halstead metric tends to overestimate the size of the effort needed on a project. [In fact,] . . . the Purdue Group suggests that the weight of empirical evidence disputes the validity of the model.

From your perspective, this suggests that Halstead's model, if used at all, could represent an upper bound on the effort estimate.

The second static model considered here is that of Bailey and Basili [1981]. In contrast to Halstead's model, their model is based on a nonlinear regression analysis. In particular, they performed a nonlinear least squares regression using 18 ($N = 18$) large projects at NASA's Goddard Space Center. The regression analysis generated a "best fit" equation minimizing the standard error estimate. This resulted in the estimation equation $E = 5.5 + 0.73 \, S^{1.16}$, with a standard error estimate of 1.25; S is the total number of lines of code.

This equation had good predictability for the 18 projects on which it was based: 78% of the predictions were within 25% of the actual effort estimate, and the mean magnitude of the relative error was only 18%. However, as Bailey and Basili point out, the model is only calibrated to the development environment on which it was based. Although they present 21 attributes clustered into three categories (methodology, complexity, and experience) designed to adjust the effort estimate to other development environments, their model should probably be considered with caution by most decision support system and expert system developers and evaluators.

This is an appropriate point to discuss Boehm's [1981] constructive cost model (COCOMO). COCOMO is a hybrid model, for it has the form of a nonlinear static cost estimation model, but all the parameters represent (experiential) judgments and not the results of regression analysis.

The basic model uses the following equation to predict effort: $E = (a)S^b$, where S is lines of code. The intermediate model, which Boehm developed to improve COCOMO's predictive validity, includes 15 adjustment factors (m_i) and is represented by

$$E = (a)(S^b) \left(\underset{i=1}{\overset{n=15}{\text{PROD}}} m_i\right)$$

There is also a detailed model, which adds additional adjustment multipliers and adjusts the size (S) estimate for software that is developed in part from existing code, but it will not be considered here.

The parameters a and b depend on the development mode of the project. There are three possible development modes for projects: organic, embedded, or semidetached. The organic mode refers to relatively small projects that typically run by themselves. Furthermore, it is assumed that it has relatively relaxed delivery requirements and a stable development environment. In contrast, the embedded mode refers to projects that are relatively large and have numerous interfaces and/or perhaps represent modules in large systems. It is also assumed that there exist rigid requirements, strict operating constraints, and a less-than-stable development environment. The semidetached mode lies somewhere in between these two extremes. Table 5.6 presents the a and b parameters for the three modes for both the basic and intermediate COCOMO models.

There are actually two intermediate versions of the COCOMO model. Intermediate 1 includes the 15 adjustment multipliers (m_i) presented in Table 5.7. Each multiplier has a scale of five or six categories that range from "very low" to "extra high." The development team selects the appropriate category for each multiplier in order to determine the scale value for the multiplier. The actual scale values for the multipliers, shown in Table 5.8, were derived from the COCOMO database by Boehm and his associates using the Delphi technique. Intermediate 2, which will not be considered here, adds a 16th multiplier for requirements volatility.

The COCOMO model appears to have considerable popularity, for it is cited in many reference texts and included in a number of empirical studies. It was derived from a database of 63 projects performed at TRW between 1964 and 1979. One of its strengths for prediction is that the database was quite heterogeneous; it

TABLE 5.6 The Parameters for the Three Modes for Both the Basic and Intermediate COCOMO Models

Mode	Basic		Intermediate	
	a	b	a	b
Organic	2.4	1.05	3.2	1.05
Semidetached	3.0	1.12	3.0	1.12
Embedded	3.6	1.20	2.8	1.20

TABLE 5.7 The Fifteen Adjustment Multipliers in Intermediate Version 1 of the COCOMO Model[a]

Product Attributes	
RELY	Required software reliability
DATA	Size of the databases
CPLX	Complexity of the system
Computer Attributes	
TIME	Execution time constraints
STOR	Storage constraints
VIRT	Virtual machine volatility
TURN	Computer turnaround (response) time
Personnel Attributes	
ACAP	Capability of the analysts
AEXP	Applications experience
PCAP	Capability of the programmers
VEXP	Virtual machine experience
LEXP	Programming language experience
Project Attributes	
MODP	Use of modern programming practices
TOOL	Use of software development tools
SCED	Existence of required development schedule

[a]From Pfleeger [1989].

included business, scientific, control, and supervisory programs written in FORTRAN, COBOL, PL/1, Jovial, and assembler languages that ranged in size from 2000 to 1 million lines of code, excluding comments. Its use should, however, be carefully considered by decision support system and expert system developers. To quote Pfleeger [1988, p. 23], ''. . . since there are many choices to be made in the COCOMO model (3 for mode, 4 to 6 for each of 15 or 16 parameters), the maximum estimated effort for a project can be more than 800 times the minimum estimated effort.''

Consistent with this warning, a recent empirical effort by Kemerer [1987] found COCOMO's predictive validity high in terms of the correlation between its predictions and the actual effort estimates for 15 independent projects, but low in terms of the magnitude of the mean relative error. That is, the predictions were in the correct direction but generally far from the mark. Moreover, Kemerer [1987, p. 423] notes that:

Paradoxically, the more advanced versions, COCOMO-Intermediate and COCOMO-Detailed, do not do as well as COCOMO-Basic in this instance. This implies that the cost drivers of the latter two models are not adding any additional explanation of the phenomenon. This is consistent with the results of Kitchenham and Taylor [1984], who evaluated COCOMO on some systems programming and real-time systems project developed by British Telecom and ICL.

TABLE 5.8   The Scale Values for the Fifteen Adjustment Multipliers in Intermediate Version 1 of the COCOMO Model[a]

Cost Driver	Very Low	Low	Nominal	High	Very High	Extra High
			Ratings			
Product						
RELY	0.75	0.88	1.00	1.15	1.40	
DATA		0.94	1.00	1.08	1.16	
CPLX	0.70	0.85	1.00	1.15	1.35	1.65
Computer						
TIME			1.00	1.11	1.30	1.66
STOR			1.00	1.06	1.21	1.56
VIRT		0.87	1.00	1.15	1.30	
TURN		0.87	1.00	1.07	1.15	
Personnel						
ACAP	1.46	1.19	1.00	0.86	0.71	
AEXP	1.29	1.13	1.00	0.91	0.82	
PCAP	1.42	1.17	1.00	0.86	0.70	
VEXP	1.21	1.10	1.00	0.90		
LEXP	1.14	1.07	1.00	0.95		
Project						
MODP	1.24	1.10	1.00	0.91	0.82	
TOOL	1.24	1.10	1.00	0.91	0.83	
SCED	1.23	1.08	1.00	1.04	1.10	

[a]From Pfleeger [1989].

It is, however, inconsistent with the findings of the Purdue Software Metrics Group, who found the basic model substantially inferior to the intermediate and detailed models. Accordingly, while decision support system and expert system developers and evaluators should seriously consider the use of COCOMO models for software cost estimation, they should do so carefully and with constant reference to Boehm's [1981] text because of the judgmental nature of the mode and adjustment multiplier scales.

5.2.3   Dynamic Cost Estimation Models

In contrast to static cost estimation models, dynamic models incorporate time as a parameter of the equation. For, to quote Fairley [1985, p. 79]:

> The number of personnel required throughout a software development project is not constant. Typically, planning and analysis are performed by a small group of people, architectural design by a larger, but still small group, and detailed design by a larger number of people. Implementation and system testing require the largest number of people. The early phase of maintenance may require numerous personnel, but the

number should decrease in a short time [in] the absence of [a] major enhancement or adaptation . . .

This point was first empirically demonstrated by Norden [1958], who showed that the rate of staff buildup and decline for engineering and development projects at IBM resembled the Rayleigh distribution in Figure 5.1. Putnam [1978] replicated Norden's findings using 50 projects from the Army Computer Systems Command, as well as 150 other projects. Moreover, Putnam used these findings to generate a model for effort estimation.

The total area (K) under the Rayleigh distribution (or curve) presented in Figure 5.1 represents the total amount of personnel time required for the entire lifecycle of a software project, including extensions and modifications to the initial program and its maintenance. In particular, Putnam observed that the cumulative effort required for the initial development effort was reached at about the peak of the curve. Using the equation for modeling the Rayleigh curve, Putnam calculated that the initial development effort represented about 40% of the total life cycle effort; specifically,

$$E = y(t) = 0.3945\ K$$

where K is the area under the Rayleigh curve for the interval of zero to infinity.

More generally, Putnam's effort estimate is affected by the difficulty of the project. Specifically, Putnam observed that out of his sample of 50 projects, the more difficult ones took substantially longer to develop than the simple ones. He hypothesized that there was a nonlinear relationship between project difficulty (D) and the productivity of the development team. Productivity (P) was defined as the total number of lines of code (S) divided by effort (E); that is,

$$P = \frac{S}{E}$$

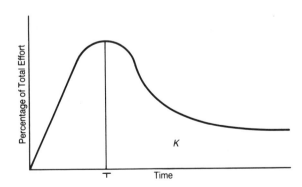

FIGURE 5.1 The Rayleigh distribution

Using a nonlinear regression analysis for the 50 projects, Putnam obtained the equation

$$P = c_1 (D^{-2/3})$$

where c_1 is a constant. Putnam also observed that difficulty (D) had an inverse relation with development time (T) that could be represented by the following equation:

$$D = \frac{K}{T^2}$$

By substitution, Putnam developed the following equation to represent his cost estimation model

$$S = c_1 \left(\frac{K}{T^2}\right)^{-2/3} E$$
$$= CK^{1/3} T^{4/3}$$

where S is measured in thousands of lines of code and C is a technology factor representing numerous factors, such as hardware constraints, personnel experience levels, the programming environment, and so on. Putnam has both (1) proposed a range of values for C when K is expressed in programmer years and T in years, and (2) indicated how C can be calibrated to a historical project for which S, K, and T are known.

Putnam developed a software package called SLIM (Software Life-cycle Methodology) incorporating his model for software cost estimation. A recent empirical evaluation of SLIM by Conte et al. [1986] found that it predicted the effort requirements for large projects reasonably well, but seriously overestimated the effort for small projects. Kemerer [1987], who only used moderate to large projects (average size was 200,000 lines of code), found that SLIM's estimates correlated highly with actual effort values, but that it overestimated the required effort in all 15 cases. Kemerer noted that this overestimation was probably due to the fact that he used projects developed in a business environment, whereas Putnam's model was developed primarily based on defense projects.

These results raise some uncertainty as to the suitability of Putnam's dynamic cost estimation model for decision support and expert systems, which are generally small in size relative to the projects on which Putnam's model was based. However, (1) its general concern with the staffing profile over time, as represented by the Rayleigh curve, and (2) the emphasis on the trade-off between development time (T) and the development effort (K), are important cost estimation issues for the development team and sponsors to consider early in development.

This concludes the overview of cost estimation models in general, and dynamic models in particular. The interested reader is referred to Jensen [1984], Londeix [1987], and Parr [1980] for variations of and extensions to Putnam's model. The reader should also consult Pfleeger [1989] for consideration of an effort estimation model for object-oriented development. For general discussions of cost estimation models, the reader is referred to Boehm [1981], Conte et al. [1986], Pfleeger [1988, 1989] and Sage and Palmer [1990].

5.3 SOFTWARE TESTING METHODS

We will overview two classes of software testing methods: static and dynamic. Static testing methods, which may be manual or automated, analyze the system's design and software without actually executing its code. Dynamic testing methods, in contrast, execute the program's code using test data. Before considering these methods, we want to make three introductory points.

First, each class of testing methods, as well as specific methods within each class, has its strengths and weaknesses, and hence represent "imperfect test methods" [Hamlet, 1988, p. 666]. As with cost estimation methods, and more generally the entire system development and evaluation cycle, the evaluator needs to use multiple methods to increase the accuracy of the feedback provided to the development team.

Second, Meyers [1979] has stated three rules that serve well as testing objectives: (1) Testing is a process of executing a program with the intent of finding an error; (2) a good test case is one that has a high probability of finding an as-yet undiscovered error; and (3) a successful test is one that uncovers an as-yet undiscovered error. As Pressman [1982, p. 290] points out, "The above objectives imply a dramatic change in viewpoint. They move counter to the commonly held view that a successful test is one in which no errors are found. Our objective is to design tests that systematically uncover different classes of errors."

The reason for this objective is, as Fairley [1985, pp. 267–268] points out, obvious:

> A well known maxim states that the number of bugs remaining in a program is proportional to the number already discovered. This is because one has most confidence in programs with no detected bugs after thorough testing and least confidence in a program with a long history of fixes.

Third, the best way to minimize the number of errors in the system, and the amount of time, effort, and money required to fix them, is to eliminate errors early in the development process. To quote Rushby [1988, pp. 49–50]:

> Recent studies [e.g., Basili and Perricone, 1984; Boehm, 1984] have shown that errors due to faulty requirements are between 10 and 100 times more expensive to fix at the implementation stage than at the requirements stage. There are two main

reasons for the high cost of modifying early decisions later in the life cycle: [1] The changes often have a widespread impact on the system, requiring many lines of code to be modified. Furthermore, it can be difficult to identify all of the code requiring attention, resulting in the modification being performed incorrectly. [2] The documentation is likely to be inadequate, exacerbating the problem of determining why certain decisions were made and assessing the impact of decisions.

Therefore, consistent with the message throughout this book, software verification and testing methods should be systematically incorporated into the decision support system and expert system design and development process as early as possible.

Again, we want to emphasize the "overview" nature of the following discussion of software testing methods. The reader interested in the greater details required for implementing these methods is referred to the general texts by DeMillo et al. [1987], Fairley [1985], Howden [1987], Pressman [1982], and Rushby [1988] (and others), as well as the references presented herein for specific methods.

5.3.1 Static Testing Methods

As DeMillo et al. [1987, p. 81] point out:

> The focus of static analysis is on requirements and design documents and on structural aspects of programs, i.e., on those characteristics of a program that are discernable without actually executing it. The tools that implement static analysis techniques are varied in scope and functionality. They range from systems which simply enforce coding standards to systems which carry out sophisticated structural error analysis.

We consider four manual, static analysis methods: requirements analyses, design analyses, code inspections, and walkthroughs. Requirements analyses typically use a checklist of evaluation criteria, such as the consistency among the different requirements specifications of the system, their necessity in achieving system goals, and their implementation feasibility with existing resources. Design analyses also use a checklist, which may actually be quite similar to that used in the requirements design, but with the focus now on elements of the software system design, such as the data flow diagrams, module interfaces, algorithms, and so forth.

Code inspections and walkthroughs involve the static analysis of the program by a group of people. The former uses a checklist of common programming errors as a reference point; the latter also uses a set of test cases for assessing the logic of the program. In addition, inspections differ from walkthroughs in that a team of trained inspectors analyzes the work products. Nevertheless, there are considerable similarities between inspections and walkthroughs. Moreover, since both can be used to analyze products throughout the software lifecycle, we have decided to describe one of them (walkthroughs) in some detail.

A walkthrough team typically consists of a reviewee and three to five reviewers. Members

> . . . may include the project leader, other members of the project team, a representative from the quality assurance group, a technical writer, and other technical personnel who have an interest in the project. Customers and users should be included in walkthroughs during the requirements and preliminary design phases, but they are usually excluded from subsequent walkthrough sessions. Higher level managers should not attend walkthroughs. Walkthrough sessions should be held in an open, nondefensive atmosphere. The presence of a vice president or department manager may inhibit the review process. . . . [Moreover,] the project leader, the senior programmers, and the walkthrough moderator should receive special training in walkthrough techniques and group dynamics to ensure the correct psychological setting. [Fairley, 1985, pp. 272–273]

The purpose of a walkthrough is, of course, to discover problem areas. Problems are not resolved at the session; they are resolved after it by the member of the development team whose work is being reviewed. The resolution may be performed independently by the reviewee or the process may involve members of the review group or others on the development team. Regardless, the reviewee must make sure that all members of the review group are notified as to how all problems identified in the walkthrough are resolved. Furthermore, this must be done in a timely fashion to keep the development effort on track.

Fairley [1985, p. 273] identifies four guidelines for effective walkthroughs. First, everyone's work, including that of the project leader, should be reviewed on a scheduled basis. This ensures that all work products are reviewed, provides a vehicle for communication among team members, and lessens the threat to any particular individual whose work is being reviewed. Second, emphasis should be placed on detecting errors. Third, the walkthrough should focus on major issues, not minor ones. To facilitate this, and to keep a positive atmosphere, one reviewer is typically designated as a moderator. And, fourth, the walkthrough session should be limited to two hours. This limits the scope of material examined, reinforces the emphasis on major issues, and provides incentives for active participation by the reviewers.

It must be emphasized that, in order to be effective, sufficient time needs to be allotted in the project schedule for walkthroughs and inspections. Neither these nor other testing methods can be considered as afterthoughts. Walkthrough sessions need to be scheduled systematically. They should be regarded as part of each team member's normal work load and not an additional commitment. The empirical data reported in the literature suggests that the additional cost for this effort will pay off substantially. In an experimental evaluation of code inspections and walkthroughs, Meyers [1979] found the methods to be effective in finding from

30% to 70% of the logic design and coding errors in typical programs. Fagan [1976] and Perriens [1977] have found error-detection rates of about 80% using code inspections at IBM. And Daily [1978] estimated that 90% of the errors found by simulator testing could be found by code inspections and design analysis.

Static analyzers are automated tools for examining a program's structure. According to DeMillo et al. [1987, p. 83]:

> Static analyzers are programs that analyze source code to reveal global aspects of program logic, structural errors, syntactic errors, coding styles, and interface consistency. They consist of a front end language processor, a data base, an error analyzer, and a report generator. The basic operation includes data collection, which creates necessary tables and graphs, error analysis, and error report generation. . . . The information revealed by static analyzers include:
>
> (1) Syntactic error messages.
> (2) Number of occurrences of source statements by type.
> (3) Cross-reference maps of identifier usages.
> (4) Analysis of how the identifiers are used in each statement (data source, data sink, calling parameter, dummy parameter, subscript, etc.).
> (5) Subroutines and functions called by each subroutine.
> (6) Uninitialized variables.
> (7) Variables set but not used.
> (8) Isolated code segments that cannot be executed under any set of input data.
> (9) Departures from coding standards (both languages standards and local practice standards).
> (10) Misuses of global variables, common variables, and parameter lists . . .

As mentioned above, static analyzers have four components: a front-end language processor, a database, an error analyzer, and a report generator. The front-end language analyzer has two parts: a lexical analyzer and a parser. For example, the DAVE system by Osterweil and Fosdick [1976] has a statement recognizer to categorize different types of statements. The source program is subdivided into units, such as the main program and subroutines, which are then decomposed into statements and then tokens. Once at this level, a number of tables containing information about variable usages, types, labels, and control flow are created and stored in the database, which is typically designed to specifically handle the type of information generated by the front-end analyzer. The error analyzer examines the database under the direction of the user, who is provided with a command or query language to communicate with the system. Although the flexibility of error analyzers varies, they are all designed to identify the types of structural errors listed above. Finally, the report generator presents the results of the error analysis. The results are reported in the form of cross-reference tables, calling sequence tables, control flow graphs, and so forth.

As Fairley [1985, pp. 277–278] points out:

There are both practical and theoretical limitations to static analysis. A major practical limitations involves dynamic evaluation of memory references at run time. In higher-level programming languages, array subscripts and pointer variables provide dynamic memory references based on prior computations performed by the program. Static analyzers cannot evaluate subscripts or pointer values; it is thus impossible to distinguish between array elements or members of a list using static analysis techniques. . . . Major theoretical limitations are imposed on static analysis by decidability theory. Decidability results can be phrased in various ways and have many profound implications. One phrasing states that, given an arbitrary program written in a general purpose programming language (one capable of simulating a Turing machine), it is impossible to examine the program in an algorithmic manner and determine if an arbitrarily chosen statement in the program will be executed when the program operates on arbitrarily chosen input data. By "algorithmic manner" we mean that it is impossible to write a computer program to perform this task for all possible programs. The term "arbitrary" is used to mean that there are programs and data for which the analysis is possible; [and] . . . not possible. . . . [Unfortunately,] there is no algorithmic way to identify all programs and data for which the analysis is possible.

For these reasons, static analyzers appear to have limited utility for testing decision support systems and expert systems. An important exception is the static analysis of the logical consistency and completeness of an expert system's knowledge base. However, even here it is not clear how valuable automated static analyzers can be for large expert systems. This issue is considered again below.

5.3.2 Dynamic Testing Methods

In dynamic testing, test data (called cases) are constructed and used to execute the software in an effort to uncover programming errors. There are four types of tests: functional, performance, stress, and structural. Functional tests are designed to evaluate the adequacy of the software in performing the functions identified in the requirements specifications. Test data are selected by specifying typical operating conditions and input values, and examining whether or not they result in the expected outcomes. Performance tests are also tied to the requirements (and design) specifications, but now the focus is on, for instance, verifying the response time under various loads, determining the amount of execution time spent in various parts of the program, and examining program throughput. Stress test are, as the name suggests, designed to overload and in many cases break the system in an effort to assess its strengths and limitations. And structural tests are designed to exercise the logic of the program by traversing various execution paths.

Three sets of terms need to be introduced as part of this overview before considering specific dynamic testing methods. The first set of terms is black-box and white-box testing. The internal structure of a program is not considered in black-box testing. Rather, the goal is to identify when the input–output behavior of the system is inconsistent with stated specifications. In contrast, the internal structure of the program is explicitly considered in white-box testing. The goal is to select test data that will assess the adequacy of the system's logic. According to these definitions, functional, performance, and stress tests represent black-box testing; structural tests represent white-box testing.

Second, we must differentiate between unit and system testing. "Unit testing comprises the set of tests performed by an individual programmer prior to integration of the unit into a larger system" [Fairley, 1985, p. 282]. The goal is to identify programming errors in the individual modules of the system. "System testing is concerned with subtleties in the interfaces, decision logic, control flow, recovery procedures, throughput, capacity, and timing characteristics of the entire system" [p. 294]. Although all four types of tests can be performed on units, the material presented by Fairley suggests that structural testing is more effective for system testing than for unit testing.

Ideally, the final system is obtained by incrementally adding pretested modules and testing the resulting assemblage. The ability to do this must be designed into the modules from the start. Additionally, aids for implementing various testing methods may not be available on the development platform. The decision as to testing methods and aids should also be included from the start so there is time to modify or write the desired testing software.

Third, we need to differentiate between integration and acceptance testing, both of which are approaches to system testing. Integration testing typically refers to the strategy selected by the development team for linking together the individual modules (i.e., units) into the overall system. Acceptance testing, which is typically performed by the quality assurance team and/or sponsoring organization, ". . . involves [the] planning and execution of functional tests, performance tests, and stress tests to verify that the implemented system satisfies its requirements" [Fairley, 1985, p. 293].

Besides the three sets of terms discussed above, two other terms need to be reviewed. The first term is *regression testing*. Once an error is identified by a test, it obviously needs to be fixed. However, debugging is a complex problem solving art. Moreover, it is imperfect in the sense that the proposed "fix" not only may or may not fix the error, it may cause errors in other segments of the program that previously operated correctly. Regression testing refers to the process whereby previously tested inputs are repeated when a fix or, more generally, any modification to the program is made. A strict regression regime would require the repetition of all previously tested inputs. While this may appear too extreme for decision support system and expert system technology, especially prototypes, it is assumed that sufficient regression testing is performed to significantly decrease the probability of substantial errors due to the debugging process itself.

The last term that needs to be overviewed is *test coverage criterion*. To quote Fairley [1985, pp. 284–287]:

A test coverage (or test completion) criterion must be established for unit testing, because program units usually contain too many paths to permit exhaustive testing. . . . Even if it were possible to successfully test all paths through a program, correctness would not be guaranteed by path testing because the program might have missing paths and computational errors that were not discovered by the particular test cases chosen. . . . An often used rule of thumb for unit test completion is 85 percent to 90 percent of branch coverage (that is, 85 percent to 90 percent of all branch alternatives have been traversed by the set of unit test cases). This coverage criterion strikes a balance between using an excessive number of test cases and leaving test completion to the intuition of each individual programmer. Typically, functional, performance, and stress tests based on the functional requirements and a programmer's intuition will achieve 60 percent to 70 percent of statement coverage. Adding branch tests to achieve 85 percent to 90 percent branch coverage is thus a significant improvement in test coverage.

Before discussing dynamic testing methods, it is important to note that the selected testing method and the resulting test cases (i.e., data) used to implement that method are firmly interwoven. It is the test designer's job to select techniques and generate test cases that will uncover the highest number of errors with the minimum reasonable number of tests and corresponding cost.

Three dynamic testing methods are overviewed below: random testing, input space partitioning, and symbolic testing. Each is considered in turn.

As the name suggests, random testing is a black-box strategy in which a program is tested by randomly selecting a subset of all possible input values. The distribution of input values can be either arbitrary or attempt to reflect the distribution actually found (or expected) in the application environment. The latter approach has the advantage that it attempts to develop an operational profile of failure intensity data approximating that that would be found if the software were in operation at the time of the testing.

More generally, the random testing method has two major advantages. First, it concentrates on finding and eliminating those faults that lead to failures on commonly occurring inputs. Second, it is consistent with the approach used intuitively by programmers to test their work. However, it does have three possible limitations. First, it can be potentially wasteful, for the same input data may be tested several times. However, it is usually easy to record inputs and, thereby, avoid repeating test cases other than for the purposes of regression testing. Second, the operational profile for failure intensities could be in error if the expected distribution of input data is in error. This can be minimized by relying on historical data if available (and appropriate) or, if necessary, using multiple experts to help construct the distribution. Third, as Rushby [1988] points out, pure random testing assumes that all failures have equal cost. In cases where certain failures are more expensive than others or potentially endanger human life, the random testing strategy should obviously be modified in order to provide early tests of those inputs that might generate especially costly failures.

In input space partitioning, test data are selected for evaluating the different subsets of the program input domain, such that each partition causes the execution of a different program control path. As discussed above in the section about test coverage, the possible input space of even simple programs can be so large that it is infeasible to examine the behavior of the program for all inputs. The result can be that only a fraction of the input space can be explored during testing. Input space partitioning attempts to address that problem by dividing the input space into different classes such that one can selectively test each class and, in turn, the larger input space.

In contrast to random testing, which randomly selects subsets of cases from the input space based on an arbitrary or operational profile of the inputs' distribution, input space partitioning subdivides the inputs into groups such that the inputs within each group are in some sense equivalent and, therefore, likely to result in similar behavior. As a result, one need only test one (or selected) member(s) from each group to test the adequacy of the program for that segment of the input space. The reason for selecting more than one member from a group is that one might not only want to test program behavior for the standard or typical member of each partitioned input group, but also for atypical members, such as those at the boundaries between groups, which would be more likely to stress the program.

Ostrand and Balcer [1988] have recently described a six-step method for partitioning the input space into categories. Their method is particularly appealing for decision support system and expert system developers because their method is oriented to specifying and generating functional tests based on the design (and possibly requirements) specifications. Because it (1) emphasizes the early focus on testing and evaluation emphasized throughout this text, and (2) extends previously developed partitioning methods, specifically, the revealing subdomain method developed by Weyuker and Ostrand [1980] and the equivalence partitioning method developed by Richardson and Clarke [1981], it is briefly covered below.

The first step in "category partitioning" is to analyze the specification so that one can identify the individual functional units that can be separately tested. Moreover, one must identify the parameters and environmental conditions that can affect each functional unit. The parameters are the explicit inputs to a functional unit; the environmental conditions are the system characteristics at the time of executing a functional unit. Once identified, the tester classifies the functional units, parameters, and environmental conditions into categories affecting program behavior.

The second step is to partition the categories into choices that include all possible values for the category. In this way, the tester can partition each category into equivalence groups from which one can select representative test cases. In the third step, the tester identifies the constraints affecting the choice of test cases. Since the choices in one category can significantly affect the choices in another, the constraints specify the permissible relations (or ground rules) for developing technically effective and economically feasible test frames for which the test cases will be developed. In the fourth step, the category, choice, and constraint information developed in the first three steps is written in a formal test specification, which is then typically processed by an automated generator to produce a set of test frames for the functional unit. In the fifth step, the tester evaluates the test frames to determine if any changes to the test specification are necessary. If they are, the fourth and fifth steps are repeated until the test frames are acceptable. Finally, in the sixth step, the test frames are converted into test cases, which are then organized into test scripts relating test cases for one or more functional units. Then, testing begins and continues based on the previously developed test coverage criteria.

The category partitioning method is new and has not yet undergone experimental evaluations. DeMillo et al. [1987] suggest that evaluations of the revealing subdomain and equivalence partitioning methods that it extends have been found to be reasonably successful. However, category partitioning, like all input space partitioning methods, is still based on a path analysis. As DeMillo et al. point out, the major problems in path analysis are that programs may contain an infinite number of paths, it may be difficult to determine all the domains (i.e., categories), and it does not detect all of the path selection, computation, or missing path errors. Further, partitioning methods assume the completeness and accuracy of the specifications on which they are based; in all too many cases, this assumption may be in error.

In contrast to random testing, input space partitioning, and most forms of testing, symbolic testing uses symbolic inputs and outputs to evaluate program accuracy. As the first two methods indicate, the usual approach to testing uses numerical data as the inputs and the human examiner to evaluate the accuracy of the outputs. With symbolic testing, symbolic constants are used as the input values and symbolic formulas or symbolic predicates are used to assess the accuracy of the outputs. For example, instead of sampling numerical test cases, one might simply use the symbolic constant X to represent data within a predefined range. Then, instead of examining whether the test cases resulted in the correct answer, one could evaluate whether the symbolic input X was propagated correctly throughout the program flow, thereby resulting in the correct symbolic predicate Y.

The underlying assumption of symbolic testing is that a program can be conceived of as a finite set of assertion-to-assertion paths. Consequently, a program can be represented symbolically by an execution tree consisting of nodes associated with the statements being executed and directed arcs indicating program flow. The objective is to demonstrate symbolically that each assertion path is accurate.

Symbolic testing can be performed manually or by an automated tool. Symbolic testing systems have been developed for FORTRAN, PL/1, and LISP. As DeMillo et al. [1987] note, these systems have been used to support test data generation, assertion checking, and path analysis, and to detect data flow anomalies. However, as both DeMillo et al. and Fairley [1985] point out, all of the automated systems are experimental. Some of the problems that need to be overcome in these specific systems, and in symbolic testing more generally, include handling of loops, evaluation of subscripts and pointers, treatment of nonlinear inequalities in path expressions, and simply dealing with the scope and details of large programs.

In closing this section, it is important to emphasize that there exist a number of other software testing methods, as well as efforts to automate them. For example, program instrumentation uses various recording instruments or probes that do not affect system functioning, such as assertion statements and history-collecting subroutines, to monitor system performance on test data. Program mutation refers to techniques for measuring test adequacy, where the latter is defined as ensuring that certain specified errors are not present in the program. And "formal verification" [Fairley, 1985, p. 297] or "mathematical verification" [Rushby, 1988, p. 41] testing uses mathematical techniques to evaluate program accuracy. The interested reader is referred to these and other texts for further information.

5.4 METHODS FOR EVALUATING A KNOWLEDGE BASE

Two classes of technical evaluation methods for assessing knowledge-base quality are considered: (1) static testing and, to a lesser extent, dynamic testing methods for determining the logical consistency and adequacy of the knowledge base; and (2) domain experts, in conjunction with empirical evaluation concepts and methods, for assessing the functional completeness and predictive accuracy of the knowledge base. Each class is considered in turn.

5.4.1 Evaluating Logical Consistency and Completeness

The concepts of static testing in conventional software testing can be readily extended to expert systems because, in both instances, the focus is on detecting anomalies in the program without actually doing so with test cases. To quote Rushby [1988, p. 92], "An anomaly in a program is nothing more than an apparent conflict between one indication of intent or purpose and another. . . ." The types of anomalies of particular interest in expert systems pertain to the logical consistency and logical completeness of the knowledge base.

Researchers [e.g., Kirk and Murray, 1988; Nazareth, 1989; Rushby, 1988] have developed taxonomies of anomalies in the knowledge base that are amenable to static testing. The taxonomy developed by Adelman et al. [1990] is listed below. We assume that the knowledge base is represented in the form of if–then production rules or can be transformed into such a representation [e.g., see Thuraisingham, 1989]. However, as Nazareth [1989, p. 257] points out, "For systems that employ more involved representation schemes, the nature of the verification task may differ."

- *Redundant Rules:* Individual rules or groups of rules that essentially have the same conditions and conclusions.

- *Subsumed Rules:* When one rule's (or rule group's) meaning is already expressed in another's that reaches the same conclusion from similar but less restrictive conditions.

- *Conflicting Rules:* Rules (or groups of rules) that use the same (or very similar) conditions, but result in different conclusions, or rules whose combination violates principles of logic (e.g., transitivity).

- *Circular Rules:* Rules that lead one back to an initial (or intermediate) condition(s) instead of a conclusion.

- *Unnecessary If Conditions:* The value on a condition does not affect the conclusion of any rule.

- *Unreferenced Attribute Values:* Values on a condition that are not defined; consequently, their occurrence cannot result in a conclusion.

- *Illegal Attribute Values:* Values on a condition that are outside the acceptable set of values for that condition.

- *Unreachable Conclusions (and Dead Ends):* Rules that do not connect input conditions with output conclusions.

Static testing for the above anomalies could be performed manually for small, well-structured knowledge bases. For even moderately sized knowledge bases, however, this approach is precluded by the amount of effort required and the probability of disagreements among testers. Therefore, researchers [e.g., Culbert and Savely, 1988; Franklin et al., 1988; Nguyen et al., 1987; Stachowitz et al., 1988] have begun developing automated static testers. However, to the best of our knowledge, no automated, knowledge-base static testers are commercially available yet.

Although a number of different technical approaches are being investigated, Gilbert [1988, p. 2] has noted that many of the automated static testers

. . . either implicitly or explicitly consider an expert system's rule base to be a graph or network. In the graph of a rule base, there are nodes that represent rules and nodes that represent the hypotheses that appear in the rules' premises and conclusions. There is an arc from a hypotheses to each rule whose premise it appears in. There is an arc to a hypothesis from each rule that asserts the hypothesis in its conclusion.

Thus, a graph can represent the knowledge base's logical structure (and flow) and, thereby, help detect the types of logical consistency and completeness errors defined above.

Although a valuable pictorial display, a graphical representation of even a moderately sized rule base can be difficult to use for error detection. Consequently, researchers have begun using matrices and Boolean algebra to automate the error-

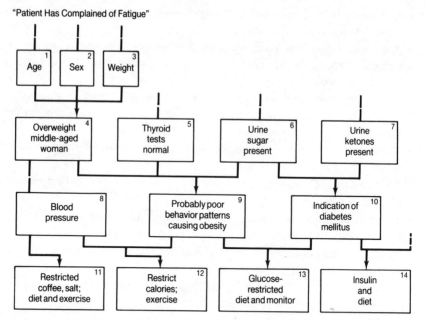

"Patient Has Complained of Fatigue"

FIGURE 5.2   The flow graph for a fragment of a fictitious rule base for diabetes diagnosis

detection process. To illustrate this, we use an example developed by Bellman and Walter [1988] to represent a common source error, which is when the same piece of information goes into different lines of reasoning. Specifically, Figure 5.2 shows the flow graph for a fragment of a fictitious knowledge base for diabetes diagnosis. Table 5.9 presents an incidence matrix for representing this graphic flow. The rows in an incidence matrix represent inputs; the columns represent outputs; and the 1's represent the connection. For instance, the information obtained for age, sex, and weight (i.e., boxes 1, 2, and 3) only goes into box 4, which, in the example, is that the patient is an overweight, middle-aged woman. Information from boxes 4–6 goes into box 9, and so forth.

The next step is to translate the incidence matrix into Boolean polynomials. The translation process for the example depends on the truth table shown in Table 5.10. We quote Bellman and Walter [1988, p. 8] to illustrate this process:

We will use "4" to mean "is an overweight, middle-aged woman," while 4' means "is anything else." Similarly, "5" means "thyroid tests normal" while 5' means "thyroid tests abnormal;" and so on. In that notation,

$$9 = 4 * 5 * 6'$$

where we use * for Boolean product (some other notations use ^). Further,

$$10 = 6 * 7$$

$$13 = 9 * 10$$

But we can substitute into the expression for 13:

$$13 = 9 * 10 = (4 * 5 * 6') * (6 * 7)$$

$$= 4 * 5 \{6' * 6\} * 7 = 0,$$

where we show { } around the factors which create the 0 product. The conclusion that $13 = 0$ means that 13 can never be set to "T". Another way of stating this is that the rules assigning 13 the value T [True] can never be utilized.

This mathematically induced result can be seen by examining the truth table shown in Table 5.10. Rule 94 (R94) asserts that 9 and 10 must be true for 13 to be true. Rule 48 asserts that 9 is true if 4 is true, 5 is true, and 6 is false. However, Rule 64 says that both 6 and 7 must be true for 10 to be true. Since 6 cannot be true and false at the same time, a logical flaw in the knowledge base has been discovered.

It is hoped that this small example will illustrate the *potential* offered by automated static testers to help determine the logical consistency and completeness of a knowledge base. We have emphasized the word *potential* for two reasons. First, no automatic static testers are currently available commercially for assessing the logical consistency and completeness of knowledge bases. Second, current "prototype" automated static testers have limitations. To quote Nazareth [1989, pp. 265–266]:

> In most cases the verification process is closely dependent on the structure of the problem domain, making translation of principles to other systems difficult. Additionally, only a subset of the errors identified [above] are covered. . . .

TABLE 5.9 An Incident Matrix Representing the Flow Graph for the Fictitious Diabetes Diagnosis Rule Base

Into: Out of \	4	9	10	11	12	13	14
1	1						
2	1						
3	1						
4	*	1					
5		1					
6		1	1				
7			1				
8				1	1		
9		*			1	1	
10			*			1	1

TABLE 5.10 A Truth Table Representing a Fragment of the Fictitious Rule Base for Diabetes Diagnosis

Assertion:	4	5	6	9		
Rule						
R 41	F	F	F	F		
R 42	F	F	T	F		
R 43	F	T	T	F		
R 44	F	T	F	F		
R 45	T	F	F	F		
R 46	T	F	T	F		
R 47	T	T	T	F		
R 48	T	T	F	T		
Assertion			6	7	10	
R 61			F	F	F	
R 62			F	T	F	
R 63			T	F	F	
R 64			T	T	T	
Assertion				9	10	13
R 91				F	F	F
R 92				F	T	F
R 93				T	F	F
R 94				T	T	T

*a*From Bellman and Walter [1988].

> The expansion of verification scope has serious implications for detection. . . . [And] the majority are directed toward applications without uncertain inference.

Kang and Bahill [1990] have developed a tool called Validator that uses test cases to determine the logical consistency and completeness of a knowledge base. The test cases can be real or imaginary. They can be developed by domain experts, knowledge engineers, users, or evaluators; or, preferably, all four to increase the probability that most segments of the knowledge base will be exercised. All that is required is that the test cases embody valid preconditions. The goal is to record rule firings, not to assess predictive accuracy. The focus is on identifying which rules never fire, and why this occurred. This should identify logical consistency and completeness errors in the knowledge base.

Kang and Bahill [1990, p. 48] discuss the following two classes of problems that result in rules not firing: "failure due to false premises" and "failure due to cutoff." Considering the former, if the premise to a rule is not satisfied by any of the test cases, then the rule will never fire. This failure can be caused by unreferenced attribute values, illegal attribute values, and unreachable conclusions (and dead ends). If a rule has an unnecessary if condition, it will still fire if the remaining if conditions are necessary and sufficient.

Failure due to cutoff implies that the system always stops before a certain rule is reached; thus, the rule never fires. This failure can be caused by redundant rules, subsumed rules, conflicting rules, and circular rules. It can also be caused if, as in most backward-chaining systems, the system stops after finding a value with complete certainty. To quote Kang and Bahill [1990, p. 48]:

Consider this set of rules:

> rule-1: if a = yes then c = 1 cf 100
> rule-2: if a = no then c = 2 cf 100
> rule-3: if b = yes then c = 3 cf X.
> rule-3 will never succeed. After the inference engine has found a value with 100% certainty, it won't seek further values. (This example presumes the user is not allowed to answer "unknown" when a value for *a* is queried.)

As this example illustrates, none of the four logical consistency errors are the problem. Instead, the problem is either (1) both preconditions for *a* incorrectly reach a conclusion with 100% certainty and, therefore, rule-3 is never reached, or (2) that *b* represents an unnecessary if condition and, more generally, rule-3 is an unnecessary rule. Deciding which of these two possibilities is the cause of the problem is for the domain expert and knowledge engineer to decide. Validator's task is simply to identify that rule-3 never fired for any test case.

Validator also identifies rules that fire all the time. As Kang and Bahill [1990, p. 48] point out, such rules are probably mistakes or are perhaps better represented as facts: "Of course, some control rules always succeed, and some rules will be designed for rare situations not exercised by the test cases at hand. Again, this technique is only advisory; the expert must make the final decision about the rule's correctness."

As this last quote illustrates, Validator leaves a lot of the evaluation of the knowledge base in the hands of whomever is using it. Moreover, it does not specifically test the knowledge base for the various types of logical consistency and completeness errors that the static testing methods described above do. Instead, it records which rules fired for which test cases, and provides cumulative statistics, most importantly identifying which rules never fired. Therefore, one might argue that it does not provide as rigorous a test of the knowledge base's logical consistency and completeness as do static testing methods. However, as mentioned before, automated static testers are not currently available; Validator is.

Performing an unaided static analysis of even a small knowledge base is a tedious task. In fact, we would recommend that two or more testers be involved in an unaided static analysis of medium to large knowledge bases because the tedious nature of the task without some automated assistance will no doubt result in errors and omissions. In addition, the use of sampling procedures would also probably be required to reduce the amount of work and, in turn, cost. Seen from this perspective, Validator is certainly a worthwhile tool for helping testers.

5.4.2 Evaluating Functional Completeness and Predictive Accuracy

By functional completeness we mean to address the range of domain-oriented questions, such as whether the knowledge base contains all desired input conditions and output conclusions, or even "knows" its knowledge limitations. Some of these questions can be answered by domain references. However, the level of domain expertise usually desired for expert systems is typically not codified in such references. Indeed, Davis [1989] has argued that one of the major contributions of expert system technology is the organization and codification impacts it has on various disciplines.

Consequently, domain experts are usually required to assess the functional completeness of the knowledge base. This is generally done by having experts perform two activities. First, one has experts examine the knowledge base and question the developers on the various conditions the system can handle or not handle. Second, one has experts use test cases, both actual and those made up by the experts, evaluators, and development team, to exercise the knowledge base. The focus is on whether the expert system is functionally complete; that is, that it has all the information it needs to operate in an operational setting.

One should remember that an expert system's level of functional completeness depends on its stage of development and, most importantly, the domain requirements resulting from the requirements analysis. The DART expert system prototype, for instance, only considered 13 of 42 possible activity nodes. This was quite acceptable in the sponsoring team's opinion because they conceptually placed a low relative weight on "functional completeness" at this stage of DART's development. A fully operational expert system would, of course, have been required to address most, if not all, of the 42 possible activity nodes.

The predictive accuracy of the knowledge base pertains to the correctness by which the facts and rules (or whatever representation scheme) relate the conditions in the test cases to the system's conclusions. An expert system could, of course, be functionally complete in terms of containing all the information needed, but perform poorly because some of the information is inaccurate. Assessing the knowledge base's predictive accuracy is essential for expert systems; otherwise, "garbage in" is literally "garbage out."

Adelman et al. [1990] identified five attributes that address the content of an expert system's knowledge base:

1. *Accuracy of Facts:* The quality of the unconditional statements in the knowledge base.

2. *Accuracy of Rules (or Whatever Representation Scheme):* The quality of the conditional statements in the knowledge base representing expert judgment.
3. *Knowledge Representation Acceptability:* Whether or not the scheme for representing knowledge is acceptable to other domain experts and knowledge engineers.
4. *Adequacy of Source:* Quality of the person(s) and/or documentation used to create the knowledge base.
5. *Modifiability of the Knowledge Base:* Extent to which there is control over changes to the knowledge base, and whether these are implemented by (selected) humans and/or the machine itself (through learning).

Conceptually, knowledge engineering is a measurement problem. Most of the problems for which we develop expert systems do not have objective, quantitative knowledge (e.g., ground truth in the form of laws) that we can, so to speak, take off the shelf and put into a system to solve a problem. Instead, we have to rely on experts to tell us, on the basis of their knowledge and experience, what information and relationships between this information are important in solving a problem (or performing a task) in the domain for which we are building the expert system.

It is not uncommon for experts to disagree not only in their conclusions, but in how they reached them. Moreover, there is considerable research [e.g., see Ebert and Kruse, 1978; Hoffman et al., 1968; Libby and Lewis, 1977] demonstrating that, under controlled settings, the predictive accuracy of different experts varies considerably. Indeed, the commonplace phrase, "Get a second opinion," heard in many problem domains for which expert systems are developed, such as medicine, is indicative of this fact. Experts often disagree with each other because they often disagree on how to combine the information into an "expert opinion."

In addition, a substantial amount of research suggests that experts and nonexperts alike are subject to systematic biases in their judgment. Lehner and Adelman [1990] have reviewed this literature from a knowledge engineering perspective. Presented below are some common biases that can significantly affect the predictive accuracy of a knowledge base. An evaluator, just like a knowledge engineer, needs to be alert for instances of their existence in a knowledge base. (Note: Keep in mind that this is a selective and small sample of a great deal of research in this area.)

Availability Bias. People often overestimate the probability of an event that is easy to recall or imagine [e.g., Tversky and Kahneman, 1973].

Confirmation Bias. People tend to seek and focus on confirming evidence, with the result that once they've formed a judgment, they tend to ignore or devalue disconfirming evidence [e.g., Wason, 1960; Tolcott et al., 1989].

Frequency Bias. People often judge the strength of predictive relations by focusing on the absolute frequency of events rather than their observed relative frequency. As Einhorn and Hogarth [1978] have shown, information on the nonoccurrence of an event is often unavailable and frequently ignored when available.

Concrete Information. Information that is vivid or based on experience or incidents dominates abstract information, such as summaries or statistical base rates. According to Nisbett and Ross [1980], concrete and vivid information contributes to the imaginability of the information and, in turn, enhances its impact on inference.

Conservatism. People often unestimate the predictive value of new information because they do not effectively use base rate information [Edwards, 1968].

Anchoring and Adjustment. A common strategy for making judgments is to anchor on a specific cue or value and then adjust that value to account for other elements of the circumstance. Usually the adjustment is insufficient. So once the anchor is set, there is a bias toward that value [Kahneman and Tversky, 1973].

"Law of Small Numbers." Problems can be framed in such a way that people, including statisticians, give undue confidence to conclusions supported by a relatively small amount of data [Tversky and Kahneman, 1971].

Hindsight Bias. After an event occurs, people will often claim they predicted the event ("I knew it all along!"), even though before the event they were uncertain [Fischhoff, 1975].

Fundamental Attribution Error. People tend to attribute success to their own skill, and failure to chance or the situation with which they were faced. However, when evaluating the performance of other people, the tendency is to attribute other people's failure to their personality traits, not the situation [Nisbett and Ross, 1980].

Biases such as these can be quite problematic from both a development and an evaluation perspective. At the very least, knowledge engineers and evaluators should be aware of their existence and look out for instances where elicited judgments may reflect a bias. For instance, the tendency to ignore base rates, which was discussed in terms of the conservatism bias above, is pervasive. A knowledge engineer or evaluator should therefore be leery of any elicited rules of the form "If observe A, then conclude B with certainty 0.80," since this rule is just as likely to be elicited if the base rate of B is 0.05 as it is if the base rate of B is 0.50. Since neither the expert nor the rule reflects base rate information, the rule is probably inappropriate.

Knowledge engineers and evaluators should also be aware that experts may be overconfident in their judgment capabilities. For example, the hindsight bias may lead experts, when recalling a past scenario, to believe their judgment processes successfully predicted the scenario outcome, when in fact they were quite uncertain. Further, the attribution error makes it likely that when their judgment fails, they will not attribute the failure to their own bad judgment.

Knowledge elicitation essentially requires that experts state how they would make a judgment in various situations. Consequently, not only may an elicited rule reflect judgmental biases, but it may also reflect biases in reporting how one would make judgments. For instance, the hindsight bias and attribution error could lead people to be overconfident in the completeness of their own knowledge. Given such overconfidence, one might speculate that experts are likely to report rules reflecting a stronger connection between pre- and postconditions than is likely to be true of their own judgments. For example, in a knowledge engineering session, an expert may suggest that the rule $P(a|$ b & c & d$) = 0.80$, even though in an actual situation where b, c, and d were known, the expert might judge $P(a) = 0.60$.

In addition, the knowledge engineer and evaluator should also be aware that elicited probability estimates often depend on the nature of the elicitation question and the scale used to measure these estimates [Hogarth, 1975]. Identical questions, asked in different ways, can lead to significant reversals in judgment or preference [e.g., Tversky and Kahneman, 1981; Slovic et al., 1988]. These results suggest that probability estimates not obtained using multiple methods may be questionable, for they may reflect the inadequacy of using only measurement procedure.

As this latter point suggests, the measurement problem inherent in developing a knowledge base is a complicated one because there are numerous sources of variability and, hence, error [Adelman, 1989]. In particular, there are five potential sources of variability in the content of a knowledge base that can influence its predictive accuracy: substantive experts, knowledge elicitation methods, knowledge engineers, knowledge representation schemes, and the problem domain itself. Unfortunately, the knowledge bases for many expert systems are developed using only one expert, one knowledge engineer, and one elicitation method for a predetermined knowledge representation scheme (or shell). The predictive accuracy of such systems have to be evaluated for actual case data, for there is minimal research demonstrating that the above sources of variability do not affect the quality of a knowledge base, and research in areas related to knowledge engineering that suggest they do.

For example, besides the research demonstrating differences in experts' judgments, there is substantial research in the field of interviewing, which is analogous in many respects to knowledge engineering, that has demonstrated significant interviewer effects [e.g., see Forsythe and Buchanan, 1989; Hammond, 1948]. In addition, research by Hammond et al. [1986; 1987] with 20 highway engineers using three knowledge elicitation methods to make aesthetics, safety, and capacity judgments found significant differences in predictive accuracy for experts, methods, problems and, most importantly, method by problem interactions. Research by Kahneman and Tversky [1984] clearly demonstrates that the way a problem is "framed," which can be critical in knowledge engineering, substantially affects people's decision-making process. Research by Dawes and Corrigan [1974] and Hammond et al. [1975] has demonstrated that the inherent predictability of prob-

Hammond et al. [1975] has demonstrated that the inherent predictability of problems varies significantly. And Leddo and Cohen's [1987] research suggests that the amount and type of knowledge elicited in a knowledge engineering session can vary depending on the expert, task, knowledge representation scheme, and elicitation method; moreover, they suggest that interactions may exist among all of these sources of variation.

Given the many different threats to the predictive accuracy of the knowledge base, multiple experts and empirical evaluation methods should be used to evaluate an expert system's predictive accuracy. The evaluation experts can include the expert(s) involved in the development effort, but should include at least one and preferably two or more experts who have not done so. Expert evaluation typically proceeds in two ways: through (1) experts' examination of the knowledge base, and (2) an assessment of the adequacy of a knowledge base's predictions for test cases.

Expert examination of the knowledge base typically focuses on whether the system exhibits "correct reasoning." The obvious concern is, of course, that the knowledge base not have mistakes. However, another concern—and one that Gaschnig et al. [1983] pointed out—is not shared by all developers: that is whether their programs reach decisions like human experts do. Many psychologists have long argued that this concern cannot be answered, for one cannot, so to speak, look inside an expert's head to obtain the correct reasoning; for example, see Hoffman [1960]. Instead, all one can do is build models of the reasoning process, and evaluate their predictive accuracy against test cases. Indeed, many researchers [e.g., Dawes and Corrigan, 1974; Einhorn and Hogarth, 1975; Levi, 1989; Stewart et al., 1988] have shown that simple linear models can often result in prediction as good as that achieved by experts or the far more complex models found in many expert systems.

This is not a resolved issue. On the one hand, Gaschnig et al. [p. 255] point out, ". . . there is an increasing realization that expert-level performance may require heightened attention to the mechanisms by which human experts actually solve the problems for which the expert systems are typically built." Additionally, Adelman et al. [1985] found that domain experts' judgments of the utility of decision support system and expert system prototypes were significantly affected by the match between how they and the system attempted to solve the problem. On the other hand, the intended users of many expert systems are not experts. Research by Lehner and Zirk [1987] indicates that nonexperts can perform extremely well with expert systems as long as they fully understand how the system is using the data to arrive at its conclusions. What all of this suggests is that, at a minimum, the system's representation and presentation schemes must be reviewed with experts and intended users.

The predictive accuracy of the knowledge base can be assessed using test cases and performance standards; that is, by an empirical evaluation. The desired standard is ground truth, the correct answers to the test cases. Procedurally, the expert system is given a set of test cases to solve. Then, the system's answers are compared to the correct answers for the test cases. The system's overall predictive accuracy can be quantified in different ways depending on the type of predictions it gives. For example, a fourfold correlation can be used to determine the level of agreement between the system's predictions and the correct answers if both are dichotomous; for instance, as for a friend versus foe identification. Pearson product-moment correlations can be used if the predictions and answers are along a continuous scale. "Scoring rules" can be used if the predictions and answers are probability estimates. A "magnitude of relative error" could also be calculated to measure predictive accuracy, as is often done to evaluate cost estimation models.

(Note: To assess the predictive accuracy of the knowledge base alone, it is assumed that the human operator is not using the system. The next chapter discusses empirical evaluation methods, such as experiments, designed to assess the predictive accuracy of the operator-controlled expert system.)

Correct answers are most desirable because substantial research (referenced above) has shown that experts often disagree with each other. And even the best expert is not accurate 100% of the time. It is usually inappropriate to expect better predictive accuracy from the system than the expert. There are, of course, exceptions, such as when the expert system incorporates knowledge from a limited, well-defined domain—such as a procedure manual—or where the system represents the expertise of several experts or is responsible for human safety. Under such circumstances, it may be quite appropriate to expect the system to be more accurate than any given expert.

Lehner [1989] has argued recently that, if possible, one should discriminate between "accuracy" and "bias." This distinction is based on signal-detection theory concepts. Specifically, accuracy refers to the degree of overlap in the distributions of belief values when the hypothesis is true as opposed to false. Bias refers to the proportion of false negatives (hypothesis true, but user says false) to false positives (hypothesis false, but user says true). The level of bias to be accepted in an expert system is a critical decision for intended users and their sponsoring organizations. As the DART evaluation demonstrated, different types of inferential errors have different implications and, thus, different importance to decision makers. It is the evaluator's job to make sure that intended users and sponsors know the amount and proportion of different types of inferential errors to which the knowledge base is susceptible throughout development.

If the correct answers do not exist or, for whatever reason, are unsuitable for the test cases, then one must rely on the judgment of an expert or the consensus judgments of a group of experts. Considerable care must be given to structuring the experts' activities. In particular, the evaluation team must ensure that the experts are "blind" as to whether the system or other experts generated the conclusions to the test cases. Otherwise, one runs the risk of having the experts' evaluation biased by this information; for example, see Chandrasekaran [1983] and Yu et al. [1979].

In closing this section, it is important to note that test-case construction is an important issue. To quote O'Keefe et al. [1987, p. 83], "The issue is not the *number* of test cases, it is the *coverage* of test cases—that is, how well they reflect the input domain. The input domain is the population of permissible input . . ." [italics theirs]. The required coverage capabilities need to be a result of the requirements analysis. For as O'Keefe et al. point out, developers frequently devote a disproportionate amount of time attempting to ensure that the system can handle the truly "expert" cases that may occur very infrequently. Furthermore, these "infrequent" cases often become the test cases. This may or may not be appropriate depending on the requirements for the system, and it can certainly be expensive.

An alternative identified by O'Keefe et al. is to select test cases randomly using a stratified sampling scheme such that the relative frequency of the cases is representative of those in the actual environment or stipulated in the requirements document. Additionally, test cases should be chosen to cover situations where a failure in the system would be especially serious. It is also important that some of the test cases simulate the most common operation of the system. Lehner and Ulvila [1989] have shown that a surprisingly small number of test cases are required to determine whether an expert system's level of predictive accuracy is sufficient to be of practical value to its users.

5.5 SUMMARY

Four classes of technical evaluation methods have been overviewed in this chapter. In particular, the focus was on methods for (1) selecting and evaluating analytical modeling methods, (2) estimating software development costs, (3) performing software testing and verification, and (4) evaluating the adequacy of an expert system's knowledge base.

Regarding the former, two taxonomies were reviewed for matching analytical methods to requirements: one was based on the SHOR paradigm, and the other on a requirements/methods matrix. Second, three categories of software cost estimation methods were reviewed: experiential methods relying on expert judgment for estimating effort and, in turn, cost; static methods utilizing regression analysis for relating cost factors to effort; and dynamic estimation methods incorporating time as a parameter of the equation. Third, two broad categories of software testing methods were covered: static testing methods in which software is analyzed, but without code execution; and dynamic testing methods in which the software is executed using sets of test data. And, fourth, two categories of methods for determining knowledge-base quality were discussed: (1) static testing and, to a lesser extent, dynamic testing methods for assessing the logical consistency and adequacy of the knowledge base; and (2) using domain experts, in conjunction with empirical evaluation concepts and methods, for assessing the knowledge base's functional completeness and predictive accuracy.

Throughout the chapter, we have tried to provide general guidelines and cautions to keep in mind when considering each class of technical evaluation methods. We have typically referred to these guidelines as "points to keep in mind." We want to close this chapter by reiterating three general points that cut across all technical methods.

First, the results of the technical evaluation can often be used to predict the results of the empirical and subjective evaluations. For how well the system is built will affect how well users can perform desired tasks with the decision support system or expert system and, in turn, what they think of it. Second, although all three classes of methods are highly applicable during the later stages of the development process, we have emphasized their application as early as possible in the process because that is when errors are easiest and cheapest to remedy. This is the "prevention versus cure" distinction so commonplace in the medical profession, and one gaining increasing support via standards and practices in software engineering. And, third, evaluators should use multiple methods whenever possible. All technical (and subjective and empirical) evaluation methods have their strengths and weaknesses. The use of two or more methods within each class will increase the probability that the evaluation effort will converge on an accurate assessment.

It obviously takes more time and money to use two methods than one. Whether the added time and money is worth it is a judgment the evaluator (and appropriate other members of the development team) will have to make on a case-by-case basis throughout development. In cases in which there is considerable uncertainty about how things are progressing and the results of errors are severe, the decision is easy; in other cases, it will be more difficult. In general, however, it should always be remembered that the total cost of the development effort will be less if errors are caught early rather than late in the process.

Chapter 6

Empirical Evaluation Methods

In contrast to (1) technical evaluation methods, which focus on how well the decision support system or expert system was built, or (2) subjective evaluation methods, which focus on how much users like it, empirical evaluation methods focus on decision makers' performance with (versus without) the system. In particular, we will overview three empirical evaluation methods: experiments, quasi-experiments, and case studies. In all cases, the methods address whether the system enhances performance. And in all cases, these empirical methods have been shown to provide valid feedback for development.

Experiments, quasi-experiments, and case studies were selected for detailed consideration because they represent a range of choices from the ". . . fully reproducible, fully-controlled artificial study, to the opportunistic, wholly unconstrained, naturalistic study" [Shrinkfield, 1983, p. 362]. In general, experiments will be most feasible during the early stages of development when one is evaluating proof-of-concept prototypes and assessing the performance adequacy of system features, such as a knowledge base or user interface. Quasi-experiments and case studies will be most feasible after the system has been transferred into its operational setting. Experiments in operational settings are, however, highly informative if administrative and cost factors permit their implementation.

It should be noted that there are other empirical evaluation models and methods [e.g., see Madaus et al., 1983, for a review], and some of their proponents strongly argue against the appropriateness of laboratory experiments [e.g., see Gupta and Lincoln, 1983; Patton, 1982]. Although we obviously disagree with this position, we do caution the reader against the uncritical application of experiments or any other empirical evaluation method. The selection of any method needs to be guided by the decision-making needs, and the practical issues of time, money, and resources. Evaluation models and methods will vary in their suitability for different contexts. Moreover, the combination of methods may ". . . provide a richer, contextual basis for interpretating and validating results" [Kaplan and Duchon, 1988, p. 575].

All the different evaluation models consider the criteria of reliability and validity (or "analogous terms" [Gupta and Lincoln, 1983, p. 326]) to be "fundamentals of design and measurement" [Patton, 1982, p. 210]. Stated bluntly, these criteria are absolutely vital to the development of all quality empirical evaluations. Neither introductory statistics nor software engineering texts consider these criteria for the range of methods addressed herein. Furthermore, few system engineering and computer science students take the experimental design courses in which they are discussed. Consequently, these fundamental criteria are stressed throughout this chapter.

The discussion will be at a general level, for this or e chapter cannot even begin to cover all the details found in experimental design and statistical analysis texts. The goal is to address the different issues that must be considered when attempting to demonstrate the performance benefits of decision support and expert systems empirically. Such a demonstration typically is, and in our opinion should be, essential for sponsors to approve the transfer of the system into an organization. After all, the bottom line is whether people can perform their tasks better, faster, and/or cheaper with than without the system.

6.1 EXPERIMENTS

Experiments are the most common and frequently thought of empirical evaluation method. They are especially appropriate when a number of people would use the decision support system or expert system, for experiments are designed to help generalize from a test sample to the larger population, which in our case would be system users and their organizations. However, experiments also can be conducted even if the system is being developed for use by one person. In this case, for example, the prospective user could solve a number of representative problems with and without the system in order to ascertain whether, in general, the user performed better with it.

One generally thinks of two kinds of experiments. The first tests the decision support system or expert system against objective benchmarks that often form performance constraints. When the system passes the benchmark, it proceeds further; when it fails, it undergoes further development or is set aside: "For example, it is not enough to know that with the aid the user can arrive at a decision in 30 min. If the organizational user required a decision in 30 min, the aid would be effective. If a decision was needed in 15 min, the aid would not be effective" [Riedel and Pitz, 1986, pp. 984–985].

The type of performance benchmarks illustrated in the above quote differs from the more traditional time and efficiency measures used to benchmark computer systems. Time and efficiency benchmarks typically get developed during requirements analyses emphasizing technical performance features. Although such performance constraints may be necessary in real-time, life-critical activities, they are unnecessary for many decision support systems and expert systems. Accordingly, we are not going to consider the timing and efficiency approach further. Readers interested in it are referred to Press [1989], who benchmarked different expert systems on the time required to load and execute different types of knowledge bases, and the amount of disk space required in source and fast-load formats.

Performance benchmarks such as those mentioned in the quote represent non-compensatory decision rules; that is, performance on other evaluation criteria does not compensate for failing the performance benchmark. Such a position may be inconsistent with the compensatory decision rule guiding the sponsoring team's intuitive decision-making processes or more formal subjective methods, such as MAUT. After all, it's quite possible that the sponsoring team might be willing to give up some time for task accomplishment (or some whatever) in order to gain even a little improvement on other measures of effectiveness, such as decision performance or personnel staffing requirements (or whatever).

The second kind of experiment, and the one that is focused on here, is a factorial design where (1) one or more factors are systematically varied as the independent variable(s), and (2) the dependent variable(s) are quantitative, objective measures of performance. As summarized in Table 6.1, there are six basic components of most factorial experiments. Each component is considered, in turn.

First, there are the participants in the experiment. (They are often called "subjects" even though they are not the subject of the test.) The participants in an experiment should be representative of the larger population to which one wants

TABLE 6.1 Some Summary Comments About Experiments

Two Typical Kinds:
    Benchmark testing
    Factorial designs

Components of Factorial Experiments
    Participants
    Independent variables
    Task
    Dependent variables (and measures)
    Experimental procedures
    Statistical analyses

General Approaches for Controlling Rival Hypotheses
    Include in experimental design
    Eliminate their ability to affect the results

to generalize. If the system is being developed for experts, then experts should be the participants in the experiment. If system users will be nonexperts, then nonexperts should be the participants. However, using experts in addition to nonexperts can provide important insights, as was illustrated with the evaluation of the DART expert system. Moreover, it is typically required for the technical evaluation of an expert system's knowledge base.

Although the following point will be discussed in greater detail later in the chapter, it is noteworthy here that if one's concern is whether or not an organizational unit performs better with the system, then organizational units should be the "participants" in the experiment. This issue is of particular concern for experiments performed in operational settings, or in high-fidelity simulations of the operational setting prior to system implementation, when the decision support system or expert system will be used by many organizational units. The concern in such settings is whether, on average, organizational units with the system perform better than those without it. The dependent measure is the performance of the organizational unit, not a particular person; for example, an expert using an expert system. It is quite possible for experts (or nonexperts) to perform better with an expert system and, at the same time, for organizational units to fail to do so because of other factors, such as organizational dynamics or the organization's formal or informal power structure, and so forth. Therefore, if one wants to know whether organizational units perform better, on average, with the system, actual or simulated units (and not a group of experts and/or nonexperts brought together for an experiment) need to be the focus of attention and, hence, the "participants."

Second, there is the experimental condition(s) or independent variable(s) of interest, such as whether the participants perform the task with—versus without— the decision support system or expert system. For instance, there were two independent variables in the DART experiment: the "degree of support" and "problem type." There were two levels on the "degree of support" independent variable. The "unaided condition" was a control group; it represented the degree of support the decision maker had without DART. The second level was the "aided" condition; it represented the support level provided by DART. The "degree of support" variable need not be limited to two levels. Indeed, it might be extremely advantageous to evaluate two or more variants of the decision support system or expert system, particularly during prototyping when there is substantial uncertainty about how sophisticated a system users need. And, in the DART experiment, there were two different problem scenarios.

Third, there is the task that the participants are to perform during the course of the experiment. The level of task difficulty should be either (1) as representative as possible of the actual setting in which the system will be used or (2) matched to the hypothesized performance capabilities of the system. The capabilities of the system depend on its stage of development [e.g., see Gaschnig et al., 1983; Marcot, 1987]. One would not expect an initial prototype to perform at the level of proficiency of an operational system and, consequently, one should not evaluate the former as if it were the latter. However, it is not always clear what performance levels a prototype should exhibit at different levels of development. Ideally, this would be stipulated in the requirements document. Unfortunately, as many researchers [e.g., Constantine and Ulvila, in press; Rook and Croghan, 1989; Rushby, 1988] have found, detailed requirements documentation is all too often unavailable for decision support and expert system technology. Thus, users, developers, and evaluators need to consider carefully what performance levels the system should exhibit at different levels of development in order to demonstrate that the development process is proceeding well.

The fourth component of experiments is the dependent variable(s) (i.e., measures of effectiveness) of interest. Objective measures (e.g., time to accomplish the task), observational measures (e.g., decision process quality), or subjective measures (e.g., user confidence in the solution) can all be used as the dependent variable(s) in an experiment, though the focus is on objective measures in this chapter. In the case of "decision quality," one can use either objective measures (i.e., the correct answer) for the task, or subjective measures (e.g., the collective judgment of two or more experts). Objective measures of decision quality are preferred to subjective ones if they exist and are appropriate for the experimental task. If experts are used to assess decision quality, attempts must be made to keep them blind as to which experimental conditions produced the solutions so that this information does not inadvertently bias their ratings.

And, fifth, there are the procedures governing the overall implementation of the experiment. Substantial care should be directed toward implementing the experiment as designed, including accurately representing the unaided as well as aided condition in order to ensure a fair test. If performance is better in the "aided" condition, one wants to be able to say that it is due to the decision support system or expert system and not some other factor. In order to do so, we need to try to control for all "plausible rival hypotheses" [Campbell and Stanley, 1966, p. 36] that might explain the obtained findings. Toward that goal, we introduce the concepts of reliability and validity. (Note: Statistical analyses, the sixth component of experimental designs, will be considered later in the subsection entitled "Statistical Conclusion Validity.")

6.1.1 Reliability and Validity Broadly Defined

Yin [1984, p. 36] defines reliability as "demonstrating that the operations of a study—such as the data collection procedures—can be repeated, with the same results." The key concept is replication. In contrast, *valid* is defined by *Webster's Dictionary* [1966] as that which is sound because it is "well grounded on principles or evidence." If an experiment is valid, its conclusions can be accepted; that is, rival hypotheses have been controlled for.

An experiment can be reliable but its conclusions invalid for numerous reasons that will be considered below. However, an experiment cannot result in valid conclusions if it is unreliable; that is, one cannot conclude that the results are well grounded if the evidence on which they are based is undependable. Consequently, the basis for good experimentation is reliable (i.e., dependable) procedures and measures. Although far from trivial, reliability is typically possible in experimentation because of high experimenter control. The experimenter can pilot-test and subsequently modify the procedures and measures used in an experiment over and over again until they produce the same results when applied to the same situation, regardless of who performs the experiment. In contrast, there exist a number of threats to the validity of an experiment's conclusions regardless of the reliability.

There are four types of validity that need to be considered when performing experiments: construct, internal, statistical conclusion, and external. Each is now discussed within the context of experiments, and again in the sections addressing quasi-experimental and case-study designs.

6.1.2 Internal Validity

Yin [1984, p. 36] has defined internal validity as "establishing a causal relationship, whereby certain conditions are shown to lead to other conditions, as distinguished from spurious relationships." That is, we want to be able to say that our independent variables, and not some other uncontrolled-for factors, caused the observed effects on our dependent variables. The "uncontrolled-for factors" represent rival hypotheses for explaining the experiment's results. Further, as Cook and Campbell [1979, p. 38] point out, "Internal validity has nothing to do with the abstract labeling of a presumed cause or effect; rather, it deals with the *relationship* between the research operations *irrespective of what they theoretically represent*" [italics theirs]. (Note: The latter issue of "theoretical representations" is considered under the subsection entitled "Construct Validity.")

There are two general approaches to controlling rival hypotheses, especially those that might be considered spurious threats to causal inference. The first is to include them in the design somehow. One way to do so is to include rival hypotheses as other independent variables in the factorial design. For example, two different problem scenarios were used in the DART experiment in an effort to minimize the degree to which the results might be scenario-dependent. Another way to include rival hypotheses in the design is through the nature of the design itself. For example, Sharda et al. [1988] used a longitudinal, factorial design in order to examine whether time was a plausible hypothesis to explain (initial) performance decrements with decision support technology, a position consistent with a learning theory perspective. The point is that the one way to control for rival hypotheses is to use an experimental design that will explicitly permit one to test their effect on performance.

Although the first approach for controlling rival hypotheses is powerful, it has two limitations. First, it suffers from sample size limitations. The number of independent variables, the levels on these variables, and, more generally, the experimental design itself must be considered with care because of their implications for the number of participants required for statistical testing purposes. The larger the number of cells in the matrix representing the factorial design's pairing of levels on the independent variables, the more participants required to fill the cells and, thus, perform the experiment.

Second, the first approach presumes that one knows all plausible rival hypotheses. This, however, is not possible; there may always be alternative hypotheses for explaining the data. That is why the philosophy of science focuses on disconfirmation, not confirmation of hypotheses. To quote Campbell and Stanley [1966, p. 34], "In a very fundamental sense, experimental results never 'confirm' or 'prove' a theory—rather, the successful theory is tested and escapes being disconfirmed. . . . An adequate hypothesis is one that has repeatedly survived such probing—but it may always be displaced by a new probe."

The second general approach for controlling for plausible rival hypotheses is attempting to eliminate any possibility that they can affect the results. In particular, one wants to control for extraneous factors that significantly impair our ability to make valid causal inferences. This second approach is exemplified by the concept of randomization. *Webster's Dictionary* [1966] states that "random applies to that which occurs or is done without careful choice, aim, plan, etc." Arbitrarily assigning test subjects to the "aided" and "unaided" conditions in a factorial design or arbitrarily determining the order in which DART test subjects worked the test problems with or without the expert system illustrates randomization.

It cannot be overstated how important randomization is in experimentation. This can be illustrated by considering the "threats to internal validity" that randomization eliminates as plausible rival hypotheses. To quote Cook and Campbell [1979, p. 56]:

> When respondents are randomly assigned to treatment groups, each group is similarly constituted on the average (no selection, maturation, or selection-maturation problems). Each experiences the same testing conditions and research instruments (no testing or instrumentation problems). No deliberate selection is made of high and low scores on any tests except under conditions where respondents are first matched according to, say, pretest scores and are then randomly assigned to treatment conditions (no statistical regression problems). Each group experiences the same global pattern of history (no history problem). And if there are treatment-related differences in who drops out of the experiment, this is interpretable as a consequence of the treatment. Thus, randomization takes care of many threats to internal validity.

(Table 6.2 more formally defines the threats to internal validity considered above.)

True experiments include randomization. When randomization is not possible, one can employ quasi-experimental designs. However, these are not as effective as experimental designs in controlling extraneous factors. As Cook and Campbell [1979, p. 56] indicate:

TABLE 6.2   Definitions of (Selected) Threats to Internal Validity

Selection:
  A threat due to the kinds of participants in one group versus another. (Note: Selection can interact with many of the other threats listed below.)

Maturation:
  A threat due to participants gaining experience or in some manner changing during the course of the research.

Testing:
  A threat potentially resulting because of the number of times participants' responses have been measured during the research.

Instrumentation:
  A threat due to changing the way the dependent variables are measured during the research.

Statistical Regression
  A threat due to selecting participants for different (and particularly extreme) groups on the basis of pretest measures with less-than-perfect reliability.

History:
  A threat due to an external event taking place during the course of the research that is not the treatment of interest.

With quasi-experimental groups, the situation is quite different. Instead of relying on randomization to rule out most internal validity threats, the investigator has to make all the threats explicit and then rule them out one by one. His task is, therefore, more laborious. It is also less enviable since his final causal inference will not be as strong as if he had conducted a randomized experiment. The principal reason for choosing to conduct randomized experiments over other types of research design is that they make causal inference easier.

Randomly assigning participants to the "aided" and "unaided" (or "with system" and "without system") conditions is the best means for essentially equating the conditions prior to beginning the experiment. Randomization significantly limits the number of rival hypotheses that can be used to explain the obtained data, which in our case would (hopefully) be markedly better performance with than without the system. Randomization does not, however, rule out all threats to internal validity. In particular, Cook and Campbell [1979, pp. 54–55] have identified four threats to internal validity that are not controlled for by randomization.

The first is the "diffusion or limitation of treatments" that may arise if members of the experimental and control groups can talk to each other during the course of the experiment and in some way obviate the effect of the treatment (e.g., the decision support system or expert system) because of the information they convey. The second threat is the "compensatory equalization of treatments." This may occur if administrators are reluctant to tolerate the perceived inequality between the experimental and control groups and, therefore, do not enforce the procedures distinguishing them. The third threat is the "compensatory rivalry by respondents receiving less desirable treatments"; that is, members of the control group act to reduce or reverse the expected difference. Cook and Campbell note that this threat is especially likely when intact organizational units are assigned to different conditions or if members of the control group perceive themselves as disadvantaged if the treatment condition is successful, both of which may happen when testing decision support and expert system technology in operational settings. The fourth threat is the "resentful demoralization of respondents receiving less desirable treatments," and represents the converse of the third threat; that is, participants receiving the treatment do not attempt to perform well.

Another threat not controlled by randomization is the unintentional confounding of the experimental treatment (e.g., the decision support system or expert system) with other factors. With this in mind, we now turn to consider construct validity.

6.1.3 Construct Validity

Yin [1984, p. 36] has defined construct validity as ". . . establishing good operational measures for the concepts being studied." Good construct validity means that we are measuring that, and only that, that we want to be measuring. Of special concern in empirical evaluations of decision support and expert systems is that the "with system" condition is not confounded by something else. If confounding exists, then the "something else" represents a rival hypothesis that could explain the obtained results.

The practice of giving control subjects placebos in medical research is a good example of trying to control for the possible confounding between the helpful concern of the physician and the chemical effects of the medication. Similarly, if one considers a decision support system or expert system as analogous to a new medication, is the positive effect of the system the result of the system or the concern of senior-level management? If it's the latter, performance will deteriorate once the system has been declared a success and its users are no longer the attention of upper management.

Possible confounding is also important when the system has a negative impact. For instance, Markus [1984] used a case-study design to show that the negative resistance to an implemented information system was not a function of the system's technical quality, but its mismatch with the organization's interaction patterns. Kaplan and Duchon [1988] used a case-study and survey research approach to demonstrate that the response to an organizationwide information system was a function of users' perception of their jobs, not the system.

If we have some idea of what "other" variables may be confounded with our experimental conditions, then we want to (1) take steps to eliminate their potential influence on our evaluation, (2) systematically incorporate them into our experimental design so that we can directly assess their effect, or (3) measure them so that we can perform a "post hoc" assessment. In choosing either of the latter two options, our goal is to measure each of these rival hypotheses (or constructs) to test their predictions with the collected data and, thereby, assess which hypotheses have been falsified. (Again, the perspective is on disconfirmation, not on confirmation, although the latter is how researchers typically report their findings.)

6.1.4   Statistical Conclusion Validity

In contrast to internal and construct validity, "[s]tatistical conclusion validity is concerned not with sources of systematic bias but with sources of random error and with the appropriate use of statistics and statistical tests" [Cook and Campbell, 1979, p. 80]. The concern is with (1) whether the study is sensitive enough to permit reasonable statements regarding the covariation between independent and dependent variables, and (2) what constitutes appropriate tests of these statements.

There are two types of potential errors when performing statistical tests. The first type, called a Type I error (alpha), is the probability of *incorrectly rejecting the null hypothesis*, which is that there is no difference in the effect of the experimental conditions on the dependent variables. For an experiment assessing a decision support system or expert system's effect on performance, it is the probability of incorrectly concluding that there is a difference in the performance levels obtained with versus without the system when, in fact, there is no difference. The second type of error, the Type II error (beta), is the probability of *incorrectly accepting the null hypothesis*. In our case, it is the probability of concluding that there is no difference in the performance levels obtained with versus without the system when, in fact, a difference exists. A test's statistical power is the complement of its Type II error level; that is, 1 − beta. Statistical power is the probability that a statistical test will *correctly reject the null hypothesis*.

One wants to set up an experiment that appropriately balances the two types of errors. Such a balance is required because the beta and statistical power values are constrained by the value set for alpha. As Baroudi and Orlikowski [1988, pp. 88–89] point out:

> The traditional belief is that the consequences of false positives are more serious than those of false negatives [Cohen, 1965]. Therefore, Type I errors are usually guarded against more stringently. The distribution of risk between Type I and Type II errors, however, needs to be appropriate to the situation at hand. Mazen et al. [1987] present a graphic illustration of a case (the ill-fated Challenger space shuttle) where the risk of incurring a Type II error (saying there was no problem when there was) far outweighed that for Type I (saying there was a problem when there wasn't).
>
> Researchers who wish to conform to the convention of protecting themselves more

against false positive claims should set alpha to .05 and beta to .20 (four times as much) [Cohen, 1977]. Accepting these recommended values for alpha and beta results in a .80 value for power (1 − beta), meaning that a statistical test having a power value of .80 has an 80% probability of detecting an effect if it exists. Cohen's prescription of a .80 conventional power level has become widely accepted as the norm . . .

Cohen [1977], as well as other texts [e.g., Bailey, 1971], provide statistical tables for calculating statistical power on the basis of the alpha level, sample size, and predicted effect of the treatment.

Baroudi and Orlikowski [1988], Cohen [1977], Cook and Campbell [1979], and other researchers [e.g., see also Bailey, 1971] have discussed ways to increase the statistical power and, more generally, the "statistical conclusion validity" of one's experiments. Five ways will be considered here.

Perhaps the most obvious way to increase statistical conclusion validity is to increase the "sample size"; that is, the number of people (or organizational units if that is the appropriate unit of analysis) participating in the experiment. The larger the sample size, the more precise the sample estimate of the values on the dependent variable for each condition, consistent with the Law of Large Numbers.

Second, one should attempt to increase the reliability of the experiment; for example, by increasing the reliability of the measurement instruments. As Cook and Campbell [1979, p. 43] note, ". . . unreliability inflates standard errors of estimates and these standard errors play a crucial role in inferring differences between statistics, such as the means of different treatment groups." Similarly, one should increase the reliability of the procedures for implementing the different conditions in the experiment. By standardizing how people receive the treatments, one decreases the error variance and, thereby, increases the probability of detecting true differences.

Third, one should give careful thought to the research design. As Kraemer and Thiemann [1987] suggest, only factors that are necessary to the research question, or that have a documented and strong relation to the response, should be included. Including marginally relevant factors decreases statistical power if not suitably compensated for by an increase in the sample size. In addition, one should try to allocate an equal number of participants to each condition. As Baroudi and Orlikowski [1988, p. 101] warn, ". . . if the group sizes are unequal, attenuation of observed effect sizes can occur, which potentially undermines the statistical power of the analysis, regardless of the total n."

Also, if possible, repeated measure (or "within subject") designs, like the one in the DART evaluation, should be used. By repeatedly measuring the test subjects, one is able to partition out the error variance due to individual (versus treatment) differences and, thus, increase the statistical power of the test. Repeated measure designs are particularly appropriate when participants are not readily available. But before using repeated measure designs where participants get the "with system" and "without system" conditions, one should make sure that participation in one condition does not inadvertently confound participation in the other. Moreover, if at all possible, the order in which participants perform the "with system" and "without system" tasks should be balanced so as not to implement an order effect into one's experiment inadvertently. And, finally, the error terms used in repeated measure designs are different than those used in "between subject" designs because they partition out the error variance due to individuals; consequently, one needs to make sure one is doing the correct analysis.

The fourth way to increase the statistical conclusion validity of one's experiments is to give careful consideration to the research question. As discussed above, decide which of the two types of error are most important, and proceed accordingly. Also, consider whether your hypothesis is directional or not. It might be, for example, that a sponsor will only consider implementing a decision support system or expert system if it can be demonstrated that it improves performance during its operational test; poorer or even equivalent levels of performance to those achieved without the system may be unimportant. In such a case, it is possible to increase the power of the test simply by moving from a two-tailed to one-tailed test, for a one-tailed test with an alpha of 0.05 has the same statistical power as a two-tailed test with an alpha of 0.10, all other things being equal. Of course, if one had decided to use a one-tailed test to determine whether the system improved performance, it would be inappropriate to test whether the system significantly decreased performance if the system did not perform up to expectations.

Fifth, one should consider the "effect size" that is of utility to the sponsors. Effect size is the difference in the performance levels achieved by the different conditions (e.g., with versus without the system). The larger the effect size that is of importance (e.g., performance improvements of 100% versus 10%, or three versus one-third standard deviations), the smaller the sample size required to find the effect. Lehner and Ulvila [1989] have shown that a surprisingly small number of test cases are required to test expert systems if users want large effects. Moreover, the focus on effect size prior to performing an experiment makes users explicitly consider their performance requirements for the system. All too often performance requirements for decision support systems and expert systems are left implicit during the early stages of development, and this can cause serious problems between sponsoring and development personnel as the initial prototypes mature. If a sponsor wants the system to have a big effect on performance, showing statistically significant but small effects with the system may not be considered an adequate return on investment in the sponsor's eyes.

Thus far, we have not indicated what statistical tests should be performed; we have simply focused on the more general issues inherent in considering statistical conclusion validity. Furthermore, we are hesitant to go into much detail about statistical tests because we know that adequate consideration of them takes substantially more space than is available here. Nevertheless, consistent with the approach taken by O'Keefe et al. [1987], we briefly review two classes of statistical tests. (Note: These tests are listed in Table 6.3 for summary purposes, as are the definitions of Type I and Type II error, and the general approaches to increasing statistical power.)

For the first class of tests, assume that one has only one factor, the degree of aiding. Moreover, assume that one has only two levels on this factor, whether the participant worked the problem with or without the decision support system or expert system, and one dependent variable (i.e., measure of effectiveness). We can use a paired (or two-sample) t-test to determine whether the difference in the average performance levels obtained in the two conditions is significant. If we have

TABLE 6.3 A Summary of Issues Involved in the Discussion of Statistical Conclusion Validity

Definitions

Type I error: The probability of *incorrectly rejecting* the null hypothesis that there is no difference between test conditions
Type II error: The probability of *incorrectly accepting* the null hypothesis that there is no difference between test conditions
Statistical power: The probability of *correctly rejecting* the null hypothesis that there is no difference between test conditions

General Approaches to Increasing Statistical Power

Increase sample size
Increase the reliability of the experiment
Give careful consideration to the research design
Give careful consideration to the research question
Consider the "effect size" that is important to the sponsors

Illustrative Types of Statistical Tests

For one independent variable with two levels and one dependent variable:
    Two-sample t-test

For more than two levels on one independent variable or two (or more) independent variables, but one dependent variable:
    Analysis of variance (ANOVA) with planned or post hoc statistical tests

For one independent variable with two levels and two dependent variables:
    Hotelling's one-sample T^2 test

For more than two levels on one independent variable or two (or more) independent variables, but two dependent variables:
    Multivariate analysis of variance (MANOVA) with ANOVAs and planned or post hoc statistical tests

more than two levels on this factor, or more than one factor, we should use an analysis of variance (ANOVA) test instead of multiple *t*-tests to control appropriately for finding differences between our conditions by chance. The ANOVA should be accompanied by either "planned" or "post hoc" statistical tests of the (average) performance levels obtained in the different conditions, depending on whether or not the observed differences were hypothesized before or after conducting the experiment, respectively.

There are, naturally, many situations where there is more than one dependent variable of interest. The second class of statistical tests deals with this case. Again, consider the case where we have only one factor, degree of support, and two levels on it. To quote O'Keefe et al. [1987, p. 87], "While a paired t-test is appropriate when systems produce a single final result, simultaneously applying a paired t-test to a number of final results is inappropriate since we can expect the final results to be correlated . . . In such cases, Hotelling's one-sample T^2 test should be used." In the case in which there are more than two levels on the factor or multiple factors, then one should use a multivariate analysis of variance (MANOVA). If the MANOVA shows a significant difference between experimental conditions, then separate ANOVAS and planned and post hoc comparison tests can be performed to examine the data statistically.

6.1.5 External Validity

In addition to internal validity, construct validity, and statistical conclusion validity, one also needs to consider external validity. To quote Campbell and Stanley [1966, p. 5], "*External validity* asks the question of *generalizability:* To what populations, settings, treatment variables, and measurement variables can this effect be generalized?" (italics theirs). Within the context of most decision support system and expert system evaluations, external validity deals with the extent to which the results obtained in an experiment conducted in the test setting will generalize to the target (i.e., operational) setting.

Test settings represent simulations of the target setting; hence, they can vary in their degree of fidelity to it. The simulated environment, the simulated decision-making organization, and even the simulated user can range between being only superficially accurate to being accurate in great detail. The more accurate the simulation along all dimensions, the greater the external validity of the experiment.

Experimentation during software and hardware development is a natural part of prototyping. To date, this experimentation typically focuses on the system–user interface [e.g., see Gould and Lewis, 1985] via "human factors evaluations" [Riedel and Pitz, 1986, p. 990]. While essential to developing a well-liked, usable system, such experiments typically have low-fidelity user-system–organization and organization–environment interfaces. Many decision support systems and expert systems are, however, used in organizations for the purposes of improving organizational decision making and, in turn, organizational performance.

Consequently, increasing the fidelity of the organizational and environment interfaces is essential in generalizing the performance results obtained in the laboratory to a real-world setting.

To increase the fidelity of the user-system–organization and organization–environment interfaces, one needs to identify the organizational structures, processes, and communication patterns (both formal and informal) affecting task performance. This includes time pressures, interruptions, the reward structure, and even whether the decision maker or a subordinate will operate the system. If a task is really performed by a group, then the group should be represented in the test setting. For some tasks, such as distributed ones, it may be possible to simulate the effects of a group by the information presented to the decision maker. For other group decision-making tasks, it may be possible to train members of the evaluation or development team to play certain roles. However, for some tasks, accurate representation of the groups may require the presence of trained personnel performing their job. There may simply be no way around this requirement from an external validity perspective. Moreover, these issues will affect the physical size and structure of the test setting. In addition, audio-and videotaping capabilities should be used as a data collection mechanism if the interactions among group members are hypothesized to affect performance.

One should also try to make participants' interaction with the decision support system or expert system as representative as possible of that that would occur in the actual operational setting. This includes the training in using the system. Insufficient training will result in the experiment being an unreliable measure of the potential value of the system; therefore, err on the side of too much versus too little training. If possible, use objective measures to demonstrate that the user has been trained to the desired level of proficiency on the system before beginning the experimental session. Also, make sure that training includes working representative problems. Not only will users be better trained to participate in the experiment, they will be better able to evaluate the system's strengths and weaknesses subjectively.

From both an experimentation and prototyping perspective, the fidelity of both the organization and environment interfaces should be improved systematically, as the user interface is typically done now, to provide maximum experimenter control for assessing the characteristics of each that have the greatest impact on system performance. Such a perspective is, however, idealistic given the time and cost constraints on most development efforts. A more practical approach for later in development may be to create a gaming simulation that is representative of the user-system–organization and organization–environment interfaces. In particular, a two-phased experimentation approach can be implemented.

The first phase is a straightforward experiment testing whether or not the system significantly improved objective process and performance measures. A positive finding in as representative a "simulated" setting as possible, especially over variations in representative problem scenarios and personnel, would provide empirical results for testing the system in its targeted operational setting. A negative finding would lead to the second phase, which would be experimentation-oriented to learning (1) why performance was not significantly better with the system, if that could not be assessed during the phase 1 experiment; and (2) whether subsequent system modifications result in improved performance. The second phase might also include modifications to aspects of the organization that are hypothesized to affect system performance. More generally, the goal of the second phase is to better assess the factors that are affecting system performance and attempt to rectify them in as representative an setting as possible before transferring the system to its operational setting.

Although a high-fidelity test setting is desirable, it is difficult to implement, takes more time, and is expensive. Accordingly, a trade-off is established between fidelity and difficulty, time, costs, and so on. Depending on the objectives of the empirical evaluation, it may or may not be desirable to fully simulate the target setting prior to testing the system in it. The evaluator needs to discuss these issues, and the trade-offs they imply, with members of the sponsoring and development team.

6.1.6 Field Experiments

Once the decision support system or expert system has demonstrated superior performance in a representative test setting, it is ready for an experiment in the target setting. Although more difficult to implement, "field experiments" also need to control for all threats to validity. For instance, regarding internal validity, organizational units (e.g., divisions/sections in a large company or governmental agency) would be *randomly* assigned to the "with system" and "without system" conditions, and performance measured after it has stabilized. The unit of analysis in most field experiments is the performance of an organizational unit; therefore, a large enough sample of units would be required for performing statistical tests.

Regarding construct validity, attention must be directed toward tightly measuring the process and performance variables of interest and controlling other variables that might be confounded with them. If one has some ideas of what these variables (or rival hypotheses) may be, then steps should be taken to eliminate their potential impact, incorporate them systematically into the experimental design, or measure them so that one can perform a post hoc assessment. If possible, a "placebo" condition would be included too.

Regarding statistical conclusion validity, one wants to have as high a level of statistical power as possible. This statement implies serious consideration of the research design, the questions being addressed (including effect size), and the relative importance of Type I and Type II errors. The issue of external validity does not have to be addressed if, and only if, the field experiment includes all aspects of the population to which we want to generalize our results.

Realize that it will be difficult to implement the above requirements in many operational settings. Evaluators should not uncritically force-fit experiments. Although experiments using randomization may be ". . . better than other available alternatives for inferring cause . . ." [Cook and Campbell, 1979, p. 342], quasi-experiments and case studies are often more feasible in the target setting. And they are powerful empirical methods.

6.2 CASE STUDIES AND QUASI-EXPERIMENTS

The sample size and randomization requirements of true experiments are not possible in many organizations. Case studies and quasi-experiments should be used in such situations. To quote Campbell and Stanley [1966, p. 34]:

> There are many social settings in which the research person can introduce something like experimental design into his scheduling of data collection procedures (e.g., the *when* and *to whom* of measurement), even though he lacks the full control over the scheduling of experimental stimuli (the *when* and *to whom* of exposure and the ability to randomize exposures) which make a true experiment possible. Collectively, such situations can be regarded as quasi-experimental designs.

All four types of validity need to be considered for these designs, just as for experiments. The reduced control of not being able to perform field experiments makes empirical evaluations in the actual setting more difficult, but it does not eliminate our ability to perform them consistent with the tenets of the scientific method: "[T]he core of the scientific method is not experimentation per se, but rather the strategy connoted by the phrase [evaluating] 'plausible rival hypotheses' " [Campbell, 1984, p. 7].

There are different types of quasi-experimental designs. Campbell and Stanley [1966] identify 10 types, not counting variations of them. The three quasi-experimental designs considered below are (1) time-series designs, where the organizational unit is measured for a period of time before and after the treatment (e.g., system implementation); (2) multiple time-series designs using a control group; and (3) nonequivalent control-group designs that obtain pretest and posttest measures at only one time for a nonrandomized sample of treatment and control groups.

Quasi-experimental designs represent a substantial advance over the "pre-experimental designs" [Campbell and Stanley, 1966] found in many "field studies" [Sharda et al., 1988]. We will first present an overview of the three preexperimental designs and, then, discuss how case-study and quasi-experimental designs represent improvements over them.

6.2.1 Preexperimental Designs

Campbell and Stanley [1966, p. 6] called the first preexperimental design "the one-shot case study." Cook and Campbell [1979, p. 96] later renamed this "the one-group posttest-only study" so that it not be confused with appropriately conducted case studies. In this approach, one organizational unit is given the treatment (e.g., the expert system) and performance is subsequently measured. There is no pretesting and there is no control group; instead, a ". . . single instance is implicitly compared with other events casually observed and remembered. The inferences are based upon general expectations of what the [performance] data would have been had the [treatment] not occurred, etc." [p. 6].

The one-group posttest-only study violates all four types of validity. First, there is no control for (or even consideration of) internal validity threats due to how participants are selected or what may have also occurred during the treatment stage, either through historical events or other changes to the participants or their organizational context. Second, nothing is measured, so it is impossible to determine what extraneous factors may have been confounded with the treatment, or to assess their effects. Third, there is no explicit measurement of performance variables or comparison with another group; thus, it is impossible to assess statistical conclusion validity. And, fourth, it provides no justified basis for predicting the effect of the treatment on another group of participants.

The second preexperimental design is the one-group pretest–posttest design, where implementation of the decision support system or expert system represents the treatment. The problem with this design is that it does not control for other factors that represent plausible rival hypotheses for explaining the improved performance between the pretest and the posttest. Three types of plausible rival hypotheses immediately come to mind. First, there may have been "other events" that occurred between the two tests that can explain the results; that is, history. Second, if the selected group represented extreme performers (e.g., the very best or very worst), then one would expect pretest–posttest differences to be affected by statistical regression to the mean. And, third, the design does not rule out other effects that are confounded with the treatment, such as the "special attention" that goes with the implementation of a decision support system or expert system.

The third preexperimental design is the "posttest-only design with nonequivalent groups" [Cook and Campbell, 1979, p. 98]. Here, the subsequent performance of the group receiving the treatment is compared with that of a group without the treatment. Since there is no pretest or randomization with this design, there is no ". . . formal means of certifying that the groups would have been equivalent had it not been for the treatment [e.g., the system]" [Campbell and Stanley, 1966, p. 12]. Or, to be more blunt, "The plausibility of selection differences in research with nonequivalent groups usually renders the design uninterpretable" [Cook and Campbell, p. 98]. The last two preexperimental designs are somewhat insidious in the sense that on the surface they represent "pretest–posttest control-group" and "posttest-only control-group" designs, respectively, which are true experimental designs because subjects are randomly assigned to at least two conditions, the treatment and the control groups.

Explicit case-study and quasi-experimental designs will now be considered in relation to the three preexperimental designs considered above. In particular, case-study designs will be juxtaposed to the one-group posttest-only design; time-series designs will be juxtaposed to the one-group pretest–posttest design; and non-equivalent control-group designs will be juxtaposed to the posttest-only design with nonequivalent control groups. The reader should keep in mind that the sampling is only from a wide variety of quasi-experimental designs. Although they are considered together here, case-study and quasi-experimental designs represent different evaluation approaches.

6.2.2 Appropriate Case Studies

Yin [1984, p. 23] has defined a case study as "an empirical inquiry that investigates a contemporary phenomenon within its real-life context; when the boundaries between phenomenon and context are not clearly evident; and in which multiple sources of evidence are used." This definition nicely fits the evaluation of decision support systems and expert systems, or more broadly, any form of information technology (or intervention) in the target setting. As Lee [1989, p. 33] points out, "There is a strong case-study tradition in the academic field of management information systems. . . . [Our concern is] to clarify the methodological basis upon which to conduct case studies."

We first consider construct validity, which is the attempt to ensure that one is measuring the concept that one wants to measure. To quote Yin [1984, p. 37]:

> To meet the test of construct validity, an investigator must be sure to cover two steps: (1) select the specific types of changes that are to be studied (in relation to the original objectives of the study) and (2) demonstrate that the selected measures of these changes *do indeed reflect* the specific types of change that have been selected [italics ours].

The reason for the italics is that the lack of experimenter control in case-study research makes it much more difficult than in an experiment to minimize the potential confounding of the treatment of interest (e.g., the system) with other variables (e.g., special attention).

Further, lack of control makes it harder to be sure one is measuring what one wants to measure. For example, in a laboratory experiment it might be easy to measure decision quality because one has a ground-truth solution to the problem scenario. In contrast, it might be quite difficult to define decision quality in the target setting because it might be in the eye of the beholder. In such settings, one needs to have two or more experts who are not part of the organization rate decision quality and then use either a consensus position or an average rating to resolve any differences of opinion. Although it may be difficult to make experts blind to the solution generated with the system in a case study, it can be done by embedding the actual solution in a range of hypothetical solutions.

The principal approach to construct validity in case-study research is twofold. First, the constructs need to be reliably measured. Again, the essence of reliability is replication; if other researchers did the same study a second time, they should obtain the same results. Second, case-study research should use multiple sources of evidence to measure the independent variable constructs. More generally, there should be a high correlation among different pieces of evidence all supposedly measuring the same construct, and no correlation among evidence measuring different constructs.

This is the concept of convergent and discriminant validation introduced by Campbell and Fiske [1959]. Quite simply, the idea is that measures of the same thing should be highly related; measures of different things shouldn't be. For instance, if the implementation of an expert system was preceded by effective training, one would expect that to be reflected in a number of ways, such as (1) behavioral measures of proficiency in using the system prior to testing (or during implementation), and (2) subjective responses to interview questions. That is, different measures of "training proficiency" would all converge on the same result. Moreover, there should be no confounding with other independent variable constructs. For example, there should be no relation between measures of training proficiency and organizational size or management attention.

Causal inference has not yet been considered. Construct validity only addresses whether one is actually measuring the variables one wants to measure, not whether there are causal relations between these variables. To do the latter, we must consider statistical conclusion validity and internal validity. The former is typically not possible in case-study research because as Lee [1989, p. 35] indicates, ". . . the study of a single case commonly yields more variables than data points—a situation that renders inapplicable the statistical controls of statistical experiments." Furthermore, many case studies generate only qualitative, not quantitative data. Accordingly, there is no way to perform a statistical test of the reasonableness of one's causal inferences.

Although one may not be able to perform statistical tests to determine statistical conclusion validity, one can still address the internal validity of case-study research. At a more conceptual level, Lee [1989, p. 40] has pointed out that

> . . . it must first be emphasized that mathematics is a subset of formal logic, not vice versa. Logical deductions do not require mathematics. *An MIS case study that performs its deductions with verbal propositions (i.e., qualitative analysis) therefore only deprives itself of the convenience of the rules of algebra; it does not deprive itself of the rules of formal logic, to which it may therefore still turn when carrying out the task of making controlled deductions* [italics his].

Yin [1984, p. 105] has emphasized the use of three modes of data analysis for case-study research: pattern matching, explanation building, and time-series analysis. We consider the first two here and the latter as a quasi-experimental design later in this chapter.

In its strongest form, pattern matching

> . . . requires the development of rival theoretical propositions articulated in operational terms. The important characteristic of these rival explanations is that each involves a pattern of independent variables that is mutually exclusive: If one explanation is to be valid, the others cannot be. This means that the presence of certain independent variables (predicted by one explanation) precludes the presence of other independent variables (predicted by a rival explanation). The independent variables may involve several or many different types of characteristics or events, each assessed with different measures and instruments. [Yin, 1984, p. 105]

Moreover, consistent with the above discussion regarding the use of multiple pieces of evidence for construct validation purposes, causal inference is enhanced if one uses different types of measures to support one hypothesis versus its plausible rivals.

The management information system (MIS) case study by Markus [1983] on resistance to system implementation is an excellent example of the use of pattern matching. First, Markus proposed three alternative theories, all documented in the literature to explain system resistance. Each led to the prediction of a different, yet specific and observable pattern of events. Conceptually, these events pitted the proposed theories against each other. Then, she collected data about each of these events. The pattern of data supported one of the theories, that the resistance was due to a person–system interaction, and not the alternative people-determined or system-determined theories.

In contrast to pattern matching, explanation building relies on iteration, where an initial set of propositions is compared to the obtained data, and subsequently revised and tested. The final explanation is seldom stipulated at the start of the study. Rather, it develops as the data are examined from a different perspective, one emerging from the analysis itself. Such an approach can be dangerous if it builds a myopic chain of evidence supporting the "new" hypothesis. Falsification, not confirmation, must be the goal; consequently, rival plausible hypotheses must be pitted against one another.

The case studies by Bourgeois and Eisenhardt [1988] and Kaplan and Duchon [1988] are excellent examples of explanation building. A quote from the latter [p. 582] captures the emergent process of this mode of analysis:

> . . . [T]he apparent inconsistency of results between the initial quantitative analysis and the qualitative data required exploration. . . . Further analysis to resolve the discrepancy led to the use of new measures developed from the quantitative questionnaire data that captured job-related responses to the computer system and that supported conclusions drawn from the qualitative data.

It should be noted that both modes of data analysis require that plausible rival hypotheses be *known* so that they can be evaluated against the data. This is, as we pointed out before, a difficult task. Moreover, it is a weakness compared to true experiments where randomization can be used to control for the spurious effects of many (but not all) *unknown* hypotheses. Nevertheless, pattern matching and explanation building are powerful modes of deduction.

Case studies have been routinely criticized on external validity grounds, for, the argument goes, how can one generalize from a sample size of one? Yet, the same criticism can be made for attempting to generalize from a single experiment; it is just as precarious. Experiments and case studies have the same external validity requirements. The more conditions for which a decision support system or expert system enhances performance, the more confidence one has that it will enhance performance in subsequent settings.

6.2.3 Time-Series Designs

We now turn to time-series designs, the first of the two quasi-experimental designs considered in this chapter. As you will remember, time-series designs were juxtaposed to the one-group pretest–posttest design where, in our case, implementation of the decision support system or expert system represents the treatment. The problem with this preexperimental design is that it does not in any way control for the effect of other plausible hypotheses that could have improved performance between the pretest and the posttest.

The "simple interrupted time series design" [Cook and Campbell, 1979, p. 209] uses the group itself as a partial control for alternative hypotheses by measuring the performance of the group *repeatedly* both before and after the treatment intervention. For example, if repeated measurements had shown that a group's performance was increasing linearly by three points on every observation, then it would be inappropriate to conclude that a decision support system or expert system had a positive effect on performance because the posttest was three points above the pretest. Similarly, if performance is known to vary with known cycles or actions, such as the time of year or the change in administrations, it would be wrong to assume that the system had significantly affected group performance without first accounting for these known causes of performance regularities.

The construct validity of a simple interrupted time-series design again depends on the extent to which one is measuring what one wants to measure. Like case studies, one should use multiple pieces of evidence to measure the independent and dependent variables. Again, the focus should be on the convergent and discriminant validity of these measures; measures supposedly measuring the same construct should be correlated, while those measuring different constructs should not. In addition, as Cook and Campbell [1979, p. 231] state:

All archived data needs close scrutiny. Operational definitions need to be critically examined, and one should not assume that the construct label applied to a particular measure is necessarily a good fit. Inquiries have to be made about shifts in definition over the time the record is kept; where possible, the nature of the shift needs documenting.

Also, special attention must be given to the reliability of the measures. Unreliability adds error into the measurement process, thereby reducing one's ability to find differences between the pretest and posttest observations. And one should be alert to possible confoundings with the decision support system or expert system.

The issues discussed above regarding the statistical conclusion validity of experiments are just as applicable to quasi-experiments. For the simple interrupted time series, this means that one wants to be able to make a reasonable statement as to whether the posttest observations represent a different pattern than the pretest ones. As the above "three-point example" illustrates, one should not use traditional statistical tests to assess mean differences. And, as McCain and McCleary [1979, p. 234] caution, one should not use ordinary least squares (OLS) regression:

> OLS regression requires an assumption that residuals, or error terms associated with each time-series observation, be independent. When naturally occurring events or behavior . . . [is] . . . observed repeatedly over time, however, events closer to each other in time tend to be more correlated with each other than with events further removed in time. . . . [Consequently,] *the estimates of standard deviations (and hence, of significance tests) are biased* [italics theirs].

Numerous texts on time-series analysis and computer programs are available to help one perform it; therefore, we will not go over the different methods here. Indeed, as with our earlier discussion of statistical tests for experimental designs, we are hesitant to discuss time-series analysis methods in any detail because adequate discussion of the topic takes considerably more space than is available here. Instead, consistent with the detailed presentation by McCain and McCleary [1979], we will only enumerate the four basic steps in the analysis for a simple interrupted time-series design.

The first step is called identification. The goal is to identify systematic components in the data (e.g., seasonal or cyclic impacts on performance) that do not depend on the treatment (i.e., decision support system or expert system). The systematic component is responsible for the correlation (called autocorrelation) in the data independent of the treatment.

The second step is estimation; the statistical parameters of the systematic component identified in step 1 are estimated to form a statistical model using appropriate nonlinear equations. The third step is diagnosis. The autocorrelation and partial autocorrelation of the residual terms are examined to diagnosis the adequacy of the estimation model built in step 2. The goal is to conclude that the residuals are unbiased, essentially behaving as white noise. If they are, then one has an adequate model for predicting regularities in the data independent of the treatment. If they don't, that is, the statistical model still has biased residuals, one repeats the process of identification, estimation, and diagnosis until an acceptable model is found.

When a predictive model with unbiased residuals is attained, one can proceed to intervention hypothesis testing. In this step, one adds an intervention component to the model. The intervention component represents the hypothesized effect of the treatment to the model; it is represented by a "transfer function." For instance, if the hypothesized effect is that of an abrupt, constant change, it would be represented by a step function. Gradual, constant change can be represented by a linear function:

> If the intervention component increases the model's predictability, the parameters of the intervention component will be statistically significant. . . . Expressing the hypothesis testing component of time series in this way illustrates that the statistical analysis does not by itself test "cause." It only asks whether a statistically significant change in the series takes place at a specified point in the series. [McCain and McCleary, 1979, p. 262]

When all is said and done, the simple interrupted time series is a weak design because of a number of threats to its internal validity, not statistical conclusion validity. The most obvious and important threat to internal validity is that some simultaneous event other than the treatment caused a change in performance. Cook and Campbell [1979, p. 211] have referred to this as a "main effect of history." Another internal validity threat is "instrumentation." As they point out, administrative changes are sometimes accompanied by changes in record keeping. Since it is not uncommon for the implementation of decision support and expert system technology to cause administrative changes as well, "changes in record keeping" is a plausible rival hypothesis. And, third, "selection" could be an internal validity threat if system implementation is also accompanied by a shift in the composition of the test group. (Note: It is assumed here that the threat to internal validity posed by seasonal or cyclical impacts on performance has been controlled for through the time-series analysis.)

In an effort to control for these threats to internal validity, Campbell and Stanley [1966] advocated the addition of a control group to the time-series design. The control group should be comparable to the treatment group, but, as Cook and Campbell [1979] demonstrated, attempting to match the groups at the point of the intervention can be difficult and sometimes cause spurious effects. What is most important is that the control group be similar to the treatment group in the sense that it can be subjected to the same historical, instrumentation, and selection effects. Consequently, a significant shift in the posttest versus pretest observations of the treatment group, but not the control group, would disconfirm the above rival hypotheses compared to the hypothesized treatment effect.

The threats to external validity for the simple interrupted time-series design still exist when a control group is added to the design. Again, this is because external validity has to do with the generalizability of the results to settings and groups different than those in the test. The broader the range of settings for which the results hold, the better the time series' (or experiment's or case study's) external validity.

6.2.4 Nonequivalent Control-Group Design

This quasi-experimental design was juxtaposed to the posttest-only design with nonequivalent groups. The latter is a preexperimental design because the treatment and control groups are only compared on a posttest. The nonequivalent control-group design adds a pretest measure for both groups in an effort to control for factors, other than the treatment, that might affect performance.

The nonequivalent control-group design is similar to the time-series design with a control group, but it utilizes only one pretest and one posttest observation per group. As a result, it is not as effective at controlling for internal validity threats. Moreover, it requires the sampling of a number of treatment and control groups; thus, it uses different statistical tests.

We will not consider the construct and external validity issues inherent in nonequivalent control-group designs, for they are similar to those for experiments, case studies, and time-series designs considered above. Rather, we consider statistical conclusion validity and internal validity, in turn.

When considering the statistical conclusion validity of nonequivalent control-group designs, one should remember that randomization is not employed. Indeed, the word *nonequivalent* is used because one cannot be sure that the populations from which the groups are sampled are the same on all pretest measures. The statistical tests used for nonequivalent control-group designs try to control for selection differences.

Reichardt [1979] reviews three principal analysis methods for controlling for selection differences measured by the pretest. The first method is analysis of covariance (ANCOVA). It examines the difference in the groups' posttest scores as a function of the pretest scores. A significant effect when pretest differences are statistically controlled for suggests that improved performance is a function of the treatment and not the groups' starting point. The second method is analysis of variance (ANOVA) with blocking or matching. Block membership (e.g., high versus low pretest score) is entered as a factor into the ANOVA so that one can test the effect of the pretest level, the treatment versus control-group condition, and interactions between the two on the posttest scores. The third method is an ANOVA with gain scores. That is, one performs an ANOVA on the experimental conditions, but now using the change in performance between the pretest and posttest as the dependent variable.

Reichardt [1979] notes that all three methods have threats to statistical conclusion validity. For example, random measurement error in the pretest can bias the estimate of the regression slope (used to estimate the pretest–posttest dependency) in the ANCOVA and, thereby, bias the estimate of a treatment effect. In the case of an ANOVA with matching, it is often difficult to match participants in the treatment and control groups in actual settings because these groups tend to differ in their extreme values. For instance, the treatment group may have a smaller number of high pretest scores. In an effort to "match" the groups, one might drop representatives with extreme values and, potentially, instill a systematic bias in the estimated treatment effect. And the statistical power of the ANOVA using gain scores, as compared to the ANCOVA or ANOVA with matching, depends heavily on the particular circumstances of the research because the former tests whether the mean pretest–posttest change is markedly different between groups, not whether the mean posttest scores are significantly different:

> The obvious conclusion is that none of the above techniques or any others should be blindly or thoughtlessly used to analyze data from nonequivalent group designs. . . . It must be remembered that a statistical technique specifies a model for the data. . . . Thus the statistical model must be carefully tailored to fit the unique characteristics and demands of the data at hand. [Reichardt, 1979, p. 186]

Cook and Campbell [1979] point out that the nonequivalent control-group design controls for all but four threats to internal validity. All the threats are a function of the selection bias built into the design by the lack of randomization. Each of the four threats is considered, in turn.

The first threat is that the nonequivalent control-group design does not control for the effects of a "selection-maturation" bias because the respondents in one group might naturally change over time irrespective of the treatment. Experience is one way this might happen when evaluating decision support systems or expert systems. For example, let's assume that an expert system was fielded for use by operational personnel with less experience than a control group of experts. In this case, one would expect the nonexpert group to improve in performance over time as they gained experience (i.e., on-the-job training), irrespective of the system. Either another group of nonexperts without the expert system, or a baseline learning curve, would be required to determine whether improved performance was due to the expert system or experience gained on the job.

The second threat is "instrumentation":

> It is not clear with many scales that the intervals are equal, and change is often easier to detect at some points on a scale than others. Scaling problems are presumably more acute the greater the nonequivalence of the experimental groups and the farther apart they are on the scale, especially if any of the group means approaches one end of the scale where ceiling or floor effects are likely. [Cook and Campbell, 1979, p. 105]

Ceiling effects are plausible for the control group of experts considered in the above example. As a result, their performance may be constrained by the nature of the measurement scale; any improvement by the treatment group may, by comparison, seem significant only because the "expert group" cannot improve its performance owing to the artificial limitations in the measurement scale. Similarly, if the experts were the treatment group receiving a decision support system or expert system, their scores may not reflect actual performance enhancements owing to the artificial constraints of the measurement scale.

The third threat to the internal validity of nonequivalent control-group designs is "statistical regression to the mean." If groups are selected on the basis of extreme pretest scores, posttest scores can be expected to move (or regress) back to the mean. This might occur in the above example if the inexperienced personnel using the expert system were selected on the basis of low performance on the pretest. Their performance on the posttest would probably improve owing to regression to the mean, irrespective of gains due to the expert system or experience.

The last threat to the internal validity of the nonequivalent control-group design is "local history," which represents an interaction of selection and history. This occurs when either the treatment or control group is exposed to events other than the treatment that might affect their performance. In the aforementioned example, this might occur if the expert and nonexpert groups worked different shifts, worked in different places, were subjected to systematic differences in administrative procedures or supervision, and so forth.

With the discussion focusing on threats to internal validity, the reader should not lose sight of the fact that the nonequivalent control-group design is a reasonably good one. It is certainly far superior to all three preexperimental designs.

6.3 SUMMARY

This chapter has reviewed, at a general level, the use of experiments, appropriate case-study designs, and two types of quasi-experimental designs for performing empirical tests and evaluations of decision support and expert system technologies. The definitions for these empirical evaluation methods are presented in Table 6.4 for summary purposes.

Although some of the specifics for implementing different empirical evaluation methods have been considered, there has been no attempt to cover all the details that would be found in experimental design and statistical analysis texts. Rather, the goal was to address the different issues that should be considered when attempting to demonstrate the performance benefits of a decision support system or expert system empirically. For that reason, the four types of validity, summarized in Table 6.5, were used as criteria for considering each method. By focusing on the threats to the different types of validity, it is hoped that readers will be able to

TABLE 6.4 Definitions of Empirical Evaluation Methods

Experiment (factorial):
   One or more factors are systematically varied as the independent variable(s); participants (or organizational units) are randomly assigned to the independent variable conditions; and the dependent variables are quantitative (and preferably, for our purposes, objective) measures of system performance.

Case Studies:
   An empirical inquiry investigating a contemporary phenomenon within its real-life context; using multiple sources of evidence; and striving to explain how or why something happened by logically linking the data to the propositions supporting one rival hypothesis versus others.

Quasi-Experimental Designs:
   Settings that permit some control over the scheduling of data collection even though one does not have complete control over the scheduling of experimental stimuli as provided by randomization. (Simple interrupted time-series design with a control group, and the nonequivalent control-group design were considered.)

TABLE 6.5 Definitions of Reliability and Validity

Reliability:
   Demonstrating that the operations of a study can be repeated with the same results.

Validity:
   Demonstrating that the results of a study are well grounded. The different types of validity:
   Internal validity: Establishing a causal relationship, whereby certain conditions are shown to lead to other conditions, as distinguished from spurious relationships.
   Construct validity: Having good operational measures for the concepts being measured.
   Statistical conclusion validity: Ensuring that the study is sensitive enough to permit reasonable statements regarding the covariation between independent and dependent variables, and using appropriate statistical tests of this covariation.
   External validity: The extent to which the results of the study can be generalized to the populations, settings, treatment variables, and measurement variables of ultimate interest.

---

better formulate research designs (i.e., strategies) for assessing the performance impact of decision support and expert system technologies. For without well-formulated and conducted empirical evaluations, one has no way of knowing whether a decision support system or expert system helps, hinders, or has no effect on performance.

━━━━━━

Managing the Evaluation Process

While writing Chapter 7, I came across the following quote by Hetzel [1984, p. 177]:

> The central theme of this book is *measurement* [italics his]. Testing is viewed as a critical support function because it provides necessary measurement information. Without this information, management is unable to assess progress or properly evaluate problems. In short, testing provides the basis for all project control.

7.1 INTRODUCTION

Measurement and control have been the themes of this book as well. The goal has been to provide you with an understanding of the methods required to perform effective evaluations, and how to incorporate these methods into the design and development process. Remember, evaluation methods are tools that sponsoring and development team members can use to obtain feedback and, thereby, improve the judgments and decisions inherent in developing decision support systems and expert systems. For that reason, evaluation represents the control mechanism that keeps the development process on track. Formal evaluation methods are means for systematically finding out what needs to be done to increase the probability that the system will be used by the people for whom it is being built and, in turn, improve organizational decision making and performance.

This chapter focuses on managing the evaluation process. This is an important topic, for if this process is not effectively managed, project control will be reduced. Further, it is an expensive process. Hetzel [1984] points out that direct testing costs for major software systems approach 25% of the development costs. Direct testing costs include reviews, program testing, systems testing, acceptance testing, test planning and design, computer time, and test resources, both human and material. This is obviously not a trivial investment. To quote Gould and Lewis [1985, p. 306], ''. . . testing still has a price. It is nowhere near as high as commonly supposed, however, and it is a mistake to imagine that one can save by not paying this price. . . . If it is not done in the developer's lab, it will be done in the customer's office.''

The failure to test and evaluate a system systematically during its development often results in ''indirect costs,'' as Hetzel [p. 174] calls them. Indirect costs include ''rewriting programs, recovery, corrective action costs, rekeying data, failures, analysis meetings, debugging, retesting,'' and so on. ''Indirect testing costs, or the costs of poor testing, are usually at least twice the direct costs and may be spectacularly higher.'' Moreover, indirect testing costs are substantially more expensive later in development. Empirical research [e.g., see Rushby, 1988] indicates that errors due to faulty requirements are between 10 and 100 times more costly to fix if detected during implementation rather than during requirements analysis.

This chapter is divided into three sections. The first overviews basic issues in managing the test and evaluation process, including the evaluator's responsibilities, the key elements for effective testing, and using test documentation as a control tool. The second section reemphasizes the multifaceted approach to test and evaluation presented in this book. Test and evaluation methods are again presented within the context of the nine-step development blueprint. By selecting methods that are best suited for answering the questions inherent at each step of development, evaluators can effectively manage testing's control function. The third section discusses the use of multiattribute utility technology (MAUT) as a means both to more effectively managing the test and evaluation process, and obtaining an overall assessment of system utility.

7.2   BASIC MANAGEMENT ISSUES

It is neither surprising nor inappropriate that the concepts of ''quality assurance'' and ''test and evaluation'' are highly correlated in the minds of most development personnel. They are even cross-referenced in library card catalogs. For the evaluator's job is to help the development team assess the extent to which they are developing a high-quality product. To quote Pressman [1982, p. 289], ''Software testing is a critical element of *software quality assurance* and represents the ultimate review of specification, design, and coding'' [italics his].

The need for software testing and evaluation will not go away by hiring smarter programmers. It should not be an afterthought thrown in at the end of development. Instead, test and evaluation should be an inherent part of the development process. Evaluators should be integral members of the development team. For simplicity, their many activities are included here under two categories: planning and execution.

7.2.1 Planning

Powell [1986] has proposed a four-step approach to test and evaluation planning. The first step is the identification of test and evaluation goals. The goals represent the sponsor's and user's requirements for the system. They can generally be formulated prior to and during the requirements analysis. The goals can be represented at a general level by an evaluation hierarchy, and at an extremely detailed level by the software requirements documentation.

In all cases, it is essential that the goals be measurable so that one can determine how well the system performs on them. The suitability of subjective, technical, or empirical evaluation methods for measuring system performance on each goal depends on the goal. For some goals, subjective evaluation methods will be the most appropriate approach; for other goals, technical or empirical methods. (Note: According to MAUT, one also needs a utility function for each goal in order to translate the measurement on a goal into a utility or value score.) Furthermore, one must have some sense of the relative importance of the goals in order to guide testing and development cost effectively.

The second step in test and evaluation planning is to determine the set of factors that might influence test and evaluation activities. Powell [1986] grouped the factors into three categories. The first is the knowledge, experience, attitudes, and expectations of members of the development and sponsoring teams, including users. The second is the project's schedule and budget, especially for test and evaluation activities. The third is available computing resources. In total, consideration of these factors is critical to tailoring test and evaluation activities to the realities of the development effort. Moreover, it can foster a reconsideration of the importance the sponsoring team places on various goals. For example, it may be inappropriate to place a high weight on performance and usability goals if the users' organization(s) will not permit a sufficient number of users to participate in an empirical and subjective evaluation of the decision support or expert system prototype.

The selection of test and evaluation methods and tools represents the third step in Powell's four-step planning approach. This book, like all methods texts, has focused on this step. In particular, the book has reviewed various subjective evaluation methods for assessing system requirements as well as users' opinions regarding system strengths and weaknesses; technical evaluation methods for selecting analytical methods for a decision support system's model base, estimating development costs, assessing how well the software was built, and evaluating the adequacy of an expert system's knowledge base; and empirical evaluation methods for assessing a decision support system's or expert system's impact on performance. The outcome of the third planning step should be the selection of the methods that will best satisfy the goals identified in step 1 given the constraints of the environment identified in step 2.

The fourth task is the development of a detailed plan specifying the proposed test and evaluation activities. The plan should identify the test and evaluation goals, and the methods (and rationale for them) that will be applied at different phases of development to help the development team determine whether the system accomplishes these goals. In addition, the plan should identify the specific tasks required to implement these methods successfully, the roles and responsibilities of different members of the development and sponsoring team, the milestones that need to be achieved and the sign-off procedures once they are attained, and as much detail about the schedule and budget as possible. As Hetzel [1984] points out, this master test plan coordinates all testing activity and imposes a testing lifecycle on the software's development lifecycle.

7.2.2 Execution

Once the master test plan is approved, it must be executed. The evaluator's specific activities include organizing the testing activities, identifying test specifications and methods, developing test cases, using the various testing methods throughout the development cycle, and documenting the test results. Coordination with members of the sponsoring and development teams is vital in performing these activities within scheduling and budget constraints and, more generally, in a manner that aids, not burdens, the development effort.

Hetzel [1984] has identified five key elements for effective testing control during development: tracking errors and failures, analyzing error trends, tracking testing costs, tracking testing status, and test documentation. Each element is considered briefly, in turn.

As Hetzel [1984, p. 178] notes, tracking errors and failures ". . . involves reliably capturing information on problems detected during testing or system operation and then analyzing and summarizing that information so that trends and significant events are recognized." Most organizations have some form of "trouble report." More generally, the American National Standards Institute (ANSI) specifies the use of two documents: a test log and a test incident report. The test log contains a chronological record of all testing activities and their results. The test incident report focuses exclusively on failures. The top half is used to record the incident, the bottom half to report the correction and, thereby, ensure that it is made.

Consistent with tracking errors is analyzing their frequency and cause from a more global perspective. The goal here is to analyze trends, not specific cases. The evaluator's goal is to assess whether there are problems in the development process, for this is critical feedback to the project manager. Hetzel [1984] suggests the use of a variety of graphs to present trend data. These include total incident frequency by project month, incidents by cause (e.g., operator error, program logic omission, line failure, etc.), incidents by system (or subsystem or module), incidents by responsible organization and/or person, and how incidents are being found (e.g., system termination, user discovered, various testing techniques, etc.). Figure 7.1, from Hetzel, presents a number of representative tracking graphs.

It cannot be overemphasized how important trend data is to effective project management. Research performed by Hammond [1971] [see also Hammond et al., 1975; Hammond and Summers, 1971] on learning complex inference tasks clearly demonstrates the superiority of general, process feedback to specific, outcome feedback. Remember, the purpose of testing is to determine how development is proceeding so that corrective actions can be taken if needed. Trend data provides

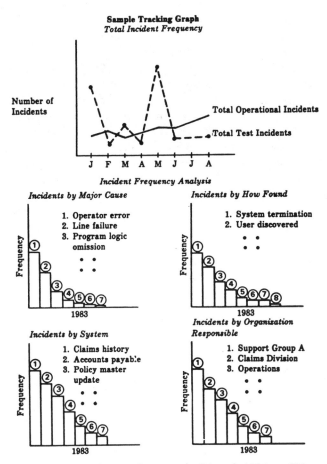

FIGURE 7.1 Illustrative incident tracking graphs [Hetzel, 1984, p. 182; reprinted with permission of QED Information Systems, Inc., 170 Linden St., Wellesley, MA 02180]

process feedback. It helps project management learn how things are going in general and reduces the probability that they will make erroneous inferences based on the outcome of a few isolated cases.

The discussion thus far has been on tracking errors and their analysis. The test and evaluation ideal is to prevent errors, not just detect them. Test and evaluation goals and measurement criteria play an essential role in error prevention, for they represent the characteristics of a good system in the eyes of the sponsor. The development team does not always stay focused on these criteria as it engages in the creative activity of giving operational shape to something that was previously only defined on paper at best and, at worst, in the ruminations of some sponsor or decision maker's mind. The evaluator's job is to help the development team stay focused. This can be particularly difficult during requirements analysis and modeling, steps 1 and 2 in the development blueprint, when it seems like one's job is to ''keep your eye on the bouncing ball.'' Nonetheless, staying focused on evaluation goals and criteria aids in providing vital project-control data that keeps the development process on track.

The third control activity identified by Hetzel [1984] is tracking testing costs. Evaluators must not only stay within their budget, but be cost-effective in their activities. It is, for example, poor management of the evaluation process to spend all one's time detecting and analyzing errors that have a minimal impact on the overall utility of the system to the sponsor.

The relative importance weights assigned by users to the different criteria in the evaluation hierarchy help one stay focused on the potential utility impact of various errors. Routinely obtaining cost estimates for fixing the various errors keeps everyone focused on potential budget implications. Hetzel [1984, p. 184] strongly urges the use of incident cost analysis graphs to display trends regarding error and failure costs. Such a graph is presented in Figure 7.2. In addition, we urge the use of ''utility'' graphs to show the system's scores on important criteria over time. As will be discussed later in this chapter, utility graphs translate the system's performance on a goal into a measurement indicating the value of that score to the sponsoring team and users. It is not cost-effective spending time and resources improving a system's score on a goal if that improvement has little utility (or value) to the user.

The fourth control element is tracking the status of testing. Substantial work is required to keep status information. This work involves keeping track of (1) the status of test design and development work, including test-case construction; (2) what has and has not been tested, including software modules and evaluation criteria, and with what methods; (3) system performance on objective and subjective criteria during testing and evaluation; and (4) what still remains to be done within the context of schedule and budget constraints. Obviously, given all that has to be done, good test plans are essential to manage the testing process effectively.

As with the first three control elements, graphs represent excellent means for tracking the status of the test and evaluation process. In particular, they tend to focus on three factors: the amount of testing planned, the amount of testing

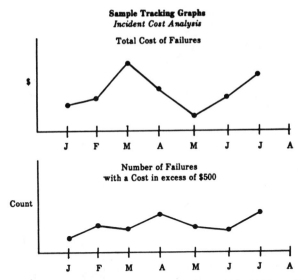

FIGURE 7.2 Illustrative incident cost analysis graph [Hetzel, 1984, p. 184; reprinted with permission of QED Information Systems, Inc., 170 Linden St., Wellesley, MA 02180]

completed, and the system's performance during testing. This point is illustrated in Figure 7.3. It shows the total number of tests planned, ready to be run, run, and run successfully over time.

Figure 7.4, from Ellis and Wygant [1989], offers another pictorial scheme for representing testing status. Panel A presents a picture of ideal test results. Most of the software requirements have been tested under various conditions, which is the reason for the high confidence rating (represented by the darker shading), and met (i.e., passed). Unfortunately, panel B represents the testing status for many

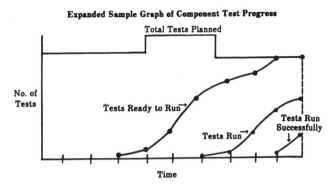

FIGURE 7.3 Illustrative graph for tracking testing status [Hetzel, 1984, p. 189; reprinted with permission of QED Information Systems, Inc., 170 Linden St., Wellesley, MA 02180]

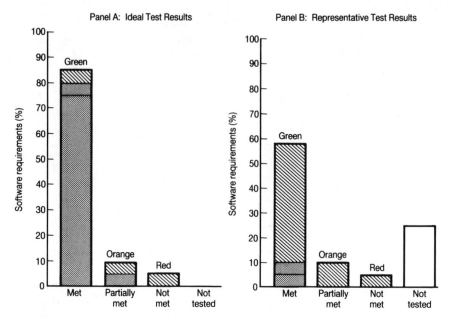

FIGURE 7.4   Illustrative graph for representing ideal and actual test performance

systems, even late in the development cycle. Here, we have a case where less than 60% of the requirements have been met, and most of these were under limited test conditions, so confidence is low. Furthermore, 25% of the requirements have not even been tested yet.

The fifth control element is test documentation. Test documentation helps to define and control the test lifecycle in a manner analogous to how program documentation helps define and control the development lifecycle. The American National Standards Institute (ANSI) has defined the following eight basic test documents: a test plan, a test design specification, a test-case specification, a test procedures specification, a test item transmittal, a test log, test incident reports, and a test summary report. The first five specify what is *to be* done; the last three specify what *has been* done.

Preparation of all eight test documents will not be cost-effective for all decision support and expert system development efforts. Moreover, tailoring will be required to impose a testing lifecycle on the development lifecycle effectively. As Hetzel [1984, p. 197] notes:

> The important step is to define which documents will be required and to establish a routine so that the documents ''control'' the work flow. At a minimum there must be a test plan, a record of test results, and a record of problems or discrepancies. These three documents establish the test work that is supposed to be done; record the testing that is actually done; and capture any problems discovered so that they are sure to be corrected. They also form the backbone of an effective system for controlling the testing work.

TABLE 7.1 **The Relative Applicability of Evaluation Methods to Different Steps in The Development Process**

Step in Development Process	Subjective Methods	Technical Methods	Empirical Methods
1. Requirements analysis	High	Medium	Medium
2. Modeling	Medium	High	Medium
3. Methods selection	Low	High	Low
4. Software selection/design/development	Medium	High	High
5. Hardware selection/configuration	Medium	High	Medium
6. System packaging	Low	High	Medium
7. System transfer	Low	High	Low
8. System evaluation	High	High	High
9. Feedback	High	High	High

7.3 THE MULTIFACETED EVALUATION APPROACH

It has been emphasized throughout this book that the goal of the test and evaluation process is to provide project-control data. From this perspective, the process itself represents a management tool. It is a mechanism that project management can use to find out how the development process is going and, if possible, identify corrective actions. To do so effectively requires that different evaluation methods be used to varying degrees to measure progress at different stages of the development process. As has been stressed repeatedly, evaluation is a multifaceted activity; experience shows that no single method is adequate either within or between steps in the development process [e.g., Beizer, 1984; Hamlet, 1988; Hetzel, 1984].

For summary purposes, refer to Table 7.1, which addresses the applicability of subjective, technical, and empirical evaluation methods to different steps in the decision support and expert system development blueprint. Table 7.2 lists the different methods, within each of the three categories, considered in this text. As can be seen, all three method categories are applicable during steps 8 and 9 (evaluation

TABLE 7.2 **Evaluation Methods**

Subjective Methods	*Technical Methods*
Multiattribute utility technology (MAUT)	Taxonomies for matching analytical
Cost-benefit analysis	methods to requirements
Dollar-equivalent technique	Software cost estimation methods
Decision analysis	Software testing methods
MAUT-based cost-benefit with optimization	Methods for evaluating a knowledge base
procedures	*Empirical Methods*
Feature-based criteria lists	Experiments
Value of information analysis	Quasi-experiments
	Case studies

and feedback, respectively) of the development process. In addition, specific methods within each category are more or less applicable to earlier steps in the development cycle.

Again, subjective evaluation methods are most applicable early in development (steps 1 and 2) because they represent an explicit means for defining the judgments of members of the sponsoring team and potential users of the system. They are, however, also applicable anywhere in the development process where members of the sponsoring and/or development team need to evaluate one option against another. In particular, as Andriole [1989] and Hopple [1988] point out, subjective evaluation methods can be used to systematically address the valuative and technical judgments inherent in evaluating the utility of available off-the-shelf software and various hardware configurations. And, as shown in the next section of this chapter, subjective evaluation methods can be used to measure and, thereby, manage the development process as seen through the eyes of sponsors and users.

Technical evaluation methods are most applicable in software design (step 4), which includes software development. They also have considerable applicability prior to programming code, in terms of (1) verifying both requirements analysis documentation and functional models of the software, (2) developing estimates of software development costs, and (3) selecting analytical methods for the model-base management system. Obviously, software test and verification methods are essential once the development process is well under way during hardware configuration, system packaging, and system transfer. And they are critical for assessing the knowledge base of expert systems.

Empirical evaluation methods are most applicable during software design (step 4) and hardware configuration (step 5). From an iterative, prototyping perspective, it is anticipated that experiments will be conducted throughout development to objectively measure the performance of the decision support system or expert system and test hypotheses for improving it. Before software development, experimental designs can be used to evaluate alternative storyboards for the system. Experimental, quasi-experimental, and case-study designs can be used after the system has been transferred to the test organization.

7.4 MAUT AS A MANAGEMENT TOOL

In closing this book, multiattribute utility technology (MAUT) will be considered as a management tool to help evaluators, developers, and sponsors track the utility of a decision support system or expert system *throughout* its design and development process. As was discussed in Chapter 4, there are five steps in using MAUT. These steps, as applied to the evaluation of decision support and expert system technology, are (1) identifying test and evaluation criteria, (2) measuring the system's performance on these criteria, (3) developing utility functions to convert performance scores on the different criteria into a common value scale,

(4) obtaining the relative importance of the different criteria, and (5) combining the utility scores on the criteria with their relative weights to assess the overall utility of the decision support system or expert system. Each of the five steps is considered, in turn.

7.4.1 Developing Evaluation Criteria

The first step is the identification of test and evaluation criteria. A value hierarchy is typically created as a means of facilitating the process of defining evaluation criteria. The top-level criterion in an evaluation hierarchy is the overall utility (or value) of the decision support system or expert system. The goal, which may or may not be achieved, is to build a system that, overall, has high utility to its users. Overall utility is disaggregated into major categories of criteria, which are further disaggregated until one is reasonably confident that one can define and obtain precise, reliable, and valid measures (or scores) of the decision support system or expert system on each bottom-level criterion in the hierarchy. These bottom-level criteria are often referred to as "attributes" in MAUT; they represent the "measures of effectiveness" against which the system gets scored.

The different methods overviewed herein address different types of test and evaluation criteria. Table 7.3 presents a framework for evaluating expert systems that not only summarizes these criteria, but attempts to integrate them by using a MAUT hierarchy. As will be discussed, this hierarchy can be used in conjunction with MAUT scoring and weighting procedures to evaluate the overall utility of an expert system to users and sponsors. Since the goal of development is the creation of high-utility technology, the goal of test and evaluation is to determine (and facilitate) the extent to which this goal has been achieved. (Note: This hierarchy also can be used to evaluate decision support systems be dropping the subbranch entitled "knowledge base" from the hierarchy.)

The hierarchy in the table has two branches. The first contains criteria for technical evaluations. These include three subbranches. The first one is for design and coding standards. Standards typically represent accepted practices (at a given time) and are designed to foster high-quality products. The IEEE Computer Society and many software development sponsors and contractors have been active developing software development standards. The ones shown in Table 7.3 are for military software, and are adaptations of the relevant standards from MIL-STD-1679 [1978], DOD-STD-1679A [1983], DOD-STD-2167 [1985], and JCMPOINST 8020.1 [1984]. Such standards obviously represent evaluation criteria, for the organization that developed the standards will consider software that does not meet its standards to be deficient, at least to some extent.

The second subbranch presents criteria for assessing the adequacy of the knowledge base or, as Rushby [1988, p. 75] has called them, the "competency requirements" of an expert system. Table 7.3 lists different criteria for assessing logical consistency and completeness, functional completeness, and predictive accuracy

TABLE 7.3 A MAUT Framework for Integrating Subjective, Technical, and Empirical Criteria When Evaluating Expert Systems[a]

Overall Test Evaluation

- Technical
- Empirical and Subjective

Technical			Empirical and Subjective	
Design and Coding Standards	Knowledge Base	Service	Performance	Usability
HoI	Logical consistency	Computer system	Ground truth	Observable
Control constructs	Redundant rules	Design	Speed	Extent of use
Size	Subsumed rules	Portability	Accuracy ($d*$)	Manner of use
Single function	Conflicting rules	Computer usage	Bias ($B*$)	Features used
Unique name	Circular rules	Setup time	Judgment	Opinions
Consistency	Unnecessary *if* conditions	Run time	Speed	Confidence
Naming convention	Logical completeness	Space requirements	Response time	Ease of use
Symbolic parameters	Unreferenced attribute values	Reliability (hardware)	Time to accomplish task	Acceptability of
Prologue	Illegal attribute values	Capacity	Quality	Person–machine interaction
Comments	Unreachable conclusions	Effect of feature use/jumping	Quality of answers	Process
Paragraphing	Functional completeness	Degradation (graceful)	Quality of reasons	Results
Single statement	All desired inputs	Handling input errors		Representation scheme
Source statement structure	Application/conclusions	System integration		Scope of application
Single entry/exit	Completely covered	Formats		Explanations
	Identified knowledge limitations	Date requirements		Adequacy of presentation/trace
Compound expression	Accuracy and adequacy	Documentation		Transparency of expert system
Complicated negative expression	Accuracy of facts	Skill requirements (includes match with users' technical background)		Organizational impact
Mixed mode questions	Accuracy of rules			Impact on work style/work load, skills, training
Nesting of control	Knowledge representation			Impact on organizational procedures, structure
Error and diagnostic messages	Accuracy of source			Input–output
Branching	Modifiability of knowledge base			
Conditional statements	Control over			
Numerical conventions	Expandability			
Significant digits				
Symbolic construction and variations				
Included/copied segments				
Self-modification of function				
Function interface				

[a]From Adelman and Ulvila [1991].
[b]HOL stands for High-Order Language.

(and adequacy). Chapter 5 addressed technical evaluation methods for measuring these criteria. In particular, we discussed the use of static testing methods for assessing the logical consistency and completeness of the knowledge base, and the use of domain experts in conjunction with empirical evaluation concepts and methods for determining the functional completeness and predictive accuracy of the knowledge base.

The third subbranch in the ''technical'' branch of the hierarchy addresses conventional software requirements, referred to as ''service requirements'' by Rushby [1988, p. 75] within the context of decision support systems and expert systems. Conventional software test and verification criteria are important for decision support systems and expert systems too, especially if the system has to be embedded in or interfaced with more conventional software modules. Service requirements include information about computer system design and portability (i.e., transferability to other hardware and software environments), computer usage (e.g., setup time, run time, space requirements, etc.), system integration, operator skill requirements, and documentation.

The second (and only other) major branch in Table 7.3 contains criteria appropriate for empirical and subjective evaluations. These are grouped according to performance and usability criteria. The performance subbranch is decomposed into criteria based on ground truth (or experts' ratings of decision quality), and the judgments of users. Both ''ground truth'' and ''judgment'' categories focus on the quality and speed aspects of performance. However, as Cats-Baril and Huber [1987] have shown, users' judgments of system performance do not always agree with more objective data. Consequently, although it is substantially more work, we urge using ground-truth data to assess performance. Moreover, we recommend here (as we have throughout the discussion of empirical evaluation methods) that experiments with aided and unaided conditions be relied on prior to transferring the system to its target setting in order to rigorously assess performance. Field experiments, quasi-experiments, and case studies should be relied on after transferring the decision support system or expert system to its operational setting.

The usability subbranch is decomposed into criteria based on evaluators' observations of participants working with the system and participants' judgments of it. In conjunction with observation methods, users' keystrokes can be recorded in an effort to better understand the extent to which the participants actually use the system during the problem-solving task, the manner in which they use it within the context of the more familiar procedures typically found in the operational setting, and the specific features of the system they used most frequently. In addition, questionnaires can be used to obtain users' opinions regarding their confidence in the system's recommendations, its ease of use, the acceptability of the person–machine interaction process, its scope of application, the adequacy of the system's explanations for its recommendations, the system's organizational impact, and specific input–output considerations.

7.4.2 Scoring the System

The second step is to test or "score" the system on each of the bottom-level attributes in the value hierarchy. If it has not already been accomplished in step 1, step 2 requires the development of an explicit measurement scale for each attribute. Depending on the attribute, the measurement scale may be in objective units (e.g., "minutes" for "ground truth: speed" in Table 7.3) or subjective units (e.g., a questionnaire rating).

How the measurement scale gets defined will, in turn, affect the type of method selected for evaluating the system on an attribute. For instance, time can be measured in "minutes" or in terms of subjective judgments. In the former case, one would perform an empirical evaluation; in the latter, a subjective evaluation. Similarly, "ease of use" can be measured subjectively by a questionnaire or objectively by the average number of actions required by users to operate the system's different capabilities. The latter measurement could be obtained by a computer program embedded in the system that counted the users' keyboard responses during an empirical evaluation.

From a management perspective, each criterion and the attributes comprising them represent a reference point that can be used to assess the system's progress throughout development. For example, one would like to see a fewer number of redundant rules, a higher percentage of accurate knowledge-base predictions, better user performance, more favorable opinions about the interface, and so forth, as the decision support system or expert system matures. Graphs can be developed to track trends on attributes over time and, thereby, facilitate management of the test and evaluation process. The goal is to identify poor performance on important attributes as early in development as possible, and fix it.

7.4.3 Developing Utility Functions

Although the natural measurement scale for an attribute depends on the nature of the attribute, a common scale is required to compare scores on one attribute with scores on another. Therefore, the third step in MAUT is to develop a utility function for each bottom-level attribute in the hierarchy. Utility (or value) functions translate the performance score on an attribute into a utility score on that attribute. By doing so, it tells all involved parties the value of the score to users and, more generally, members of the sponsoring team.

As was discussed in Chapter 4, utility functions tend to be linear increasing or decreasing in form. However, they can be U-shaped or inverted U-shaped functions to various degrees, or even a step function such that the utility score on an attribute remains zero until a certain level of performance is achieved on that attribute. As this last type of utility function implies, it is not enough for evaluators to track the performance score on each attribute; they must also track its utility (or value) score to determine whether the system is performing well in the eyes of sponsors and potential users.

Two points must be kept in mind when developing utility functions. First, the measurement scale one uses can affect the utility scores one obtains during development. Consider, for example, the attribute "redundant rules" listed under the "knowledge base: logical consistency" criterion in Table 7.3. Let's assume for illustrative purposes that we defined the measurement scale for this attribute as the number of redundant rules found in the knowledge base. Further assume that we do not have an automated static tester that can do an exhaustive analysis of the knowledge base; therefore, we are sampling from portions of the knowledge base. And, finally, assume that all redundant rules are corrected once they are found.

We know that zero (0) redundant rules is the best that an expert system can do on this scale; thus, it would get the best utility score (e.g., 100) for that attribute. However, until we first attempt to assess the number of redundant rules in the knowledge base, we have no idea of an appropriate endpoint for the measurement scale and, therefore, the worst utility score (e.g., 0) for the attribute. Moreover, that endpoint may change over time. For instance, one might find only two redundant rules when one measures this attribute for the first time early in the development process. However, later in development when the knowledge base has become quite large (e.g., 10 times the size when we first measured it), there may be 10 redundant rules. What do we do?

One potential solution is to select an endpoint a priori (e.g., 20 redundant rules) when one begins testing. However, no empirical data exists regarding the number of redundant rules to expect in expert systems; so, we really have no way to select a reasonable endpoint a priori. Furthermore, in our example, this approach would result in a higher utility score early in development (2 versus 10 redundant rules on the 0 to 20 scale) even though the knowledge base was 10 times larger later in development.

A better solution would be to define the measurement scales as the percentage of redundant rules found in the knowledge base, where a lower percentage results in a higher utility score. Assuming for illustrative purposes that (1) there were 10 rules when the knowledge base was first tested and 100 rules later in development, and (2) the use of linear utility functions, one would have obtained utility scores of 80 (i.e., $100 - 2/10$) and 90 (i.e., $100 - 10/100$) for the redundant rule attribute early and later in development, respectively. More generally, care must be given to defining the attributes' measurement scales because they can affect their utility scores.

The second point to keep in mind is that linear functions are often good approximations of nonlinear functions. As previously discussed, utility functions may be strongly nonlinear in shape. Figure 4.2 presented a good example, for 50% of the utility was, in that case, lost at the 12% point on the measurement scale (i.e., if the expert system was set up after 5 minutes); 75% of the utility was lost at the 25% point (i.e., after 25 minutes). As this case illustrates, representatives of the user and/or sponsoring community may be able to and desire to generate nonlinear utility functions. But they may find the development of nonlinear utility functions with which they are comfortable to be quite difficult for other attributes. In such cases, one may want to assume linear utility functions. To quote Edwards et al. [1975, p. 156], ". . . linear approximations to monotonic nonlinear functions are likely to be unimportant relative to test–retest unreliability, interrespondent differences, and the like." The use of linear utility functions by representatives of the user community certainly represents a good place to begin.

7.4.4 Obtaining Relative Importance Weights

The fourth step in applying MAUT is to obtain relative importance weights on the criteria and attributes in the hierarchy. These weights are used to determine the relative value of a utility score on one attribute versus the utility score on another. In this way, utility scores on one attribute are made comparable to utility scores on other attributes. In a sense, it is MAUT's approach for making "apples and oranges" comparable.

For instance, considering Table 7.3, what is the relative importance of the five attributes measuring the "logical consistency of the knowledge base"? The answer to this question indicates the relative value of the best utility score on each of these five attributes. For example, let's assume that "conflicting rules," "circular rules," and "unnecessary *if* conditions" each get a relative weight of 0.30, and that "redundant rules" and "subsumed rules" each get a weight of 0.05, so that the relative weights on the five attributes sum to 1.0. These relative weights mean that a utility score of 100 on "conflicting rules" is worth six times as much as a utility score of 100 on "redundant rules." In contrast, a 100 score on "conflicting rules" is worth the same amount as a 100 on "circular rules" because these two attributes have the same relative weight. By assigning relative importance weights to the attributes measuring a criterion, the value of utility scores on one attribute can be compared in relation to others.

It is, of course, possible that the most important attribute measuring a criterion is not critical overall because that criterion is not very significant relative to the other criteria. Continuing the example, the "logical consistency of the knowledge base" may be more, less, or just as important as the other criteria measuring the utility of the knowledge base. Let's assume for illustrative purposes that "logical completeness," "functional completeness," and "accuracy and adequacy" are all given relative, proportional weights of 0.3 and that "logical consistency" is given a relative weight of 0.1, so that the four weights sum to 1.0. One can now compute the relative importance of each of the attributes measuring "logical consistency" with respect to the knowledge base subcategory by multiplying the proportion weights at the criteria and attribute levels.

Continuing our example, "conflicting rules" has a cumulative proportional weight of 0.03; 0.1 for the criterion weight times 0.3 for the attribute weight. This means that a utility score of 100 on "conflicting rules" turns into a score of 3 points (on a 100-point scale) on the "knowledge base" subcategory. Or, to put it differently, a utility score of 100 on conflicting rules is worth 3% of the best possible score (i.e., a 100) on the "knowledge base" subcategory. A utility score of 100 on "redundant rules" is worth one-half of one percent (i.e., 0.1×0.05) on the "knowledge base" subcategory.

Similarly, the broad subcategory entitled "knowledge base" may be more, less, or just as important as the two other "technical evaluation" subcategories: (1) "design and coding standards," and (2) "service requirements." Likewise, the "technical evaluation" category may be more, less, or just as important as the "empirical and subjective evaluation" category. Consequently, one must also obtain the relative, proportional weights on all criteria moving up the hierarchy.

By multiplying the relative weights from the top to the bottom of the hierarchy, one can obtain overall (i.e., cumulative) relative weights on the bottom-level attributes. These weights will sum to 1.0; hence, the cumulative relative weight on a bottom-level attribute indicates its total, relative worth when assessing the overall utility of the decision support system or expert system. For instance, a cumulative relative weight of 0.01 on a bottom-level attribute means that a score of 100 on that attribute will result in 1 point on the overall utility score for the system. Similarly, a score of 50 on that attribute will result in a score of 0.05 on overall utility, and so on.

The cumulative weights for the bottom-level attributes must be examined to make sure that they have not been inadvertently skewed by the weights at higher levels of the hierarchy. Skewing can occur because it is difficult to know the cumulative impact of assigning relative importance weights at each level of a large hierarchy. By examining the cumulative weights, one can assess these implications and, in turn, make any changes in the relative weights at higher levels of the hierarchy that will most accurately represent users' and sponsoring team members' trade-offs for the measures used to evaluate the system.

7.5.5 Obtaining an Overall Utility Score

The fifth step in applying MAUT is to obtain overall utility scores at each level of the hierarchy. A performance score on an attribute is converted into an overall utility score on that attribute by first translating the performance score into a utility score on that attribute and, then, multiplying the utility score by the cumulative, proportional importance weight for that attribute. An overall utility score for a criterion (e.g., "logical consistency") is obtained by adding the overall utility scores for the attributes comprising it (e.g., "redundant rules," "subsumed rules," "conflicting rules," "circular rules," and "unnecessary *if* conditions"). One continues the addition all the way up the hierarchy to obtain an overall utility score for the decision support system or expert system.

Equation 1 can be used to calculate the overall utility score for a system based on its scores on the bottom-level attributes:

$$U(a) = w_1 u(x_1) + \cdots w_n u(x_n) \tag{1}$$

where

U(a) is the overall utility for system a;

there are n bottom-level attributes;

each w indicates the cumulative proportional weight on each attribute; and

each u(x) is the utility scale value for the system's score on that bottom-level attribute.

Four points must be made in concluding this subsection. First, the use of relative weights assumes an additive decision rule for combining utility scores on different attributes. This is a compensatory decision rule because high utility values on certain attributes can compensate for low utility values on other attributes and still result in a good score overall.

Such a decision rule may or may not reflect the value position of the sponsoring team. For instance, as Riedel and Pitz [1986] point out, it might be more appropriate to use a noncompensatory rule to ensure that a decision support system or expert system gets a low score on the global measure of effectiveness if it fails to achieve the necessary performance level on critical bottom-level attributes. This perspective can be handled arithmetically by (1) a zero/one utility score to reflect whether or not the system passed the threshold on the critical attributes, and (2) the use of a multiplicative combination rule to obtain the overall utility score. The interested reader is referred to Hogarth [1987] and Keeney and Raiffa [1976], who review different types of decision rules. We have emphasized an additive decision rule because of its simplicity and robustness in many decision situations.

Second, sensitivity analysis can be used to assess the extent to which the overall utility score depends on the system's performance scores for certain attributes, the utility functions for certain attributes, or the relative importance weights at different levels of the hierarchy. Sensitivity analysis is often referred to as "what if" analysis, for the focus is on determining if certain changes will result in different results. As such, it can provide important management guidance to the development team. Continuing our example, a sensitivity analysis might show that even if the "logical consistency" criterion was just as important as the other "knowledge base" criteria, improved performance on the five attributes defining "logical consistency" would have a minimal impact on an expert system's overall utility score. One reason for this might be that the expert system is performing substantially worst on other more important criteria (i.e., "usability"); consequently, it would be more valuable to direct work there.

Third, the type of measurement scale can affect the relative importance placed on bottom-level attributes and upper-level criteria in the hierarchy. For example, one might place a high relative weight on "performance" in Table 7.3 if one thinks one will have "ground truth" measures of performance attributes.

However, one might give a much lower relative weight to this criterion if one will only have "judgment" measures of the performance attributes. The problem gets more complicated because the appropriate measurement scale for an attribute may vary depending on the stage in the development process. For instance, only "judgment," not "ground truth" measures of "performance" are usually possible early in the development process.

If the relative weights are a function of the measurement scale, which in turn may be a function of the system's stage of development, then the model for evaluating the utility of the system's performance will not be stable throughout development. Although there is nothing to preclude the use of different value models at different points in the development process, it makes it more difficult to use the value model as a management tool. What one would like is a value model that stays stable such that changes to the overall utility measures for the decision support system or expert system are only due to its hopefully better scores on the performance scales for the bottom-level attributes. Table 7.3 attempts to deal with this problem by having subjective and objective measures of selected attributes in the hierarchy from the beginning of development. The overall relative importance weights placed on these attributes indicates their importance from the user's perspective after the completion of the system or prototype.

Fourth, representative users should be members of the development team from the outset of development in an effort to build a stable value model. More generally, the application of MAUT illustrates the different responsibilities of technical personnel and users on the development team. In particular, measurement of the decision support system or expert system on evaluation criteria other than usability, which requires users' input, are the province and responsibility of technical members of the evaluation team. Similarly, the technical judgments necessary to improve the system's performance on these criteria are the province and responsibility of team members with the appropriate technical background and training. In contrast, the selection of the evaluation criteria and attributes, and the specification of utility functions and relative importance weights, are the province and responsibilities of future users, or their representatives from the sponsoring team, for these tasks represent the valuative component inherent in evaluating (and developing) decision support and expert system technology.

Measurement and valuation tasks should not be confused during evaluation. The former indicates "what is"; the latter, "what ought to be." Technical personnel should not overstep the bounds of their technical competency and make value judgments regarding what the system ought to look like. Likewise, other than in the use of subjective evaluation methods, users should not overstep their bounds and play the role of pseudoexperts. To do otherwise confuses the roles and responsibilities of members of the development team and reduces the extent to which test and evaluation methods can provide effective feedback for guiding development.

7.5 SUMMARY

The first of the chapter's four sections reviewed introductory points regarding the importance of managing the test and evaluation process. The second section overviewed basic issues in testing management, including the testing specialist's responsibilities, the key elements for effective testing, the use of test documentation as a control tool, Powell's [1986] four-step approach to test and evaluation planning, and Hetzel's [1984] five key elements for testing control. The third section reemphasized the multifaceted approach to test and evaluation presented in this book. The fourth section presented an overview of the use of MAUT as a tool for managing the test and evaluation process.

The goal of this text has been to provide you with an understanding of the methods required to perform effective evaluations of decision support and expert systems and how to incorporate these methods into the development process. A broad survey of different evaluation methods has been provided because different methods are required for addressing the many different types of judgments and decisions inherent in the development process. The objective to which their use is directed is twofold: to increase the probability (1) that the decision support system or expert system will be used efficiently by the decision maker(s) for whom the system is being built, and (2) that the system is capable of improving organizational decision making and performance. This is the final objective of any decision support system or expert system development effort that is not purely for research purposes—it has also been the objective of this book.

References

Ackoff, R. L. (1967) "Management Misinformation Systems." *Management Science*, 14: 147–156.

Adelman, L. (1982) "Involving Users in the Design of Decision-Analytic Aids: The Principal Factor in Successful Implementation." *Journal of the Operational Research Society*, 33: 333–342.

Adelman, L. (1984) "Real-Time Computer Support for Decision Analysis in a Group Setting: Another Class of Decision Support Systems." *Interfaces*, 14: 75–83.

Adelman, L. (1987) "Supporting Option Generation." *Large Scale Systems*, 13: 83–91.

Adelman, L. (1989) "Measurement Issues in Knowledge Engineering." *IEEE Transactions on Systems, Man and Cybernetics*, SMC-19: 483–488.

Adelman, L., and M. L. Donnell (1986) "Evaluating Decision Support Systems: A General Framework and Case Study," in S. J. Andriole (ed.), *Microcomputer Decision Support Systems: Design, Implementation, and Evaluation*. Wellesley, MA: QED Information Sciences.

Adelman, L., and K. Gates (1983) *Evaluation of the Duplex Army Radio/Radar Targeting Aid (DART)* (Report 83-84). New Hartford, NY: PAR Technology Corporation.

Adelman, L., and J. W. Ulvila (1991) "Evaluating Expert System Technology," in S. J. Andriole and S. M. Halpin (eds.), *Information Technology For Command and Control*. New York: IEEE Press.

Adelman, L., M. L. Donnell, R. H. Phelps, and J. F. Patterson (1982) "An Iterative Bayesian Decision Aid: Toward Improving the User-Aid and User-Organization Interfaces." *IEEE Transactions on Systems, Man and Cybernetics*, SMC-12: 733–742.

Adelman, L., P. J. Sticha, and M. L. Donnell (1984) "The Role of Task Properties in Determining the Relative Effectiveness of Multiattribute Weighting Techniques." *Organizational Behavior and Human Performance*, 33: 243–262.

Adelman, L., F. W. Rook, and P. E. Lehner (1985) "User and R&D Specialist Evaluation of Decision Support Systems: Development of a Questionnaire and Empirical Results." *IEEE Transactions on Systems, Man and Cybernetics*, SMC-15: 334–342.

Adelman, L., P. J. Sticha, and M. L. Donnell (1986a) "An Experimental Investigation of the Relative Effectiveness of Two Techniques for Structuring Multiattributed Hierarchies." *Organizational Behavior and Human Decision Processes*, 37: 188–196.

Adelman, L., D. A. Zirk, P. E. Lehner, R. J. Moffett, and R. Hall (1986b) "Distributed Tactical Decision Making: Conceptual Framework and Empirical Results." *IEEE Transactions on Systems, Man and Cybernetics*, SMC-16: 794–805.

Adelman, L., J. W. Ulvila, and P. E. Lehner (1990) *Testing and Evaluating C3I Systems That Employ AI* (Vol. 1). Reston, VA: Decision Science Consortium, Inc.

Albrecht, A. J. (1979) "Measuring Application Development Productivity." *Proceedings of the IBM Application Development Symposium*, Monterey, CA.

Albrecht, A. J., and J. E. Gaffney (1983) "Software Function, Source Lines of Code, and Development Effort Prediction." *IEEE Transactions on Software Engineering*, SE-9: 639–648.

Andreu, R., and Corominas, A. (1989) "SUCCES92: A DSS for Scheduling the Olympic Games." *Interfaces*, 19: 1–12.

Andriole, S. J. (1982) "The Design of Micro-Computer Based Personal Decision Aiding Systems." *IEEE Transactions on Systems, Man and Cybernetics*, SMC-12: 463–469.

Andriole, S. J. (1987) "Storyboard Prototyping For Requirements Verification." *Large Scale Systems*, 12: 231–247.

Andriole, S. J. (1989a) *Handbook for the Design, Development, Evaluation, and Application of Interactive Decision Support Systems*. Princeton, NJ: Petrocelli.

Andriole, S. J. (1989b) *Storyboard Prototyping for Systems Design: A New Approach to User Requirements Validation and System Sizing*. Wellesley, MA: QED Information Sciences, Inc.

Andriole, S. J., H. H. Black, G. W. Hopple, and J. R. Thompson (1986) "Intelligent Aids for Tactical Planning." *IEEE Transactions on Systems, Man and Cybernetics*, SMC-16: 854–864.

Andriole, S. J., M. Akey, T. R. Butler, K. Dunkelberger, and P. J. Millis (1987) "Some Principles of Decision Support Systems Design and Development and a Combat Support System Case Study." *Large Scale Systems*, 12: 5–31.

Bahill, A. T., P. N. Harris, and E. Senn (1988) "Lessons Learned Building Expert Systems." *AI Expert*, 3: 36–45.

Bailey, D. E. (1971) *Probability and Statistics: Models for Research*. New York: Wiley.

Bailey, J. W., and V. R. Basili (1981) "A Meta-Model for Software Development Resource Expenditures." *Proceedings of the 5th International Conference on Software Engineering*, pp. 107–116.

Bailey, J. W., and Pearson (1983) "Development of a Tool for Measuring and Analyzing User Satisfaction." *Management Science*, 29: 530–545.

Baroudi, J. J., and W. J. Orlikowski (1988) "The Problem of Statistical Power in MIS Research." *MIS Quarterly*, 87–106.

Basili, V. R., and B. T. Perricone (1984) "Software Errors and Complexity: An Empirical Investigation." *Communications of the ACM*, 27: 42–52.

Beam, W. R., J. D. Palmer, and A. P. Sage (1987) "Systems Engineering and Software Productivity." *IEEE Transactions on Systems, Man and Cybernetics*, SMC-17: 163–186.

Beizer, B. (1984) *Software System Testing and Quality Assurance*. New York: Van Nostrand Reinhold.

Bellman, K. L., and D. O. Walter (1988) "Analyzing and Correcting Knowledge-Based Systems Requires Explicit Models." *Proceedings of the AAAI-88 Workshop on Validation and Testing Knowledge-Based Systems*, St. Paul, MN, August 20.

Bender, P. S., R. W. Brown, M. H. Isaac, and J. F. Shapiro (1985) "Improving Purchasing Productivity at IBM with a Normative Decision Support System." *Interfaces*, 15: 106–115.

Berliner, D. B., D. Angell, J. W. Shearer (1964) *Behaviors, Measures, and Instruments for Performance Evaluation in Simulated Environments*. Paper presented at the Workshop on the Quantification of Human Performance. Albuquerque, NM.

BETAC Corporation, Enemy Sortie Capability and Measurement Aid: Final design plan and functional description (Arlington, VA, 1985).

Boar, B. (1984) *Application Prototyping: A Requirements Definition Strategy for the 80's*. New York: Wiley.

Boehm, B. (1981) *Software Engineering Economics*. Englewood Cliffs, NJ: Prentice-Hall.

Boehm, B. (1984) "Verifying and Validating Software Requirements." *IEEE Software*, 1: 75–88.

Bourgeois, L. J., and K. M. Eisenhardt (1988) "Strategic Decision Processes in High Velocity Environments: Four Cases in the Microcomputer Industry." *Management Science*, 34: 816–835.

Brown, R. V., A. S. Kahr, and C. R. Peterson (1974) *Decision Analysis for the Manager*. New York: Holt, Rinehart & Winston.

Buede, D. M. (1988) *Decision Software: A State of the Art Review*. Reston, VA: Decision Logistics.

Buede, D. M., and L. Adelman (1987) *Decision Support Systems: Design, Use, and Evaluation*. Coursebook for seminar sponsored by the U.S. Army Logistics Management Center, Fort Lee, VA.

Buede, D. M., G. Yates, and C. A. Weaver (1985) "Concept Design of a Program Manager's Decision Support System." *IEEE Transactions on Systems, Man and Cybernetics*, SMC-15: 457–468.

Campbell, D. T. (1984) "Foreward," in R. K. Yin (ed.), *Case Study Research: Design and Methods*. Beverly Hills, CA: Sage.

Campbell, D. T., and D. W. Fiske (1959) "Convergent and Discriminant Validation by the Multitrait-Multimethod Matrix." *Psychological Bulletin*, 56: 81–105.

Campbell, D. T., and J. C. Stanley (1966) *Experimental and Quasi-Experimental Designs for Research*. Chicago: Rand McNally.

Carlson, E. D. "An Approach for Designing Decision Support Systems," in W. C. House (ed.), *Decision Support Systems: A Data-Based, Model-Oriented, User-Developed Discipline*. Princeton, NJ: Petrocelli.

Casey, J. (1989) "Picking the Right Expert System Application." *AI Expert*, 4(9): 44–47.

Cats-Baril, W. L., and G. P. Huber (1987) "Decision Support Systems for Ill-Structured Problems: An Empirical Study." *Decision Sciences*, 18: 350–372.

Chandrasekaran, B. (1983) "On Evaluating AI Systems for Medical Diagnosis." *AI Magazine*, 4: 34–37.

Chapnick, P. (1988) "When We Look Back." *AI Expert*, 3(12): 5–6.

Cholawsky, E. M. (1988) "Beating the Prototype Blues." *AI Expert*, 3(12): 42–49.

Clymer, J. (1985) "A Sampling of Artificial Intelligence Software." *Personal Computing*, November: 104.

Cohen, J. (1965) "Some Statistical Issues in Psychological Research," in B. B. Woleman (ed.), *Handbook of Clinical Psychology*. New York: McGraw-Hill.

Cohen, J. (1977) *Statistical Power Analysis for the Behavioral Sciences*, revised edition. New York: Academic.

Cohen, J., and C. Cohen (1975) *Applied Multiple Regression/Correlational Analysis for the Behavioral Sciences*. Hillsdale, NJ: Lawrence Erlbaum.

Cohen, M. S., and A. N. S. Freeling (1981) *The Impact of Information on Decisions: Command and Control System Evaluation*. Reston, VA: Decision Sciences Consortium, Inc.

Constantine, M. M., and J. W. Ulvila (in press). "Knowledge-Based Systems in the Army: The State of the Practice and Suggested Improvements." *Expect Systems with Applications*.

Conte, S. D., H. E. Dunsmore, and V. Y. Shen (1986) *Software Engineering Metrics and Models*. Reading, MA: Benjamin/Cummings.

Cook, T. D., and D. T. Campbell (1979) *Quasi-Experimentation: Design and Analysis Issues for Field Settings*. Chicago: Rand McNally.

Culbert, C., and R. T. Savely (1988) "Expert System Verification and Validation." *Proceedings of AAAI-88 Workshop on Validation and Testing Knowledge-Based Systems*, St. Paul, MN, August 20.

Daily, E. B. (1978) "Software Development." *Proceedings of European Computing Review*, Infotech International.

Dalkey, N. C., and O. Helmer (1963) "An Experimental Application of the Delphi Method to the Use of Experts." *Management Science*, 9: 458–467.

Davis, A. M., E. H. Bersoff, and E. R. Comer (1988) "A Strategy for Comparing Alternate Software Development Life Cycle Models." *IEEE Transactions on Software Engineering*, 14: 1453–1461.

Davis, R. (1989) "Expert Systems: How Far Can They Go." *AI Magazine*, 10: 65–77.

Dawes, R. M., and B. Corrigan (1974) "Linear Models in Decision Making." *Psychological Bulletin*, 81: 95–106.

Deadline Newsletter (1988). "Synopsis of *Software Metrics: Establishing a Company-Wide Program* by Robert B. Grady and Deborah L. Caswell." Vol. 1, 5–11.

Dearden, J. (1972) "MIS is a Mirage." *Harvard Business Review*, 50: 90–99.

DeBrabander, B., and G. Theirs (1984) "Successful Information System Development in Relation to Situational Factors Which Affect Effective Communication Between MIS-Users and EDP-Specialists." *Management Science*, 30: 137–155.

Delbecq, A. L., and A. H. Van de Ven (1971) "A Group Process Model for Problem Identification and Program Planning." *Journal of Applied Behavioral Science*, 7: 466–492.

Delbecq, A. L., A. H. Van de Ven, and D. H. Gustafson (1975) *Group Techniques for Program Planning: A Guide to Nominal Group and Delphi Processes*. Glenview, IL: Scott, Foresman.

DeMillo, R. A., W. M. McCracken, R. J. Martin, and J. F. Passafiume (1987) *Software Testing and Evaluation*. Menlo Park, CA: Benjamin/Cummings.

DOD-STD-1679A: Software Development (Section 5.3, Programming Standards), February 1983.

DOD-STD-2167: Defense System Software Development (Section 30.3), Detailed Requirements section of General Design and Coding Standards), June 4, 1985.

Ebert, R. J., and T. E. Kruse (1978) "Bootstrapping the Security Analyst." *Journal of Applied Psychology*, 63: 110–119.

Edwards, W. (1968) "Conservatism in Human Information Processing," in B. Kleinmuntz (ed.), *Formal Representation of Human Judgment*. New York: Wiley.

Edwards, W. (1977) "How to Use Multiattribute Utility Measurement for Social Decision Making." *IEEE Transactions on Systems, Man and Cybernetics*, SMC-7: 326–340.

Edwards, W., M. Guttentag, and K. Snapper (1975) "A Decision-Theoretic Approach to Evaluation Research," in E. L. Struning and M. Guttentag (eds.), *Handbook of Evaluation Research*. Beverly Hills, CA: Sage.

Eils, L. C., and R. S. John (1980) "A Criterion Validation of Multi-Attribute Utility Analysis and of Group Communication Strategy." *Organizational Behavior and Human Performance*, 25: 268–288.

Einhorn, H. J., and R. M. Hogarth (1975) "Unit Weighting Schemes of Decision Making." *Organizational Behavior and Human Performance*, 13, 171–192.

Einhorn, H. J., and R. M. Hogarth (1978) "Confidence in Judgment: Persistance of the Illustration of Validity." *Psychological Review*, 85: 395–416.

Einhorn, H. J., and W. McCoach (1977) "A Simple Multi-Attribute Procedure for Evaluation." *Behavioral Science*, 22: 270–282.

Eliot, L. B. (1989) "Mass Market Applications: They're Here." *AI Expert*, 4(12): 9–14.

Ellis, J. O., and M. N. Wygant (1989) *A System Oriented Methodology to Support Software Testing*. White Sands Missile Range, NM: USA Test and Evaluation Command.

Fagan, M. E. (1976) "Design and Code Inspections to Reduce Errors in Program Development." *IBM Systems Journal*, 15: 182–211.

Fairley, R. E. (1985) *Software Engineering Concepts*. New York: McGraw-Hill.

Farr, L., and H. J. Zagorski (1965) "Quantitative Analysis of Programming Cost Factors: A Progress Report," in A. B. Frielind, (ed.), *ICC Symposium Proceedings on Economics of Data Processing*. Amsterdam: North-Holland.

Figgins, T., S. Barth, and K. Gates (1983) *DART Functional Description*. Contract #F30602-81-C-0263. Rome Air Development Center, Griffiss Air Force Base, NY.

Fischhoff, B. (1975) "Hindsight/Foresight: The Effect of Outcome Knowledge on Judgment Under Uncertainty." *Journal of Experimental Psychology: Human Perception and Performance*, 4: 330–344.

Forsythe, D., and B. Buchanan (1989) "An Empirical Study of Knowledge Elicitation: Some Pitfalls and Suggestions." *IEEE Transactions on Systems, Man and Cybernetics*, SMC-19: 435–442.

Franklin, W. R., R. Bansal, E. Gilbert, and G. Shroff (1988) "Debugging and Tracing Expert Systems." *International Hawaii Conference on System Sciences*.

Gaschnig, J., P. Klahr, H. Pople, E. Shortliffe, and A. Terry (1983) "Evaluation of Expert Systems: Issues and Case Studies," in F. Hayes-Roth, D. A. Waterman, and D. B. Lenat (eds.), *Building Expert Systems*. Reading, MA: Addison-Wesley.

Gelperin, D., and B. Hetzel (1988) "The Growth of Software Testing." *Communications of the ACM*, 31: 687–695.

Geoffrion, A., and R. F. Powers (1983) "Management Support Systems," in W. C. House (ed.), *Decision Support Systems: A Data-Based, Model-Oriented, User-Developed Discipline*. Princeton, NJ: Petrocelli.

Gilbert, E. (1988) *Static Analysis Tools for Expert Systems*. Arlington, VA: Booz, Allen & Hamilton.

Ginzberg, M. J. (1977) "Steps Toward More Effective Implementation of MS and MIS." *Interfaces*, 8: 57–63.

Girill, T. R., C. H. Luk, and S. Norton (1988) "The Impact of Usage Monitoring on the Evolution of an Online-Documentation System: A Case Study." *IEEE Transactions on Systems, Man and Cybernetics*, SMC-18: 326–332.

Gould, J. D., and C. Lewis (1985) "Designing for Usability: Key Principles and What Designers Think." *Communications of the ACM*, 28: 300–311.

Grady, Robert B., and D. L. Caswell (1987) *Software Metrics: Establishing a Company-Wide Program*. Englewood Cliffs, NJ: Prentice-Hall.

Gulliksen, H. (1950) *Theory of Mental Tests*. New York: Wiley.

Gupta, E. G., and Y. S. Lincoln (1983). "Epistemological and methodological bases of naturalistic inquiry," in G. F. Madaus, M. S. Scriven, and D. L. Stufflebeam, (eds.), *Evaluation Models: Viewpoints on Educational and Human Services Evaluation*. Boston, MA: Kluwer-Nijhoff, 1983.

Halstead, M. (1977) *Elements of Software Science*. Amsterdam: Elsevier.

Hamlet, R. (1988) "Special Section on Software Testing." *Communications of the ACM*, 31: 662–667.

Hammond, K. R. (1948) "Subject and Object Sampling: A Note." *Psychological Bulletin*, 45: 530–533.

Hammond, K. R. (1971) "Computer Graphics as an Aid to Learning." *Science*, 171: 903–908.

Hammond, K. R., and L. Adelman (1976) "Science, Values, and Human Judgment." *Science*, 194: 389–396.

Hammond, K. R., and D. A. Summers (1972) "Cognitive Control." *Psychological Review*, 79: 58–67.

Hammond, K. R., T. R. Stewart, B. Brehmer, and D. O. Steinmann (1975) "Social Judgment Theory," in M. F. Kaplan and S. Schwartz (eds.), *Human Judgment and Decision Processes*. New York: Academic.

Hammond, K. R., R. M. Hamm, and J. Grassia (1986) "Generalizing Over the Conditions By Combining the Multitrait-Multimethod Matrix and the Representative Design of Experiments." *Psychological Bulletin*, 100: 257–269.

Hammond, K. R., R. M. Hamm, J. Grassia, and T. Pearson (1987) "Direct Comparison of the Relative Efficacy of Intuitive and Analytical Cognition in Expert Judgment." *IEEE Transactions on Systems, Man and Cybernetics*, SMC-17: 753–770.

Harmon, P., R. Maus, and W. Morrissey (1988) *Expert Systems Tools and Applications*. New York: Wiley.

Hehnen, M. T., S. C. Chou, H. L. Scheurman, G. J. Robinson, T. P. Luken, and D. W. Baker (1984) "An Integrated Decision Support and Manufacturing Control System." *Interfaces*, 14: 44–52.

Hetzel, W. (1984) *The Complete Guide to Software Testing*. Wellesley, MA: QED Information Sciences, Inc.

Hoffman, P. J. (1960) "The Paramorphic Representation of Clinical Judgment." *Psychological Bulletin*, 57: 116–131.

Hoffman, P. J., P. Slovic, and L. G. Rorer (1968). "An Analysis-of-Variance Model for the Assessment of Configural Cue Utilization in Clinical Judgment." *Psychological Bulletin*, 69: 338–349.

Hogarth, R. M. (1975) "Cognitive Processes and the Assessment of Subjective Probability Distributions." *Journal of the American Statistical Association*, 70: 272–289.

Hogarth, R. M. (1987) *Judgment and Choice*. New York: Wiley.

Hopple, G. W. (1988) *The State-of-the-Art in Decision Support Systems*. Wellesley, MA: QED Information Sciences.

Howden, W. E. (1987) *Functional Program Testing and Analysis*. New York: McGraw-Hill.

Huber, G. P. (1980) *Managerial Decision Making*. Glenview, IL: Scott, Foresman.

Huber, G. P. (1986) "The Decision-Making Paradigm of Organizational Design." *Management Science*, 32: 572–589.

Jr., E. G., Hurst, D. N. Ness, T. J. Gambino, and T. H. Johnson (1983) "Growing DSS: A Flexible, Evolutionary Approach," in J. L. Bennett (ed.), *Building Decision Support Systems*. Reading, MA: Addison-Wesley.

JCMPOINST 8020.1: Independent Software Nuclear Safety Analysis (Change 2, Appendix F, Section 3.6 (3), Specification and Design Audit and Analysis), March 3, 1984.

Jensen, R. W. (1984) "A Comparison of the Jensen and COCOMO Schedule and Cost Estimation Models." *Proceedings of the International Society of Parametric Analysis*, pp. 96–106.

Kahneman, D., and A. Tversky (1973) "On the Psychology of Prediction." *Psychological Review*, 80: 237–251.

Kahneman, D., and A. Tversky (1984) "Choices, Values, and Frames." *American Psychologist*, 39: 341–350.

Kahneman, D., P. Slovic, and A. Tversky (eds.) (1982) *Judgment Under Uncertainty: Heuristics and Biases.* New York: Cambridge University Press.

Kang, Y. and A. T. Bahill (1990). "A Tool for Detecting Expert System Errors." *AI Expert*, 5: 46–51.

Kaplan, B., and D. Duchon (1988) "Combining Qualitative and Quantitative Methods in Information Systems Research: A Case Study." *MIS Quarterly*, 12: 571–586.

Keen, P. G. W. (1980) "Decision Support Systems: Translating Analytic Techniques into Useful Tools." *Sloan Management Review*, 21: 33–44.

Keeney, R. L., and H. Raiffa (1976) *Decisions with Multiple Objectives.* New York: Wiley.

Keim, R. T., and R. Janaro (1982) "Cost/Benefit Analysis of MIS." *Journal of Systems Management*, September: 20–25.

Kelly, C. W. (1979) *Program Completion Report: Advanced Decision Technology Program (1972–1979)* (Tech. Rep. TR 79-3-93). McLean, VA: Decisions and Designs, Inc.

Kemerer, C. F. (1987) "An Empirical Validation of Software Cost Estimation Models." *Communications of the ACM*, 30: 416–429.

Keyes, J. (1989) "The Citibank Pension Expert." *AI Expert*, 4: 61–65.

King, W. R., and D. I. Clelland (1975) "The Design of Management Information Systems: An Information Analysis Approach." *Management Science*, 22: 286–297.

Kirk, D. B., and A. E. Murray (1988) *Verification and Validation of Expert Systems for Nuclear Power Applications.* McLean, VA: Science Applications International Corporation.

Kitchenham, B., and N. R. Taylor (1984) "Software Cost Models." *ICL Technical Journal*, 4: 73–102.

Klein, G. A., and C. Brezovic (1988) "Evaluation of Expert Systems," in S. J. Andriole and G. W. Hopple (eds.), *Defense Applications of AI.* Lexington, MA: Lexington Books.

Klein, G. A., and J. Weitzenfeld (1982) "The Use of Analogues in Comparability Analysis." *Applied Ergonomics*, 13: 99–104.

Kraemer, H. C., and S. Thiemann (1987) *How Many Subjects?: Statistical Power Analysis in Research.* Beverly Hills, CA: Sage.

Lay, P. M. W. (1985) "Beware of the Cost/Benefit Model for IS Project Evaluation." *Journal of Systems Management*, June: 30–35.

Leddo, J. M., and M. S. Cohen (1987) "A Cognitive Science Approach to Elicitation of Expert Knowledge." *Proceedings of the 1987 Joint Directors of Laboratories Conference*, McLean, VA: Science Applications International Corporation, 1987.

Lee, A. S. (1989) "A Scientific Methodology for MIS Case Studies." *MIS Quarterly*, 13: 33–50.

Lehner, P. E. (1989) "Toward a Mathematics for Evaluating the Knowledge Base of an Expert System." *IEEE Transactions on Systems, Man and Cybernetics*, SMC-19: 658–662.

Lehner, P. E., and L. Adelman (1990) "Behavioral Decision Theory and Its Implications for Knowledge Engineering." *Knowledge Engineering Review*, 5: 5–14.

Lehner, P. E., and J. W. Ulvila (1989) *A Note on the Application of Classical Statistics to Evaluating the Knowledge Base of an Expert System.* Reston, VA: Decision Sciences Consortium, Inc.

Lehner, P. E., and D. A. Zirk (1987) "Cognitive Factors in User/Expert-System Interaction." *Human Factors*, 29: 97–109.

Lehner, P. E., L. Adelman, J. O. Crowley, and J. R. McIntyre (1985a) *Enemy Performance Assessment Aid: Final Functional Description and Design Plan* (Tech. Rep. 85-110). New Hartford, NY: PAR Technology Corporation.

Lehner, P. E., J. R. McIntyre, L. Adelman, K. Gates, P. Luster, M. Probus, and M. L. Donnell (1985b) *An Intelligent Aid for Estimating Enemy Courses of Action* (Tech. Rep. 84-131). New Hartford, NY: PAR Technology Corporation.

Lehner, P. E., M. R. Probus, and M. L. Donnell (1985c) "Building Decision Aids: Exploiting the Synergy Between Decision Analysis and Artificial Intelligence." *IEEE Transactions on Systems, Man and Cybernetics*, SMC-15: 469–474.

Levi, K. (1989) "Expert Systems Should be More Accurate than Human Experts: Evaluation Procedures from Human Judgment and Decisionmaking." *IEEE Transactions on Systems, Man and Cybernetics*, SMC-19: 647–657.

Libby, R., and B. L. Lewis (1977) "Human Information Processing Research in Accounting." *Accounting, Organizations, and Society*, 21: 245–268.

Liebowitz, J. (1986) "Useful Approach for Evaluating Expert Systems." *Expert Systems*, 3: 86–96.

Liebowitz, J., and D. A. De Salvo (eds.) (1989) *Structuring Expert Systems: Domain, Design, and Development*. Englewood Cliffs, NJ: Yourdon.

Londeix, B. (1987) *Cost Estimation for Software Development*. Reading, MA: Addison-Wesley.

Machie, R. R., and C. D. Wylie (1985) *Technology Transfer and Artificial Intelligence*. Goleta, CA: Essex Corporation.

Madaus, G. F., M. S. Scriven, and D. L. Stufflebeam (eds.) (1983). *Evaluation Models: Viewpoints on Educational and Human Services Evaluation*. Boston, MA: Kluwer-Nijhoff.

Marcot, B. (1987) "Testing Your Knowledge Base." *AI Expert*, 2: 42–47.

Markus, M. L. (1983) "Power, Politics, and MIS Implementation." *Communications of the ACM*, 26: 430–444.

Markus, M. L. (1984) *Systems in Organizations: Bugs and Features*. Marshfield, MA: Pitman.

Mazen, A., L. Graf, C. Kellogg, and M. Hemmasi (1987) "Statistical Power in Contemporary Management Research." *Academy of Management Journal*, 30: 369–380.

McCain, L. J., and R. McCleary (1979) "The Statistical Analysis of the Simple Interrupted Time-Series Quasi-Experiment," in T. D. Cook and D. T. Campbell (eds.), *Quasi-Experimentation: Design and Analysis Issues for Field Settings*. Chicago: Rand McNally.

Medlin, S. M., and L. Adelman (1989) "Automated Cost-Benefit Analysis: A Powerful Decision Support Tool for HRD Managers." Twelfth Annual Conference on Teaching Public Administration, Charlottesville, VA.

Meyers, G. (1979) *The Art of Software Testing*. New York: Wiley.

MIL-STD-1679: Weapon System Software Development (Section 5.3, Programming Standards), December 1, 1978.

Morton, M. S. Scott (1980) Book review of *Decision Support Systems: Current Practice and Continuing Challenges* by Steven L. Alter, *Sloan Management Review*, 21: 77.

Nachmias, D., and C. Nachmias (1976) *Research Methods in the Social Sciences.* New York: St. Martin's.

Nazareth, D. L. (1989) "Issues in the Verification of Knowledge in Rule Based Systems." *International Journal of Man-Machine Studies*, 30: 255–271.

Nelson, E. A. (1966) *Management Handbook for the Estimation of Computer Programming Costs.* Santa Monica, CA: System Development Corporation.

Newquist, H. P., III (1988) "Tales from the Hearth of AI." *AI Expert*, 3(12): 61–63.

Nguyen, T. A., W. A. Perkins, T. J. Laffey, and D. Pecora (1987) "Knowledge Base Verification." *AI Magazine*, 8: 69–75.

Nisbett, R., and Ross, L. (1980) *Human Inference: Strategies and Shortcomings of Social Judgment.* Englewood Cliffs, NJ: Prentice-Hall.

Norden, P. (1958) "Curve Fitting for a Model of Applied Research and Development Scheduling." *IBM Journal of Research and Development.* Vol. 2, Number 3.

O'Connor, M. F. (1989). "Planning for Integrated System Evaluation: An Application to SDI," in S. E. Johnson and A. H. Levis (eds.), *Science of Command and Control: Coping With Complexity (Part II).* Fairfax, VA: AFCEA International Press.

O'Connor, M. F., and W. Edwards (1976) *On Using Scenarios in the Evaluation of Complex Alternatives* (Tech. Rep. DDI/DT/TR-76-17). McLean, VA: Decisions and Designs, Inc.

O'Keefe, R. M., O. Balci, and E. P. Smith (1987) "Validating Expert System Performance." *IEEE Expert*, 2: 81–90.

Osterweil, L. J., and L. D. Fosdick (1976) "DAVE: A Validation Error Detection and Documentation System for Fortran Programs." *Software Practice and Experience*, 6: 473–486.

Ostrand, T. J., and M. J. Balcer (1988) "The Category-Partition Method for Specifying and Generating Functional Tests." *Communications of the ACM*, 31: 676–686.

Parr, F. N. (1980) "An Alternative to the Rayleigh Curve Model for Software Development." *IEEE Transactions of Software Engineering*, SE-6: 291–296.

Patton, M. Q. (1982). *Practical Evaluation.* Beverly Hills, CA: Sage.

Perriens, M. P. (1977) *An Application of Formal Inspections to Top-Down Structured Program Development.* Gaithersburg, MD: IBM Federal Systems Division.

Pfleeger, S. L. (1988) *An Overview of Cost Models for Object-Oriented Development.* Fairfax, VA: George Mason University.

Pfleeger, S. L. (1989) "An Effort Estimation Model for Object-Oriented Development." (Ph.D. dissertation.) Fairfax, VA: School of Information Technology and Engineering, George Mason University.

Phelps, R. H. (1986) "Decision Aids for Military Intelligence Analysis: Description, Evaluation, and Implementation," in S. J. Andriole (ed.), *Microcomputer Decision Support Systems: Design, Implementation, and Evaluation.* Wellesley, MA: QED Information Sciences.

Pitz, G. F., and J. McKillip (1984) *Decision Analysis for Program Managers.* Beverly Hills, CA: Sage.

Powell, P. B. (1986) "Planning for Software Validation, Verification, and Testing," in S. J. Andriole (ed.), *Software Validation, Verification, Testing and Documentation.* Princeton, NJ: Petrocelli.

Press, L. (1989) "Expert System Benchmarks." *IEEE Expert,* 4: 37–44.

Pressman, R. S. (1982) *Software Engineering: A Practitioner's Approach.* New York: McGraw-Hill.

Putnam, L. H. (1978) "A General Empirical Solution to the Macro Software Sizing and Estimating Problem." *IEEE Transactions on Software Engineering,* SE-4: 345–361.

Ramsey, H. R., and M. E. Atwood (1979) *Human Factors in Computer Systems: A Review of the Literature.* Englewood, CO: Science Applications, Inc.

Reichardt, C. S. (1979) "The Statistical Analysis of Data from Nonequivalent Group Designs," in T. D. Cook and D. T. Campbell (eds.), *Quasi-Experimentation: Design and Analysis Issues for Field Settings.* Chicago: Rand McNally.

Richardson, D. J., and L. A. Clarke (1981) "A Partition Analysis Method to Increase Program Reliability." *Proceedings of the 5th IEEE International Conference on Software Engineering,* pp. 244–253.

Riedel, S. L., and G. F. Pitz (1986) "Utilization-Oriented Evaluation of Decision Support Systems." *IEEE Transactions on Systems, Man and Cybernetics,* SMC-16: 980–996.

Riemenschneider, R. A., A. J. Rockmore, and T. A. (1983) *A Route Planning Aid: System Specifications* (PAR Report #83-135). New Hartford, NY: PAR Technology Corporation.

Rockmore, A. J., L. Hemphill, R. A. Riemenschneider, M. L. Donnell, and K. Gates (1982) *Decision Aids for Target Aggregation: Technology Review and Decision Aid Selection* (PAR Report #82-32). New Hartford, NY: PAR Technology Corporation.

Rook, F. W., and J. W. Croghan (1989) "The Formulation of Knowledge Acquisition Methods: A Systems Engineering Conceptual Framework." *IEEE Transactions on Systems, Man and Cybernetics,* SMC-19: 586–597.

Rushby, J. (1988) *Quality Measures and Assurance for AI Software* (NASA Contractor Report 4187). Washington, DC: National Aeronautics and Space Administration (Code NTT-4).

Ruttman, L. (1980) *Planning Useful Evaluations: Evaluability Assessments.* Beverly Hills, CA: Sage.

Saaty, T. L. (1980) *The Analytic Hierarchy Process.* New York: McGraw-Hill.

Sage, A. P. (1986) "An Overview of Contemporary Issues in the Design and Development of Microcomputer Decision Support Systems," in S. J. Andriole (ed.), *Microcomputer Decision Support Systems: Design, Implementation, and Evaluation.* Wellesley, MA: QED Information Sciences.

Sage, A. P. (1987) "Collective Enquiry," in M. Singh (ed.), *Systems and Control Encyclopedia.* Oxford, England: Pergamon.

Sage, A. P. (1991) *Decision Support Systems Engineering.* New York: Wiley.

Sage, A. P., and J. D. Palmer (1990) *Software Systems Engineering.* New York: Wiley.

Sage, A. P. and C. C. White, III (1980) *Evaluation of Two DDI Decision Aids Developed for DCA:C140* (Document No. 33737-W114-RU-00). Falls Church, VA: TRW Defense and Space Systems Group.

Sage, A. P., and C. C. White, III (1984) "ARIADNE: A Knowledge-Based Interactive System for Decision Support." *IEEE Transactions on Systems, Man and Cybernetics*, 14: 279–296.

Schein, E. H. (1970) *Organizational Psychology*. Englewood Cliffs, NJ: Prentice-Hall, 1970.

Shank, R. C., and R. P. Abelson (1977) *Scripts, Plans, Goals, and Understanding: An Inquiry into Human Knowledge Structures*. Hillsdale, NJ: Lawrence Erlbaum.

Sharda, R. (1984) "Linear Programming on Microcomputers: A Survey." *Interfaces*, 14: 27–38.

Sharda, R., S. H. Barr, and J. C. McDonnell (1988) "Decision Support System Effectiveness: A Review and an Empirical Test." *Management Science*, 34: 139–159.

Sherif, M., and C. I. Hovland (1961) *Social Judgment: Assimilation and Contrast Effects in Communication and Attitude Change*. New Haven: Yale University Press.

Shrinkfield, A. J. (1983). "Designing Evaluations of Educational and Social Programs by Lee Cronbach: A synopsis," in G. F. Madaus, M. S. Scriven, and D. L. Stufflebeam, (eds.), *Evaluation Models: Viewpoints on Educational and Human Services Evaluation*. Boston, MA: Kluwer-Nijhoff, 1983.

Shycon, H. N. (1977) "All Around the Model—Perspective on MS Applications." *Interfaces*, 7: 40–43.

Simon, H. A. (1960) *The New Science of Management Decisions*. New York: Harper & Row.

Slagle, J. R., and M. R. Wick (1988) "A Method for Evaluation Candidate Expert System Applications." *AI Magazine*, 9: 44–53.

Slovic, P., B. Fischhoff, and S. Lichtenstein (1988) "Response Mode, Framing, and Information-Processing Effects in Risk Assessment," in D. Bell, H. Raiffa, and A. Tversky (eds.), *Decision Making: Descriptive, Normative, and Prescriptive Interactions*. Cambridge: Cambridge University Press.

Smith, D. L. (1988) "Implementing Real World Expert Systems." *AI Expert*, 3(12): 51–57.

Spetzler, C. S., and C. A. S. Stael von Holstein (1975) "Probability Encoding in Decision Analysis." *Management Science*, 22: 340–358.

Sprague, R. H., Jr. and E. D. Carlson (1982) *Building Effective Decision Support Systems*. Englewood Cliffs, NJ: Prentice-Hall.

Stachowitz, R. A., C. L. Chang, and J. B. Combs (1988) "Research on Validation of Knowledge-Based Systems." *Proceedings of the AAAI-88 Workshop on Validation and Testing Knowledge-Based Systems*, St. Paul, MN, August 20.

Steiner, I. D. (1972) *Group Process and Productivity*. New York: Academic.

Stewart, T. R., W. R. Moninger, J. Grassia, R. H. Brady, and F. H. Merrem (1988) *Analysis of Expert Judgment and Skill in a Hail Forecasting Experiment*. Boulder, CO: Center for Research on Judgment and Policy at the University of Colorado.

Stumpf, S. A., R. D. Freedman, and D. E. Zand (1979) "Judgmental Decisions: A Study of Interactions Among Group Membership, Group Functioning, and the Decision Situation." *Academy of Management Journal*, 22: 765–782.

Symons, C. R. (1988) "Function Point Analysis: Difficulties and Improvements." *IEEE Transactions on Software Engineering*, SE-14: 2–10.

Thuraisingham, B. (1989) "From Rules to Frames and Frames to Rules." *AI Expert*, 4(10): 31–39.

Tolcott, M. A., and V. E. Holt (eds.) (1987) *Impact and Potential of Decision Research on Decision Aiding: Report of a Department of Defense Roundtable Workshop*. Washington, D.C.: American Psychological Association.

Tolcott, M. A., F. F. Marvin, and P. E. Lehner (1989) "Expert Decision Making in Evolving Situations." *IEEE Transactions on Systems, Man and Cybernetics*, SMC-19: 606–615.

Tong, R. M., N. D. Newman, G. Berg-Cross, and F. Rook (1987) *Performance Evaluation of Artificial Intelligence Systems*. Mountain View, CA: Advanced Decision Systems.

Turban, E. (1990) *Decision Support and Expert Systems*. New York: Macmillan.

Tversky, A., and D. Kahneman (1971) "The Belief in the 'Law of Small Numbers'." *Psychological Bulletin*, 76: 105–110.

Tversky, A., and D. Kahneman (1973) " Availability: A Heuristic for Judging Frequency and Probability." *Cognitive Psychology*, 5: 207–232.

Tversky, A., and D. Kahneman (1974) "Judgment Under Uncertainty: Heuristics and Biases." *Science*, 185: 1124–1131.

Tversky, A., and D. Kahneman (1981) "The Framing of Decisions and the Psychology of Choice," *Science*, 211: 453–458.

Ulvila, J. W., P. E. Lehner, T. A. Bresnick, J. O. Chinnis, Jr., and J. D. E. Gumula (1987) *Testing and Evaluating C^3I Systems That Employ Artificial Intelligence*. Reston, VA: Decision Sciences Consortium, Inc.

Van Duyn, J. (1982) *DP Professional's Guide to Writing Effective Technical Documentation*. New York: Wiley.

von Winterfeldt, D., and W. Edwards (1986) *Decision Analysis and Behavioral Research*. New York: Cambridge University Press.

Wagner, G. R. (1981) "Decision Support Systems: The Real Substance." *Interfaces*, 11: 77–86.

Wason, P. (1960) "On the Failure to Eliminate Hypotheses in a Conceptual Task." *Quarterly Journal of Experimental Psychology*, 12: 129–140.

Watson, S., and D. M. Buede (1987) *Decision Synthesis: The Principles and Practice of Decision Analysis*. Cambridge, England: Cambridge University Press.

Webster's Seventh New Collegiate Dictionary (1966) Springfield, MA: G. & C. Merriam.

Weiss, J. J., and G. W. Zwahlen (1982) "The Structured Decision Conference: A Case Study." *Hospital and Health Services Administration*, 27: 90–105.

Weitzel, J. R., and L. Kerschberg (1989) "A System Development Methodology for Knowledge-Based Systems." *IEEE Transactions on Systems, Man and Cybernetics*, SMC-19: 598–605.

Weyuker, E. J., and T. J. Ostrand (1980) "Theories of Program Testing and the Application of Revealing Subdomains." *IEEE Transactions on Software Engineering*, SE-6: 236–246.

Wohl, J. G. (1981) "Force Management Decision Requirements for Air Force Tactical Command and Control." *IEEE Transactions on Systems, Man and Cybernetics*, SMC-11: 618–639.

Wohl, J. G., E. E. Entin, D. Serfaty, R. M. James, and J. C. Deckert (1987) *Human Cognitive Performance in ASW Data Fusion*. Burlington, MA: ALPHATECH, Inc.

Wolfgram, D. D., T. J. Dear, and C. S. Galbraith (1987) *Expert Systems for the Technical Professional*. New York: Wiley.

Wolverton, R. W. (1974) "The Cost of Developing Large-Scale Software." *IEEE Transactions on Computers*, C-23: 615–636.

Yin, R. K. (1984) *Case Study Research: Design and Methods*. Beverly Hills: Sage.

Yu, V. L., L. M. Fagan, S. M. Wraith, W. J. Clancey, A. C. Scott, J. F. Hanigan, R. L. Blum, B. G. Buchanan, and S. N. Cohen (1979) "Antimicrobial Selection by a Computer: A Blinded Evaluation by Infectious Disease Experts." *Journal of the American Medical Association*, 242: 1279–1282.

Index

Abelson, R. P., 218
Acceptance testing, 140
Accuracy vs. bias, 155
Ackoff, R. L., 18, 207
Activity node identification, 24, 25–27
Additive decision rule, 63, 204
Adelman, L.
  1976, 212
  1982, 18, 28, 46, 104, 207
  1983, 25, 207
  1984, 63, 71, 207
  1985, 31, 46, 103, 116, 154, 208, 215
  1986, 14, 19, 20, 25, 31, 48, 59, 207, 208
  1987, 44, 62, 110, 207, 209
  1089, 71, 153, 207, 215
  1990, 144, 150, 151, 208, 214
  in press, 207
Air Force. *See* U.S. Air Force
Akey, M., 208
Albrecht, A. J., 122, 126, 208
Algorithmic methods, 16, 43
Analysis of co-variance (ANCOVA), 183–184

Analysis of variance (ANOVA), 172, 183–184
Analytical methods, 2, 43–44
  categorization of, 110–113
  characteristics of, 114–120
  computer science (CS), 43, 110, 111, 117, 118
  decision analysis (DA), 43, 66–71, 110, 111, 114–115, 118, 119
  ease of use of, 115
  epistemological basis of, 114–115
  evaluating, 43–44, 109–120
  flexibility of, 116
  management science (MS), 43, 110, 111, 118, 119
  matching to requirements, 43–44, 109–120
  operations research (OR), 43, 110, 111, 114–115, 118, 119
  and requirements/methods matrix, 114–120
  selection of, 43–44
  and SHOR paradigm, 110–114
  structure of, 115–116
  transparency vs. safety of, 116

Discovering Antarctica

The Land

June Loves

CHELSEA HOUSE
PUBLISHERS

A Haights Cross Communications Company

Philadelphia

Chelsea House Publishers
1974 Sproul Road, Suite 400
Broomall, PA 19008-0914

The Chelsea House world wide web address is www.chelseahouse.com

Library of Congress Cataloging-in-Publication Data Applied for.
ISBN 0-7910-7023-9 17.95 j

First published 1998 by
MACMILLAN EDUCATION AUSTRALIA PTY LTD
627 Chapel Street, South Yarra, Australia, 3141

Acknowledgements
The author would like to thank Rod Seppelt and Maria Turnbull of the Australian Antarctic Division for their assistance.

Cover: Jean-Paul Ferrero/AUSCAPE

Jean-Paul Ferrero/AUSCAPE, pp. 18 (top left), 22–23 (top), 23 (bottom); Great Southern Stock, p. 5 (top) © Tresize, 13 © M. Pole, 21 © Tresize, 14 © Tresize; Rod Ledingham, pp. 12, 15 (left), 17 (top), 26; Colin Monteath/AUSCAPE, pp. 18–19 (center), 22 (bottom), 29 (bottom); D. Parer & E. Parer-Cook/AUSCAPE, pp. 5 (bottom), 9, 10, 16–17, 20; Getty Images, p. 15 (right); Tui De Roy/ AUSCAPE, p. 18 (bottom), 19 (right); Galen Rowell-Explorer/AUSCAPE, p. 24 (bottom); Michael Whitehead/AUSCAPE, pp. 21 (top), 24 (top).

Words that appear in **bold type** can be found in the Glossary on page 31.

Contents

Introduction

Antarctica is a massive continent that surrounds the **South Pole**. It is the fifth largest continent in the world. Antarctica is covered with vast sheets of ice and snow that are several miles thick. Beneath this frozen layer is a rocky base that is **visible** in a few coastal areas, in some of the larger mountain ranges, and on the nunataks, or isolated mountaintops.

▶ Antarctica has many ice shelves. These huge, floating cliffs of ice may be many thousands of years old.

An Island Continent

Antarctica is an island continent. It is very isolated and is considered to be the most **remote** land on Earth.

▼ Antarctica has an area of 5.5 million square miles (14.25 million square kilometers) which is mostly covered in ice and snow.

Where Is Antarctica?

Antarctica is at the south end of Earth. It lies within the Antarctic Circle, an imaginary line around the South Pole at nearly 66.5 degrees south latitude. The South Pole is at 90 degrees south latitude.

This image shows the Antarctic continent, which lies at the southern end of Earth and surrounds the South Pole.

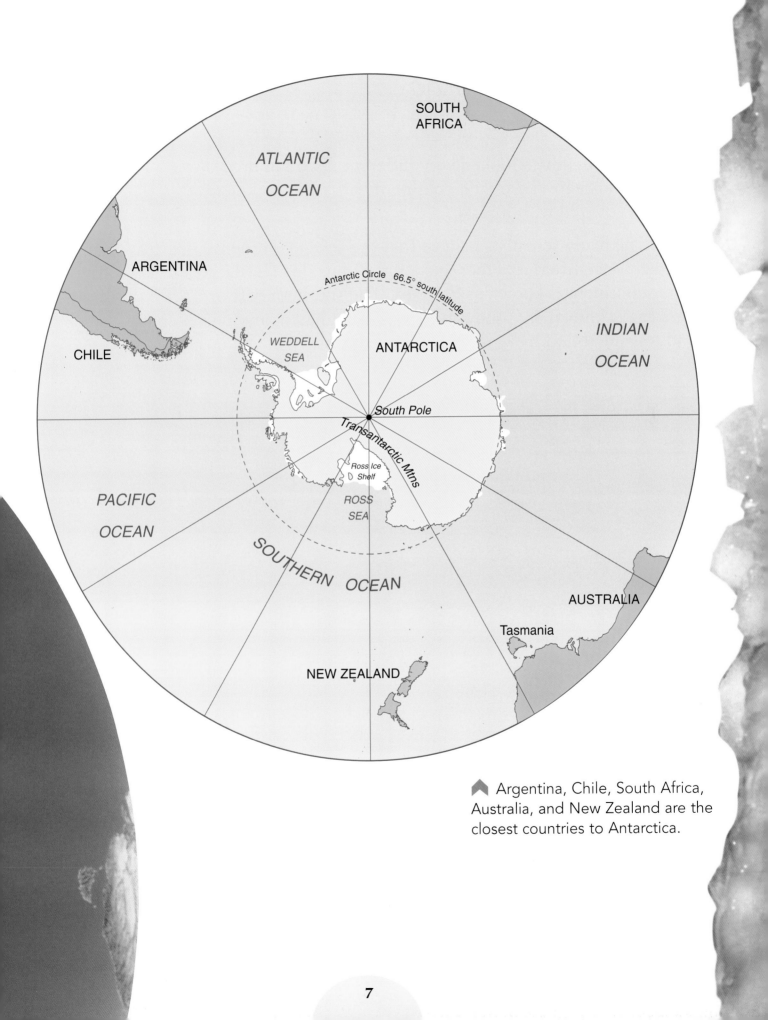

SOUTH
AFRICA

ATLANTIC

OCEAN

ARGENTINA

Antarctic Circle   66.5° south latitude

INDIAN

OCEAN

CHILE

WEDDELL
SEA

ANTARCTICA

South Pole

Transantarctic Mtns

Ross Ice
Shelf

PACIFIC

OCEAN

ROSS
SEA

AUSTRALIA

SOUTHERN   OCEAN

Tasmania

NEW ZEALAND

▲ Argentina, Chile, South Africa,
Australia, and New Zealand are the
closest countries to Antarctica.

Antarctica Long Ago

Gondwana

Long ago, Antarctica looked very different. Two hundred million years ago, the frozen continent had a warm climate and was covered with forests.

Today, many scientists believe that the seven continents of Earth once fitted together like a jigsaw puzzle. This large super-continent is known as Pangaea. The southern part of Pangaea is known as Gondwana. Gondwana had many trees and was **inhabited** by reptiles and **amphibians**.

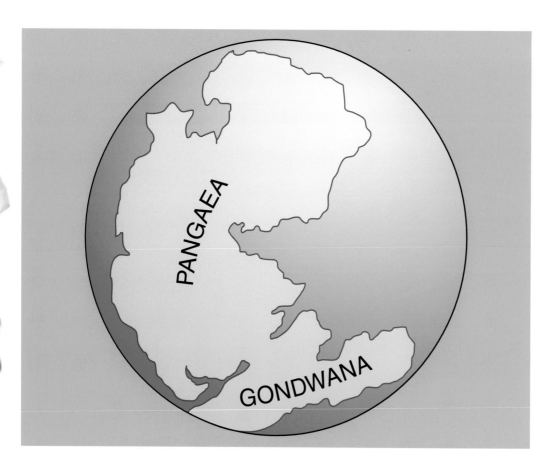

◄ Scientists believe that Antarctica was once part of Gondwana, the southern region of the super-continent Pangaea.

About 140 million years ago, the super-continent began to break up. In Gondwana, the different parts moved away from each other and eventually formed what we now call South America, Africa, Madagascar, India, Australasia, and Antarctica.

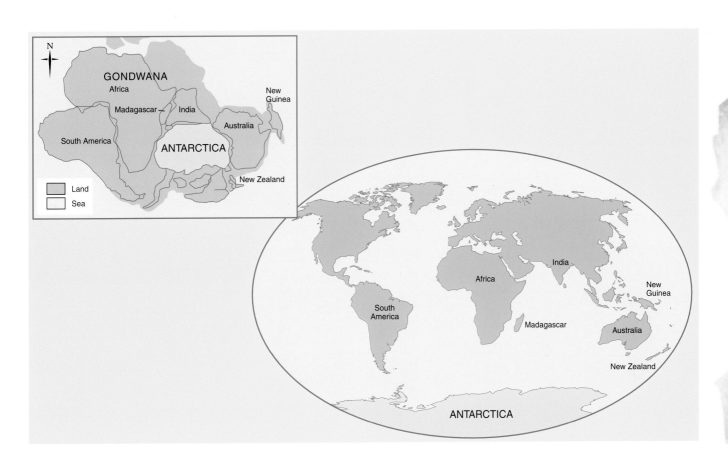

The map on the left shows how the continents are thought to have fitted together in Gondwana. The map on the right shows the location of these continents today.

Coal in Antarctica

Layers of coal 13 feet (4 meters) thick have been found in Antarctica. This coal formed from trees and other plants that grew millions of years ago.

The types of rocks and fossil plants and animals that scientists have found in Antarctica suggest that the continent was warmer and wetter in the past.

Climate and Weather

Antarctica is the coldest place on Earth. Temperatures rarely rise above freezing and often fall below minus 58 degrees Fahrenheit (minus 50 degrees Celsius). Along the coast of Antarctica, temperatures are warmer.

Wind

Antarctica is the windiest continent on Earth. Strong gales near the coast often reach 120 miles (190 kilometers) per hour, and winds up to 200 miles (320 kilometers) per hour have been reported.

Precipitation

Antarctica is the world's driest continent. **Precipitation**, which falls mainly as snow, equals less than 5 inches (12.5 centimeters) of rain per year.

▲ Antarctica's climate is hostile for people. Scientific research workers in Antarctica need special clothing and equipment to cope with the strong winds and freezing temperatures.

▲ The high Antarctic **plateau** is the world's largest and driest desert.

Whiteouts

Whiteouts happen in cloudy conditions when the color of the sky and the color of the surface of the ice become the same. There are no horizons, shadows, or contrasts between objects. These conditions make it difficult to judge distances correctly.

Antarctic Temperatures

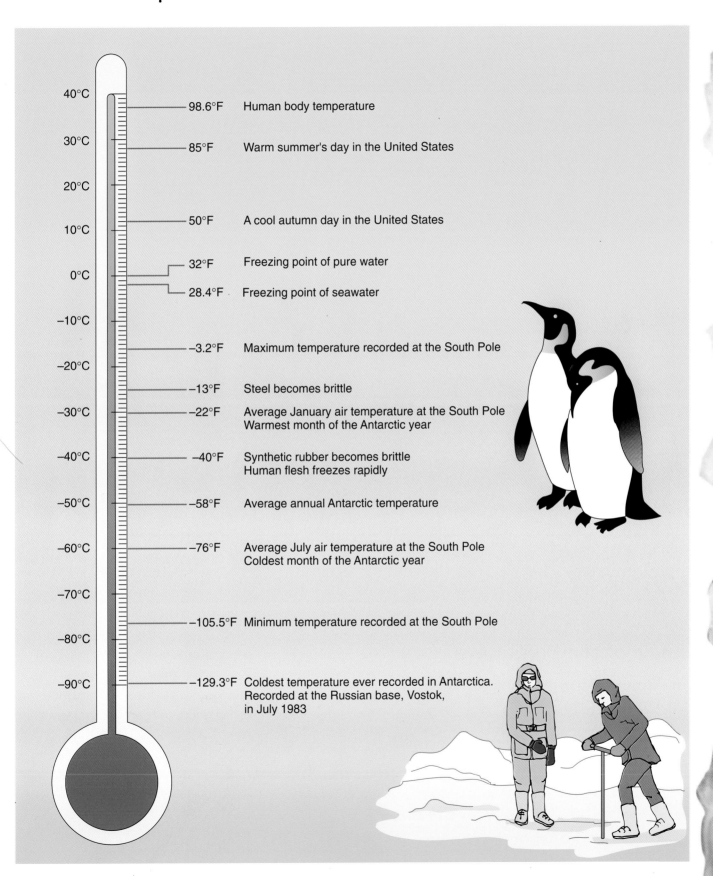

40°C	
30°C	98.6°F — Human body temperature
20°C	85°F — Warm summer's day in the United States
10°C	50°F — A cool autumn day in the United States
0°C	32°F — Freezing point of pure water
	28.4°F — Freezing point of seawater
−10°C	−3.2°F — Maximum temperature recorded at the South Pole
−20°C	−13°F — Steel becomes brittle
−30°C	−22°F — Average January air temperature at the South Pole / Warmest month of the Antarctic year
−40°C	−40°F — Synthetic rubber becomes brittle / Human flesh freezes rapidly
−50°C	−58°F — Average annual Antarctic temperature
−60°C	−76°F — Average July air temperature at the South Pole / Coldest month of the Antarctic year
−70°C	−105.5°F — Minimum temperature recorded at the South Pole
−80°C	
−90°C	−129.3°F — Coldest temperature ever recorded in Antarctica. Recorded at the Russian base, Vostok, in July 1983

Why Is Antarctica So Cold?

Antarctica's severe climate is caused by the constant snow cover and ferocious winds. Antarctica is also a long way from the equator, where temperatures are warmer. The Antarctic continent is very high, which makes temperatures colder.

Another reason Antarctica is so cold is because, for half the year, the sun does not shine on the South Pole. Antarctica faces away from the sun as Earth travels around it. The continent is dark 24 hours a day during this time.

Angle of the Sun's Rays

In Antarctica, the sun is either low in the sky or below the horizon.

Because of the angle of the sun's rays, the sun has to heat more atmosphere and a bigger area of land than when it is high in the sky, making the temperatures cooler.

▲ Ice and snow cover most of Antarctica even in summer. The whiteness of the snow and ice reflects 80 percent of the sun's heat back into space.

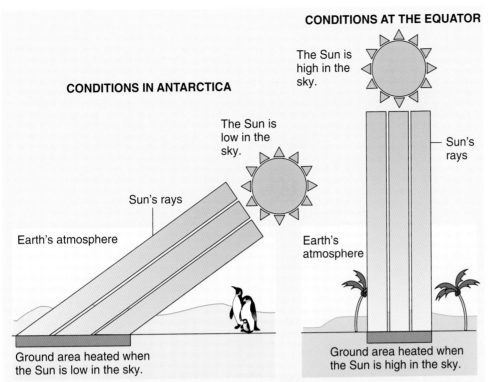

CONDITIONS IN ANTARCTICA

CONDITIONS AT THE EQUATOR

The Sun is high in the sky.

The Sun is low in the sky.

Sun's rays

Sun's rays

Earth's atmosphere

Earth's atmosphere

Ground area heated when the Sun is low in the sky.

Ground area heated when the Sun is high in the sky.

This diagram shows the effect of the angle of the sun's rays on temperature.

When the Sun is low in the sky, its rays are spread over a bigger area of the ground, which weakens the warming effect of the Sun. The Sun's rays must also pass through a greater area of Earth's atmosphere to reach the ground. The atmosphere absorbs much of the heat, which also weakens the warming effect of the Sun. These conditions help to create the freezing temperatures in Antarctica.

Blizzards are a combination of very strong winds and falling or drifting snow. A severe blizzard can cut **visibility** to less than a few feet. Blizzards can last for many days.

The Antarctic Ice Cap

Antarctica is covered by a giant sheet of ice called the Antarctic ice cap.

The ice cap is made of snow collected over 100,000 years and **compressed** into ice. At its deepest, the ice is more than 14,500 feet (4,500 meters) thick.

Under this sheet of ice is a rocky foundation. Only around 2 percent of this rocky foundation is visible in Antarctica.

The Antarctic ice cap covers all but 2 percent of the rocky foundation below.

Movement of the Ice

The ice cap is dome-shaped. It flows like water, but moves very slowly.

The ice cap moves from the highest parts of Antarctica to the sea at the edge of the continent. Rivers of ice called glaciers drain the center of Antarctica and flow slowly to the coast.

Snow and Ice

Both snow and ice are made of tiny water crystals. These crystals start as water droplets that have **evaporated** from the surface of the ocean. They rise into the air and form a cloud. If it is cold enough, the droplets freeze and form ice crystals. These grow and stick together to make snowflakes that fall to Earth.

Snowfall

Not all the snow that falls in Antarctica each year melts. It is blown around, piles up, and slowly turns into ice.

⬆ Snowflakes come in an **infinite** variety of **symmetrical** shapes. No two snowflakes are the same. Most snowflakes have six sides.

◀ Sastrugi is hard, **sculptured** snow that looks like frozen surf. It is shaped by the winds and can be up to 10 feet (3 meters) high. This type of snow can cause great difficulty for travelers.

Glaciers

Glaciers are rivers of ice. Antarctica has the world's biggest glaciers.

All Antarctic glaciers were formed when snow collected in small hollows high on the Antarctic plateau. Over time, more snow fell and slowly the snow at the bottom was pressed into ice. This base gradually spread out into a tongue of ice and became a glacier. The glaciers continue to grow today.

Glaciers and Ice Shelves

As one glacier slides downhill towards the ocean, it is joined by other glaciers. When glaciers flow into the ocean, they can form huge, floating ice shelves.

▲ Many of Antarctica's glaciers flow into the sea.

Crevasses are deep cracks in a glacier, caused by the movement of the ice. Some crevasses can be 100 feet (30 meters) wide and many more feet deep. They are often covered with bridges of snow that hide the danger below.

Moraines

As a glacier slides down a hill or mountain, it grinds out a wide, U-shaped valley. If the ice later melts, it leaves behind the rock and soil that have been ground out and pushed along by the glacier. This is called a moraine.

The Lambert Glacier

The Lambert Glacier in Antarctica is the biggest glacier in the world. It ends at the Amery Ice Shelf and is 250 miles (402 kilometers) long and up to 40 miles (64 kilometers) wide. It was discovered by the crew of an Australian aircraft operating from Mawson Station in 1956.

Icebergs and Ice Shelves

Icebergs are floating lumps of ice. They have different shapes, sizes, and colors. Icebergs float because the ice is less **dense** than sea water.

Some icebergs are made when ice breaks off (calves) from ice shelves. Other icebergs are made by the collapse of ice cliffs, or when glaciers flow directly into the sea.

Iceberg Shapes

> Irregular icebergs are smaller icebergs that have broken off from ice cliffs or glaciers.

> Tabular icebergs have a square, table-like shape. They have recently calved from ice shelves. As they grow older, they lose their square shape and become rounder.

> Rounded icebergs are old icebergs that have tilted or **capsized**. Often their undersides have been sculptured by the water, resulting in beautiful shapes.

Icebergs are frozen fresh water. Some people have talked of towing icebergs to countries where fresh water is needed.

The Movement of Icebergs

Icebergs are moved more by the ocean currents than by the wind. This is because four-fifths of an iceberg is below the surface of the ocean, so the water has much more to push against than the wind. Icebergs generally travel from east to west around Antarctica, not far from shore. They eventually move north into the open ocean and melt as they move towards warmer areas.

Ice Shelves

Ice shelves are huge, floating slabs of ice. Many ice shelves are found in Antarctica. They are formed when ice meets the sea, making a shelf of ice. Some ice shelves are **permanent** and may have been in Antarctica for many thousands of years.

Ross Ice Shelf is Antarctica's largest ice shelf. It fills a bay and reaches far out into the sea. On the edge of the sea, the Ross Ice Shelf is made of ice cliffs.

The early expeditions used the Ross Ice Shelf as their starting point as they attempted to reach the South Pole for the first time.

Sea Ice

By late winter, ice covers more than 7 million square miles (19 million square kilometers) of the oceans surrounding Antarctica and completely encloses the continent.

Sea ice forms as winter approaches. The oceans begin to cool and the surface freezes. Greasy-looking slicks of ice appear on the surface of the ocean. This ice is moved around by gentle wind and waves and made into pancake-shaped circles, called pancake ice. The pancake ice joins with ice from below the surface of the sea. Snow covers it on top. These thickening layers of ice are broken into pack ice.

Pancake ice is formed by the movement of the wind and waves.

Pack Ice

Pack ice covers huge stretches of the oceans surrounding Antarctica and moves constantly. In winter, the frozen surface of the sea may extend more than 250 miles (400 kilometers) from the edge of the Antarctic continent.

When spring comes, the sun, wind, and waves soften the pack ice, causing great cracks. Eventually, the pack ice melts for the summer.

▶ Pack ice develops great cracks during spring and melts during the summer months.

Dangers of Pack Ice

When the pack ice breaks up during spring, it is moved around the oceans by the wind and the currents. This means it is impossible to know where the ice will be, making it very dangerous for sea travel.

Fast Ice

Close to the shore, the movement of the oceans creates fast ice. Fast ice stays attached to the Antarctic continent for a long period of time. It moves very slightly, up and down, with the tides.

▶ Fast ice reaches out into the sea and can support people and large vehicles, such as aircraft.

Mountains

Antarctica has many mountains, including three active volcanoes.

In many places, the mountain ranges of Antarctica are almost completely hidden by ice. Isolated nunataks, or peaks, show through the ice and snow.

Transantarctic Mountains

The Transantarctic Mountains are one of the world's greatest mountain chains. They divide the Antarctic continent into East and West Antarctica.

▲ The Transantarctic Mountains are almost completely covered by ice.

◄ The Olympus Range forms part of the Transantarctic Mountains.

Vinson Massif

The highest mountain in Antarctica is Vinson Massif, which is 16,860 feet (5,139 meters) high. It is part of the Ellsworth Mountain Range.

Volcanoes

Long ago, chains of volcanoes were formed on the Antarctic Peninsula. Now only Mount Erebus on Ross Island, Mount Melbourne beside the Ross Sea, and Deception Island off the Antarctic Peninsula are active.

Facts about Mount Erebus

Mount Erebus is an active volcano that is 12,448 feet (3,794 meters) high. It is one of the few volcanoes in the world that has a **molten lava** lake in its **crater**.

The active volcano Mount Erebus pours out a continuous fountain of steam.

23

Lakes and Oases

There are both freshwater and saltwater lakes in Antarctica. Shallow freshwater lakes may freeze to the bottom in winter. Many lakes have a permanent layer of ice on the surface. Some of the most saline (salty) lakes rarely freeze at the surface.

◀ Deep Lake is the most salty of the saltwater lakes in the Vestfold Hills. Only a few single-celled plants and animals can survive in the salty conditions.

Saltwater Lakes

Saltwater lakes are found in the Vestfold Hills. These lakes have salt levels up to ten times that of sea water. These lakes formed at the end of the last ice age, about 18,000 years ago.

Freshwater Lakes

Freshwater lakes support slightly more **species** of plankton, algae, and mosses than saltwater lakes. However, since some freshwater lakes freeze solid during the winter, the growth of these plants is limited to the short summer.

Oases

In Antarctica, oases are large areas of land that are mainly free of ice. They are cold deserts where snow does not gather.

Antarctic oases often have freshwater and saltwater lakes. These lakes often have a permanent ice cover.

▶ The McMurdo dry valleys of southern Victoria Land are large Antarctic oases.

Seasons at the South Pole

Close to both the North and South Poles, the sun remains above the horizon for almost half of the year and below the horizon for the other half. This means that for half of the year it is always dark and for the other half it is always light.

The seasons in the southern hemisphere are opposite from those in the northern hemisphere. In spring and summer, from September to March, Antarctica has 24 hours of sunlight. Winter and autumn days, from March to September, have 24 hours of darkness. This is because, as Earth **rotates** in its **orbit** around the sun, its **axis** is **tilted** at 23.5 degrees towards the sun.

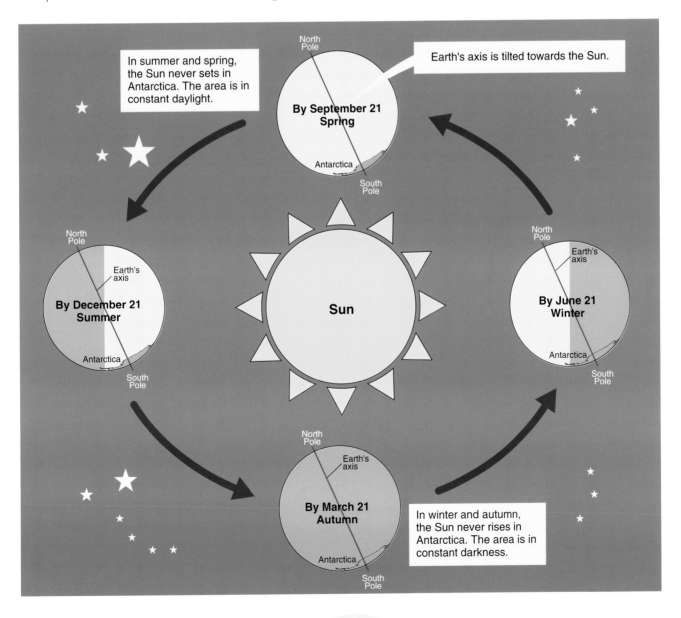

In summer and spring, the Sun never sets in Antarctica. The area is in constant daylight.

Earth's axis is tilted towards the Sun.

North Pole

By September 21
Spring

Antarctica

South Pole

North Pole

Earth's axis

By December 21
Summer

Antarctica

South Pole

Sun

North Pole

Earth's axis

By June 21
Winter

Antarctica

South Pole

North Pole

Earth's axis

By March 21
Autumn

Antarctica

South Pole

In winter and autumn, the Sun never rises in Antarctica. The area is in constant darkness.

Auroras

Auroras look like curtains of glowing lights in the night sky. They are caused by explosions on the sun's surface, which send tiny particles called electrons to Earth.

Each electron has an electric charge. The electrons **collide** with very cold gases in Earth's upper atmosphere. This makes the gases glow different colors. For example, oxygen glows green, while nitrogen glows pink. The glow of the aurora is very similar to an ordinary fluorescent tube or neon light.

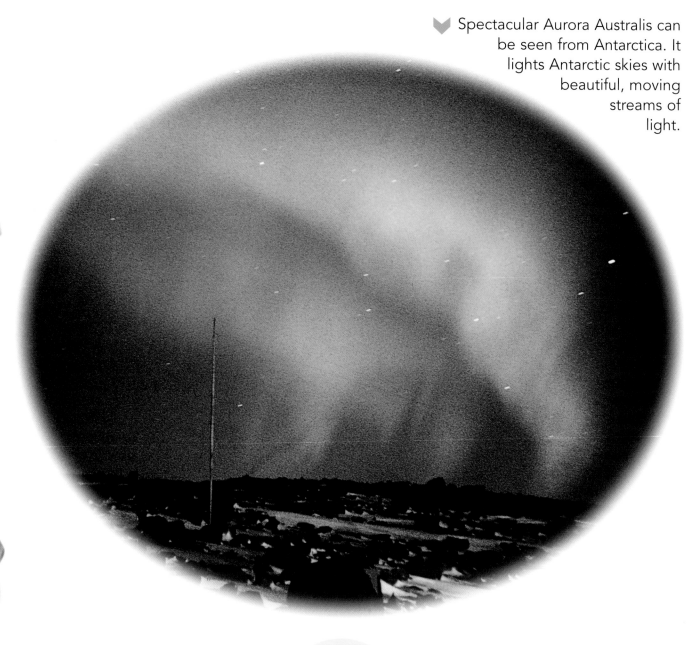

Spectacular Aurora Australis can be seen from Antarctica. It lights Antarctic skies with beautiful, moving streams of light.

Mineral Resources and Meteorites

There are mineral resources in Antarctica, although only about 1 percent of the land not covered with ice has been explored for mineral **deposits**.

Low-grade iron ore is present in the Prince Charles Mountains, and traces of other minerals, such as gold, copper, tin, and cobalt, have been reported.

There are also coal deposits in the Transantarctic Mountains and in the Prince Charles Mountains.

The Antarctic Treaty

Under the **Antarctic Treaty** (1991) there is an agreement to ban mining activities in Antarctica for 50 years.

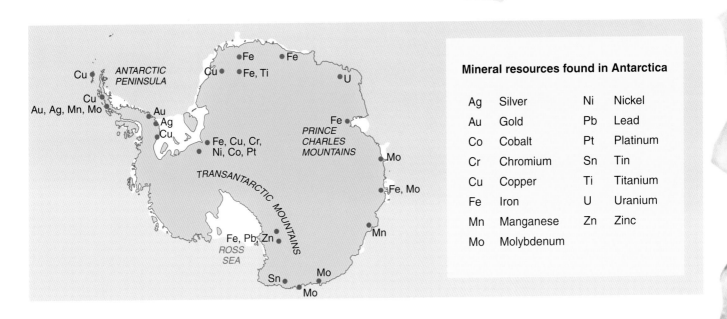

Mineral resources found in Antarctica

Ag	Silver	Ni	Nickel
Au	Gold	Pb	Lead
Co	Cobalt	Pt	Platinum
Cr	Chromium	Sn	Tin
Cu	Copper	Ti	Titanium
Fe	Iron	U	Uranium
Mn	Manganese	Zn	Zinc
Mo	Molybdenum		

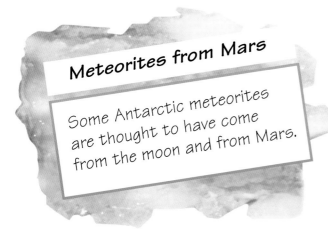

Meteorites from Mars

Some Antarctic meteorites are thought to have come from the moon and from Mars.

Meteorites

Meteorites are masses of stone or metal which have reached Earth from outer space. Meteor **fragments** have been found on the ice in Antarctica. Meteorites are important because they tell us something about other planets.

Sub-Antarctic Islands

The sub-Antarctic islands are islands in the oceans surrounding Antarctica. They are close to the Antarctic Convergence, which is the **boundary** between cold Antarctic water and warmer sub-Antarctic water. The islands have different landscapes and climates. Many animals and birds live on and visit these islands.

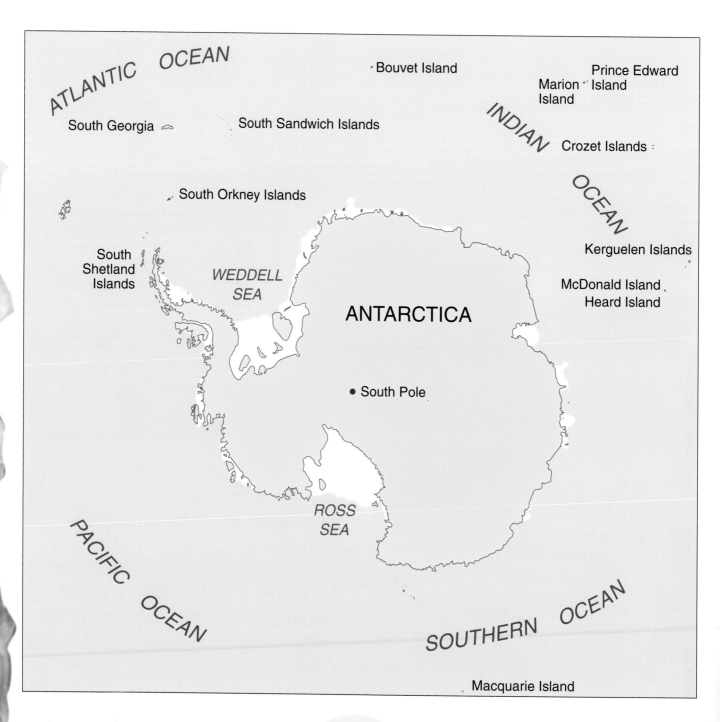

ATLANTIC OCEAN

Bouvet Island

Prince Edward Island
Marion Island

South Georgia   South Sandwich Islands

INDIAN

Crozet Islands

OCEAN

South Orkney Islands

Kerguelen Islands

South Shetland Islands   WEDDELL SEA

McDonald Island
Heard Island

ANTARCTICA

• South Pole

ROSS SEA

PACIFIC OCEAN

SOUTHERN OCEAN

Macquarie Island

A World Laboratory

Antarctica has always been a place of mystery and challenge for people. There are many issues concerning the development of Antarctica, and most of these involve the presence of people on the continent.

Today, Antarctica is very important for the world because of the knowledge and understanding it can provide. It is of great value as a world laboratory for scientific work and as a place of peace and stability.

Managing Antarctica so that it keeps its special qualities and meets the different aims of peoples and nations is of great importance.

◥ People are working to preserve the Antarctic land so that it can support the fascinating mix of wildlife found there.

➤ The future of humans on Earth may depend on the information gained by scientific workers in Antarctica.

Antarctic Fact File

The Land
Antarctica is a huge, frozen continent surrounding the South Pole. It has an area of 5.5 million square miles (14.25 million square kilometers) and is the fifth largest continent.

People
No **indigenous** humans have ever lived in Antarctica. Today, scientists, support workers, and visitors stay in Antarctica for varying lengths of time.

Animals
No native land mammals live permanently in Antarctica. Seals, whales, and penguins all inhabit the waters around Antarctica. Other seabirds live in and visit Antarctica.

   The largest animal that lives permanently in Antarctica is a midge, a kind of wingless fly no more than one-half inch (12 millimeters) long.

Plants
Antarctica has no trees or bushes. Only two kinds of flowering plants, and simple plants such as mosses and lichens, can grow in Antarctica.

Coldest Place on Earth
Antarctica is the coldest place on Earth. The lowest temperature ever recorded was minus 129.3 degrees Fahrenheit (minus 89.6 degrees Celsius) at the Russian base, Vostok, in July 1983.

   Antarctica's annual average temperature is minus 58 degrees Fahrenheit (minus 50 degrees Celsius).

Windiest Place on Earth
Winds have been recorded at 200 miles (320 kilometers) per hour at Commonwealth Bay.

Driest Place on Earth
Precipitation, which falls mainly as snow, equals less than 5 inches (12.5 centimeters) of rain per year. This makes Antarctica a frozen desert.

Highest Continent on Earth
Antarctica is the highest of all continents. Its average **elevation** is 7,546 feet (2,300 meters) above sea level.

Highest Mountain
Antarctica's highest mountain is Vinson Massif in the Ellsworth Mountain Range. It is 16,860 feet (5,139 meters) above sea level.

The Antarctic Ice Cap
The Antarctic ice cap is a thick sheet of ice which covers almost all of the continent. At its deepest, the ice is more than 14,700 feet (4,500 meters) thick.

   Antarctica holds 70 percent of the world's fresh water in the form of ice.

Ross Ice Shelf
The Ross Ice Shelf is a huge, floating cliff of ice 30 to 45 miles (50 to 70 kilometers) above sea level. Along the coast, pieces break off the ice shelf and form icebergs.

Glossary

amphibian
a cold-blooded animal that can live on land or in water

Antarctic Treaty
an agreement between many countries to protect Antarctica

axis
the imaginary line around which Earth rotates

boundary
edge

capsize
to turn over and sink

collide
to crash into

compressed
squeezed or squashed

crater
the cup-shaped dip at the mouth of a volcano

dense
solid

deposit
a layer of material at a particular place

elevation
height

evaporate
when moisture leaves a body of liquid and goes into the air

fragment
a part of something

infinite
never-ending

inhabit
to live in

indigenous
having always lived in a certain place

low-grade
poor quality

molten lava
lava that is in a liquid form

orbit
to travel around something

permanent
always there

plateau
a raised surface of flat land

precipitation
moisture that falls from the sky to Earth

remote
a long way from anything else

rotate
to spin around on an axis

sculptured
formed into a shape, like a sculpture

South Pole
the southernmost end of Earth

species
type

symmetrical
where both halves of an object are the same

tilt
lean

visibility
the ability to see ahead

visible
able to be seen

Index